THE ENCYCLOPEDIA OF WEALTH BUILDING OPPORTUNITIES

MONEY MANUAL NO. 1—REAL ESTATE WEALTH BUILDING OPPORTUNITIES
How To Buy And Sell Real Estate
For Maximum Profits

MONEY MANUAL NO 2—INVESTMENT OPPORTUNITIES FOR THE 1980'S
Wealth Building Strategies In The Stock Market,
Gold, Silver, Diamonds...

MONEY MANUAL NO. 3—SECRETS OF THE MILLIONAIRES
How The Rich Made It Big

MONEY MANUAL NO. 4—THE DYNAMICS OF PERSONAL FINANCIAL PLANNING
How To Save, Invest, And Multiply Your Money.

MONEY MANUAL NO. 5—HOW TO START MAKING MONEY IN A BUSINESS OF YOUR OWN
A Guide To Money Making Opportunities

MONEY MANUAL NO. 6—A TREASURY OF HOME BUSINESS OPPORTUNITIES
How to Make Money Without Leaving Home.

MONEY MANUAL NO. 7—HOW TO ACHIEVE TOTAL SUCCESS
How To Use The Power Of Creative Thought

THE DYNAMICS
OF PERSONAL
FINANCIAL PLANNING

PUBLISHED BY:

GEORGE STERNE
PROFIT IDEAS
8361 Vickers, Suite 304
San Diego, CA 92111

ACKNOWLEDGEMENT

The Publisher wishes to express thanks to Russ von Hoelscher for his contribution of research and writing to this book.

THE DYNAMICS OF PERSONAL FINANCIAL PLANNING

TABLE OF CONTENTS

FOREWORD

In today's changing economy, diligent personal money management is essential. Financial independence, or at least reasonable financial security, should be the goal of every productive person who wants to someday reach maturity with dignity.

America's per capita income is one of the highest ever obtained by man, yet out of every one hundred citizens who reach the age of sixty-five, ninety percent are flat broke. Only slightly more than one in every one hundred (about eleven per thousand) have obtained financial security. All others must continue to work for a living or are partially or totally dependent on friends, relatives, or public charity. The "average person" reaching retirement age during the 1980's will have earned over a half million dollars in his or her life-time. At age sixty-five, 98.9% will have too little or absolutely nothing left after forty to fifty years of making money. Something is definitely not right.

Since you have no choice but to participate in *the money game* it is vital that you learn the rules and play to win! This book was written to help you be a BIG WINNER.

In addition to advice on protecting your money, you will discover new ways to put your money to work earning more money. "Money Making Money" is a strategy you can prosper with. Also, this book will help you get the most for every dollar you spend. You absolutely must become a wise buyer if you wish to receive maximum value and enjoyment from everything you purchase.

Learn *THE DYNAMICS OF PERSONAL FINANCIAL PLANNING* and you will know the joy of money and the satisfaction of reaching financial independence. Money won't solve your problems, but it will remove one of life's biggest—the lack of same!

This book is about you, your money, and how you can reach FINANCIAL FREEDOM. Are you interested?

CHAPTER ONE

YOUR PERSONAL MONEY
GAME PLAN

Money management and financial planning is personal business. Everyone has different financial objectives, money making ability, assets, and their own unique temperament. Your money plans, therefore, must be uniquely designed to fit your singular needs and goals.

While some may complain that we have become too beholden to the power of money, this complaint, valid or not, in no way alters the fact that money (purchasing power) is essential in today's society.

For most people, the chief source of money is their salary. Money management is essential to today's worker. After a lifetime of productive wage earning, all but a small percentage of wage earners end up broke, or nearly broke. A sad commentary on how we manage, or mismanage our money.

While the advice in this book should help people worldwide to manage, save, invest, and multiply their money, there is no doubt that Americans are in the enviable position of being able to pick from a huge buffet of financial vehicles and capital preservation strategies, unmatched anywhere else in the *Free World*. Albeit true, to benefit from this huge array of vehicles and techniques, you must become aware of them and choose the ones that are right. For your individual objectives, you must define your personal *money game plan*.

YOUR FINANCIAL SUCCESS
IS GUARANTEED IF . . .

FINANCIAL FREEDOM. (Don't those two words conjure up uplifting thoughts?) It is possible if you're willing to start with, stay with, and stick with the knowledge in this volume. Are you willing to be financially free? Don't balk at my question. The fact is that 90% of all adults spend little or no time charting a financial game plan. "Economics" is perceived as a dull and boring topic by the vast majority. Is it any wonder then why these same people end up at the mercy of some form of charity in their senior years?

Your financial success is guaranteed if you are willing to learn *THE DYNAMICS OF PERSONAL FINANCIAL PLANNING* and then practice these dynamics in all your financial affairs.

THE WEALTH SECRET

A simple but powerful secret for the accumulation of wealth is found in these eight magic words.

"A Part of All I Earn, I Keep."

It would be nice if EVERYTHING we earned would be ours to keep, but this just isn't so. Much of the money we earn belongs to the IRS, the mortgage company, the grocery store, schools, churches, insurance companies, and various other merchants, professionals, and politicians.

Most people try to retain a little money from their regular earnings after paying off the government, various debts and expenditures to professionals and merchants. It's the "pay myself last" syndrome and it doesn't work. If you allow yourself to be last in line, you will usually pay yourself little or nothing. You must learn to pay yourself first! You earn the money and you deserve a cut right off the top!

THE 10% FACTOR

Consider this: Regardless of how large or meager your personal earning power is today, your standard of living would not drastically change if you earned 10% less than you now do. By paying yourself 10% off the top, you will soon have a valuable "chunk of money" that in turn can go to work to make much more money for you. And *money making money* is the silver lining that leads to financial freedom.

FIVE MAJOR REASONS WHY PEOPLE FAIL

There are five major reasons why so many are losing "the money game." They are:
(1) The wrong attitude about money.
(2) Failure to set financial goals.
(3) Ignorance concerning making money make money.
(4) Ignorance about how to use tax laws.
(5) Procrastination.

FAILURE TO SET FINANCIAL GOALS

You may not plan to fail, most people don't, but if you fail to plan, you probably will not be successful. Successful people are always goal setters and goal achievers. To get from here to there you need a road map and goals can chart the path and give you an easy to follow "map to success."

Goal setting and goal achieving are essential to any man or woman who wants success in money managing, financial planning, or any other worthwhile endeavor.

Setting and achieving goals can become the art and science

13

of productive living. Once we realize goal-achievement is governed by definite mental laws—not by luck, chance or the "breaks"—we can start believing in ourselves and our goals.

Every person is a goal-setter in many respects, whether they realize it or not. Some goals are major goals, and others are merely minor objectives. There are day-to-day, hour-to-hour goals, and there are long range (weeks, months, years) planned goals. There are positive and negative goals, and it's important to pursue the one and banish the other.

Setting goals comes easy to most people but achieving them only becomes natural once you understand the process. It is my intent to show you how to set goals that are both high and realistic—and then show you how to achieve them. You can do it! It's not difficult when you apply the correct mental techniques. In fact, it can be fun as well as rewarding. The longer you work on it, the easier it will become. Like almost anything worthwhile in life, in the beginning it takes real determination and a good measure of effort. Later on it becomes so natural, so second-nature, that you'll find yourself "going with the flow."

The Law of Visualization in Goal Setting

A basic, proven law of mental science is that a desire consistently held in mind tends to become objectified in form. The form can be something that can be seen, such as a new car, a fabulous home, a beautiful boat, new clothes, money, etc., or it can be an attitude of mind or quality of character—unseen, but no less real. Because of this fact, we should put our goals to "mind," and think about them often.

Goals Must Be "Seen" as Already Accomplished

How can one "see" a goal accomplished when it's not yet

a reality? To begin with you can use the incredible power of mental visualization. That which we can see ourselves doing, having and being, can be manifested.

Goal Setting + Desire + Faith = Goals Achieved

After we have first set the goal or goals to mind and visualized them in our mind's eye, we have both consciously and subconsciously started our march toward goal achievement. Now let's greatly enhance our probability for successful goal achievement by adding two more powerful abstract motives: Desire and Willpower.

A strong will power aroused by a burning desire gives the total person a powerful thrust forward. Now the creative energy is in high gear and we are determined to succeed.

There may be many obstacles to overcome on down the road, but now we can label them challenges—not merely problems—and our desire and willpower is prepared for the task at hand. We will claim success! We don't intend to be sidetracked very long, and we will not give up! Our desire and faith is equal to every obstacle (challenge).

YOUR FINANCIAL GAME PLAN

Success and security in personal money management is not the result of chance, fate or luck. Our self-image, desire, faith and goal setting makes for good luck and happy financial landings. This book is a step-by-step blueprint to financial success. Follow its advice, set high yet realistic goals (remember: you have to keep it believable to yourself) and financial freedom will be yours.

MONEY MAKING MONEY

The third big reason that so many are losing the financial game is that they fail to realize the importance of the vital concept — MONEY MAKING MONEY.

When it comes to teaching financial matters, or for that matter, financial survival, our school system has a very poor track record. Even college students are lacking in the basics of understanding personal money management techniques. Our school system is doing a somewhat adequate job of teaching the know-how of various vocations. They are instructing students on how to prepare themselves to be proficient in the career of their choice, from basic mechanics to advanced computer technology. They are offering great opportunities to obtain knowledge in a vast array of fields from the professions to sales and distribution, and from engineering to nuclear science. Yet, they are not teaching the one vital subject that everyone needs to know to live abundantly and securely — and that is how to manage money.

This lack of financial knowledge is destroying the great American success dream. There has never been an economic system to rival the great potential of free enterprise, to bring the most good to the largest number of people, but to successfully participate in this marvelous system, you must understand how it works.

Since schools are definitely not doing a good job teaching how to take advantage of our free enterprise system, it is crucial that every person takes the time and makes the effort to obtain this essential knowledge. Reading this book is a major step in the right direction. Continue to learn by reading other good sound financial books. Magazines like *MONEY, THE WALL STREET JOURNAL,* and *THE FINANCIAL SECURITY DIGEST,* CAN ALSO HELP ACCELERATE YOUR FINANCIAL EDUCATION.

Understanding personal economics will allow you to learn how to achieve financial independence.

Multiplying money is how the rich got rich and also how they continue to become richer. There is a right (perhaps several), investment for you. This book will help you discover it. For now, simply realize the vast importance of first saving money daily, weekly, or monthly, and then making that money multiply.

YOU MUST UNDERSTAND TAX-AVOIDANCE

The fourth reason why so many go down the drain financially, is because most people fail to learn and apply tax law. While it is often wise to consult with a competent accountant and/or a tax attorney, it is a mistake to remain personally ignorant concerning tax law and tax avoidance. Don't confuse tax avoidance with tax evasion. You have every right to avoid taxes legally. Tax evasion on the other hand is illegal and not recommended.

Understanding tax law will help you differentiate between "money earned" and "money kept." Money strategies built around "keepable income" will be found throughout this book.

Contrary to what you may have read in your newspaper or viewed on any television news show, your taxes will not be cut appreciably within the next several years. The Reagan sponsored **Economic Recovery Act** offered a little relief to some Americans, but the heavy spending by past and present congresses will not permit a major tax break. Even without further liberal tax legislation, taxes are bound to rise due to general inflation, the big financial mess Social Security is wallowing in, and increased military spending.

The massive tax increase, mislabeled "windfall profits tax" (on which there can be a tax without a profit) is nothing

17

more than a sales tax on gasoline and other petroleum products. Uninformed citizens cheer when the government slaps big industry with new taxes, not realizing the burden is in turn passed on to them. When you hear a politician preaching "soak the rich," or "make the big corporations pay more," you can be certain that the burden will soon filter down and fall squarely on the shoulders of all citizens. It's a shame that a large portion of the public still buys this hogwash. The real cause of high taxes is what government spends. When government spends more money than it takes in, which has been the case in recent history, citizens pay the difference in the form of inflation and the interest expense on the national debt.

Tax avoidance through adequate tax planning can save most people a bundle by sharply reducing their tax burden. Tax planning and tax saving loopholes need not be the exclusive domain of the super rich. This book will prove that average citizens can greatly reduce and in some cases completely wipe out their tax burden. You owe it to yourself to learn and use the tax saving tactics found in this book. Money saved is money earned.

PROCRASTINATION

Last, but certainly not least in the quintet of major reasons that so many people fail in their quest to obtain financial freedom, or at least reasonable financial security, is that arch-enemy of forward progress, *procrastination.* There is no doubt that procrastination can be your greatest deterrent to reaching your financial goals. Time is the issue. How will you use this precious commodity. If you use your time wisely, you will reap great benefits and the peace of mind that comes with freedom from all money worries. If you misuse your time, you probably will fall short of financial freedom and eventually have to rely on some sort of charity.

Procrastination is an insidious enemy of your goal to be able to retire in financial dignity. Sometimes you may confuse goals and obligations. A larger home, a boat, travel to foreign lands—all of these can be your goals. But preparing to retire in financial dignity is more than a goal. It is your obligation, a debt that you owe yourself and others—your family, your community, and other taxpayers. With proper financial planning and sound money management, it is a debt that you can pay, making your retirement years happy instead of haphazard, comfortable instead of depressing.

I have observed that in the early years of life, when spending habits are formed, thoughts of retirement are far away and have little relationship to current needs and even less to future needs. The habit becomes reinforced with the same passing of time that brings retirement closer. Then when retirement time is so near as to be of immediate concern, it is often too late to make adequate preparation.

Procrastination always stands in the shadows, awaiting its opportunity to spoil your chances for success. Don't allow it to steal your dreams!

FINANCIAL FREEDOM FORMULA

**Here is a formula that can
make you financially successful.**

**Ideas + Desire + Time + Money + The American
Free Enterprise System = Your Opportunity
to be Financially Free.**

THE IDEA

Everything begins in our minds, or as Jack Ensign Addington so aptly titled his important book on the subject

Psychogenesis, *Mind and Beginning or in the Beginning, Mind.* The conscious and/or subconscious decisions made in our mind determines what we will have, be, and do in our lives.

Financial freedom starts with an idea concerning a life that is financially free. The more real, vivid, and alive that idea becomes, the greater our desire will be to make it a reality.

DESIRE

Once an idea is born, desire must step in and "feed the thought," if it is to grow strong and exert itself. Financial freedom is a very reachable objective and yet it takes desire backed by faith and enthusiasm to give us the drive power to climb the mountain and claim the victory. Nothing worthwhile is ever accomplished without a heaping helping of desire.

TIME

The younger you are, the less money you will need to reach financial independence. It only takes a small amount of money to compound to a large sum if you have time for it to grow. A savings of only $40 per month started at age 25 is equivalent to $120 per month started at age 35, $400 at age 45 and $1,700 at age 55. This is based on an anticipated age 65 retirement.

If you have a lump sum of $20,000 here is the difference time makes in multiplication of your money using a very conservative compound interest rate of 6%.

20

Years	At 6 percent
10	$ 35,816
20	64,142
30	112,868
40	205,714

I hope these figures convince you that the time to get started in order to reach your predetermined goal is right now! While the universe appears relatively unconcerned about our definition of time, it is a big factor in making financial plans here on Earth.

MONEY

The real challenge is to have your *money making money*. The rate of return (ROR) is the key-to-the-kingdom of financial freedom. Your ROR will be determined by how wisely you put your money to work for you. Let's look at the difference in multiplication on our $20,000 lump sum, comparing a 6% interest against a 12% interest.

Years	At 6 percent	At 12 percent	Difference
10	$ 35,816	$ 62,116	$ 26,300
20	64,142	192,924	128,790
30	112,868	599,198	484,330
40	205,714	1,861,018	1,655,304

HANDLING DOLLARS

There are only three things you can do with your dollars—spend, loan, or hold on to. If you spend them, make darn certain you enjoy what they bring you because spent dollars have lost their option power. If you decide not to spend your dollars (and here we are discussing money over and above

21

your normal living cost), you have two options: loan or keep. You may loan dollars at various interest rates, the lower rates usually being the safest (banks, savings and loans, government bonds); the higher interest rate (unsecured loans to entrepreneurs, etc.) usually being the riskiest.

You may also put your dollars in an "ownership" position. You can own shares of American or foreign industry, real estate, energy, commodities, precious metals, diamonds, gemstones, rare coins, or stamps, art objects and antiques.

Throughout this book we will be discussing how to profit by owning or loaning dollars.

WHICH IS SAFER — OWNING OR LOANING?

There is no easy answer to this question since the *ROR* MUST BE THE DECIDING FACTOR. However, the safety of receiving, let us say, 6% from a bank or savings and loan association, can mean little or nothing if inflation is higher than the interest you are receiving. It will take approximately twelve years for one dollar to become two at a 6% return.

Likewise, owning investments (shares in industry, real estate, etc.) are dependent on how well you selected the independent investment vehicle. I know men and women who have tripled their money in less than one year (a fantastic *ROR*) through real estate investing, while others bought real estate that appreciated very slowly, if at all. The past two 1981-1982 years have not been good for real estate. 1983-1984 offers a cloudy outlook, although this writer believes the overall investment trend will be positive, especially in high growth areas.

Gold and silver give us a dramatic view of volatile precious metal markets. A few years ago, gold was selling at $850 per ounce and silver had risen to $52 per ounce. 1982 saw these two precious metals clobbered by recession and other factors. As this is being written, (the end of 1983) gold is approximately $430 per ounce and silver is near $12 per ounce, — huge declines from their lofty highs, but much higher than 1982 lows of $300 and $5 respectively.

Safety is relative to your ROR. Savings offer limited yields, however, even inflation ravaged savings can be superior to owning stocks, real property, precious metals or anything else that sharply declines in value.

Faced with an elaborate buffet of investment opportunities, the individual must consider all factors to choose wisely. This book will help you decide what methods best suit your temperment and individual problems.

WEALTH MULTIPLICATION

Think about this: you have two job offers. Both will last only one month, one week and one day.

One month	=	30 days
One week	=	7 days
One day	=	1 day
		38 days

Your first job offer is a $1,000 a day for the 38 days. Your second offer is one cent (1¢) the first day and doubled each day thereafter until day 38. Take your choice! See the following chart for the results—

DAY	OFFER ONE DOLLARS	OFFER TWO DOLLARS
1	$ 1,000	$ .01
2	1,000	.02
3	1,000	.04
4	1,000	.08
5	1,000	.16
6	1,000	.32
7	1,000	.64
8	1,000	1.28
9	1,000	2.55
10	1,000	5.10
11	1,000	10.20
12	1,000	20.40
13	1,000	40.80
14	1,000	81.60
15	1,000	163.20
16	1,000	326.40
17	1,000	650.00
18	1,000	1,300.00
19	1,000	2,600.00
20	1,000	5,200.00
21	1,000	10,400.00
22	1,000	20,800.00
23	1,000	41,600.00
24	1,000	83,200.00
25	1,000	165,750.00
26	1,000	331,500.00
27	1,000	663,000.00
28	1,000	1,326,000.00
29	1,000	2,652,000.00
30	1,000	5,304,000.00
31	1,000	10,608,000.00
32	1,000	21,216,000.00
33	1,000	42,432,000.00
34	1,000	84,864,000.00
35	1,000	169,728,000.00
36	1,000	339,456,000.00
37	1,000	678,912,000.00
38	1,000	1,357,824,000.00
	Total $38,000	Total $2,715,648,602.80

IT'S MIND BOGGLING, BUT 1¢ MULTIPLIED ONLY 38 TIMES REPRESENTS TWO BILLION, SEVEN HUNDRED AND FIFTEEN MILLION, SIX HUNDRED AND FORTY-EIGHT THOUSAND, SIX HUNDRED AND TWO DOLLARS AND EIGHTY CENTS.

24

Million Dollar Multiplication — starting with only one thousand dollars — you're half way to a million by the fifth multiple. Starting with just one thousand dollars, you could reach millionaire status by doubling your money only ten times. And you're half way there by the time you reach only your fifth multiple ($32,000). Here's how it works:

10th multiple: time is measured in
    Years—Months—Weeks—Days—Minutes—Seconds

Time with an *S* = *Times*, representative of the amount of times something happened. Not necessarily in time years.

Example: *I drove my car 13 times.*

The 10th times multiple: take $1,000 and double it 10 times. I bought 10 houses this year and doubled my investment each time. I was half way to my million dollar mark, when I reached only— $32,000.

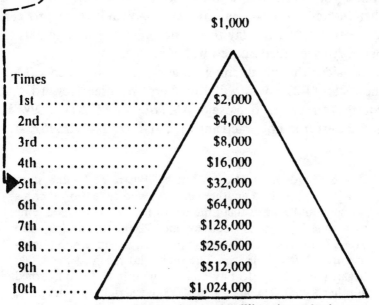

$1,000

Times
1st $2,000
2nd..................... $4,000
3rd $8,000
4th $16,000
5th $32,000
6th $64,000
7th $128,000
8th $256,000
9th $512,000
10th $1,024,000

This makes me a millionaire today!

25

KNOW THE TRUTH

Please don't be misled into thinking that this book is going to make you a billionaire, or even a mere millionaire. Wealth multiplication and double-your-money concepts are much easier printed on paper than turned into reality through your efforts. Easy to accomplish they may not be, but the concept is valid, and the potential to do it in the *real world* is available. That's the beauty of our free-enterprise system, it truly does offer everyone who will earn and learn the opportunity to pyramid and prosper through wealth multiplication.

Handle your dollars wisely. A portion of every dollar should be spent for the necessities of life, a portion for luxuries, a portion should be given away, and a portion should be invested. You are the steward of every dollar that comes your way, and if you're not a responsible steward of that money, you will miss great opportunities to prosper. You can't refuse to play the money game. Everyone participates. All are called but few will win.

Consider the enlightening bible story of the talents (Matthew 25: 14-29); you will find here the great reward that comes from productive use of *MONEY MAKING MONEY,* and the error in not practicing the *LAW OF INCREASE.*

The Kingdom of Heaven can be illustrated by the story of a man going into another country, who called together his servants and loaned them money to invest for him while he was gone. He gave $5000 to one. $2000 to another, and $1000 to the last—dividing it in proportion to their abilities— and then left on his trip. The man who received the $5000 began immediately to buy and sell with it and soon earned another $5000. The man with $2000 went right to work, too, and earned another $2000.

But the man who received the $1000 dug a hole in the ground and hid the money for safekeeping. After a long time their master returned from his trip and called them to him to account for his money. The man to whom he had entrusted the $5000 brought him $10,000.

His master praised him for good work. "You have been faithful in handling this small amount," he told him, "so now I will give you many more responsibilities."

Then the man with the $1000 came and said, "Sir, I knew you were a hard man, and I was afraid you would rob me of what I earned, so I hid your money in the earth and here it is." But his master replied, "Wicked man! Lazy slave! Since you knew I would demand your profit, you should at least have put my money into the bank so I could have some interest. Take the money from this man and give it to the man with the $10,000. For the man who uses well what he is given shall be given more, and he shall have abundance. But the man who is unfaithful, even what little responsibility he has shall be taken from him."

Let's analyze what the master considered good stewardship. He praised the two who "bought and sold" with the money entrusted to them, and gave them more. He severely reprimanded the one who dug a hole and buried the money, saying, "You should at least have put the money into the bank so I could have some interest." Note, however, that this was not what he recommended. Had the servant lived in the United States during the period when our banks paid 3 percent interest, in order for the money to have doubled, the master would have to have taken a twenty-four-year trip. Even if he had earned up to 5 percent, it would have taken 14.4 years. At 8 percent it would have been a nine year trip. The lesson here is loud and clear. Use any money you receive wisely. For the person who uses well what they have been given shall be given more and they shall enjoy abundance.

Now that we have covered some of the basics and hopefully have convinced you how important the concepts of *MONEY MAKING MONEY* and *PERSONAL FINANCIAL PLANNING* are, let's get into the specifics.

CHAPTER TWO

CAVEAT EMPTOR

LET THE BUYER BEWARE!

There is hardly an item or a service available today that you cannot be taken on. The following list of the top twenty complaints received at the United States Office of Consumer Affairs points out the fact that even products or services considered to be reputable are vulnerable to complaints by the consumer.

1. Automobiles
2. Business
3. Mail order
4. Appliances
5. Credit
6. Utilities
7. Housing
8. Advertising
9. Pricing
10. Health Care
11. Services
12. Travel
13. TV/Radio/Video
14. Periodicals
15. Insurance
16. Furniture
17. Home repairs
18. Tires
19. Mobile Homes
20. Computers

The Council of Better Business Bureaus reports the ratio of compaints settled to complaints received.

Lowest Percent of Complaints Settled

Legal services   Waterproofing Companies
Reupholstering   Auto Repair-Except transmission
Business opportunities   Market Research
Work at home opportunities Home Remodeling
Vacation certificates   Automotive
Paving contractors   Service stations
Miscellaneous Home Repair Hair Products

This list does not indicate that these industries had or did not have many complaints, only that of the complaints officially received, many were not resolved by the Better Business Bureaus.

General Rules for Shopping

The best way to avoid having to make a complaint is to shop with care. Getting the most real value for your dollar means being familiar with the several principles that the well-advised shopper uses when shopping.

Decision to Buy

The decision to buy should come from within. Don't be talked into something that you will regret later. The item or service must fit some physical or psychological need **and** your budget. As emotional as advertising tends to make buying, the best shoppers make cold, calculated decisions and then enjoy the benefits of the purchase.

Evaluations of the Buy

Once you have decided that you are going to buy, you should learn what you can about the potential purchases. Of

30

course, you will find that for smaller purchases you will not spend much time in the evaluation of which brand to buy. It simply is not worth the time and effort to spend hours shopping for a two dollar purchase. The best means of evaluation are listed below:

1. SHOPPING — as many stores and brands as you have time for.

2. CONSUMER MAGAZINES — will prepare you for what you see on the shelf.

3. FRIENDS' ADVICE — the more people you poll about a particular purchase the better your chances of getting reliable information. Not all people will be good shoppers as you will see.

The Other Considerations

1. Who the seller is — does he stand behind his product.

2. Time of year — chart below shows the best times of year for purchases.

3. Sales — be careful that it is on your list, some stores are **always** having sales. If you have really shopped around you should know a true sale and value.

4. Convenience stores — are expensive because they charge for convenience.

5. List — use a list of the items you are ready to purchase.

6. Cash — use cash money; doesn't earn interest in your

checking account and cash avoids overextension of credit and the budget.

7. Credit — only when convenience dictates.

8. Checks — if you are afraid to carry too much cash for a large purchase.

9. Quality — good equals poor quality; better equals good quality; best equals extravagant quality.

The following is a list of the most common times that particular items come on sale. If you can put off a needed purchase until the sale arrives you may find some good bargains.

Appliances — January, March, July, October
Autos — August, September, November, December
Bedding — January, August
Bicycles — January, September
Building materials — June
Carpets — February, July
Clothing — January, August
Fishing equipment — April, October
Furniture — January, July
Housewares — January, August
Stereos — January, May
TV's — May, June
White goods — January, May, August

Shopping to Eat

Would it be surprising to you if I told you that almost 25% of the money spent in the supermarket is for non-food items.

Paper, soap, health, beauty aids, liquor, etc. account for close to 25% of the tab at the checkout stand. So when itemizing your preliminary budget you will find that supermarket money will be projected most accurately by adding an allowance of 30% to your pure food budget amount. You will notice that supermarkets are becoming more like the old general store. Everything from oil for your car to perfumes is being offered at the local supermarket. So beware of those aisles that do not have the items you want on your list.

The facts show that nearly a majority of Americans are getting a poor diet. The culprit seems to be sugar. People are increasing the amount received from starches. Too much sugar is not good for you. A high sugar breakfast for example will give you a quick burst of energy then let you down with the 11 o'clock droopies. A protein and starch cereal will also give you a quick burst of energy but will not let you down with that burned out feeling later.

Food Buying Guidelines

1. Plan — your meals and your shopping.

2. List — use a list. It is convenient and saves time.

3. Shop — once a week on a full stomach. Shopping for food on an empty stomach only courts temptations for expensive gourmet items and snacks.

4. Buy — items that you may purchase at convenience stores can be purchased at substantial discounts in the supermarket.

5. Snacks — are expensive in general.

6. Prices — National brands are more expensive than store brands usually.

7. Economy sizes are economical if all the contents are used without wasteful leftover or spoilage.

8. Seasons — create cheap prices in the summer for fruits and various other items for vegetables. Satisfy yourself during the peak of the harvest when it's cheapest.

9. Meat — is expensive and too many of us indulge in huge amounts of pork and beef. Check the amount of fat and bone compared to the meat. Eat less red meat and more fish and fowl.

10. Compare — brands of the same item. Sometimes cheaper is better.

11. Clerks — watch them and count your change.

Restaurants

From fast food to chateaubriand restaurants cost more than home prepared food. The reason is simple, you are paying for the service provided in the preparation and serving of a meal. The same meal at a restaurant can cost from 10 to 100% more than the same food prepared at home. Restaurants can be economical when what you are ordering is the kind of dish that would involve the purchase of numerous food items that you would not normally buy and that will have portions unused and wasted due to the specialized nature of the dish. Restaurants are also economical if time is money for you and the time wasted preparing a meal could be better spent earning money. In other words if you were in and out of a restaurant in 20 minutes and it would have taken you an hour to prepare and eat the meal yourself, the difference of 40 minutes at $15 per hour would mean that you could spend much more for your meal in a restaurant and the difference to you would be winding up with more money than if you had taken a full hour with self service (assuming that the 40 minutes is extra work).

Liquor is one of the biggest items in restaurants. If you can nurse your drink or avoid alcoholic drinks altogether while dining, you will realize a considerable saving. Wine is one of the real profit makers for restaurant owners. With the price usually double of what normal retail prices are, you may want to have your wine at home.

Organic Food

Organic food is probably better for you if you can afford it. The strict definition of organic food is that food that is grown without the use of pesticides and chemical fertilizers. The theory is that such foods will be pure food, free of any contaminants and therefore your health will be maintained at its highest. The problem is that food grown under such conditions has a much lower productivity factor, so it costs more. Another problem is that with the development of sincere and professional organic growers and distributors has come a plague of frauds by those who label foods as organic that do not meet the true criteria. Be sure you buy your organic food from a reputable organic market and read the labels for contents to be sure that what you buy is indeed pure. Just because a label says "organic" does not guarantee anything. Study the labels of the various foods you buy regularly until you know which ones are indeed organic or as close as you can get.

The excessive amounts of fat, sugar, salt, cholesterol and

alcohol that make up the eating habits of too many people have been related to cancer of the stomach, breast, prostrate, liver and intestines. Another study indicates that those people contracting heart disease, angina, diabetes, and arthritis, were able to overcome the symptoms of these diseases in 90 days on a low fat, low sugar, high carbohydrate diet and a program of regular moderate exercise.

I take the time to go through the basics of a diet because properly prepared, a good diet will save you plenty in the way of shopping bills, by eliminating junk food and the potential savings in medical bills is astronomical!

Carbohydrates

Carbohydrates are grain products, vegetables, and sweets. The complex carbohydrates are grain and vegetables and are most important in your diet. Sugar use has been linked to diabetes and cholesterol. To the extent that grain and vegetables replace calories in your diet obtained from sugar and fats, they are most important. Contrary to popular belief that grain products will put weight on, is the fact that a lack of these products will contribute to a need to replace these essentials with harmful substitutes such as sugar and fat products.

Fat

Fat is an important part of the diet and is a necessary part of the diet. The problem in America with fats is the excessive use in the diet to the exclusion of complex carbohydrates. The excessive use of fat, especially animal fat in beef, veal and pork leads to high cholesterol and obesity, the most common causes of heart problems.

Protein

The highest source of protein are meat, fish, poultry, eggs, milk, and grains. The most efficient sources of protein are grains.

Vitamins

Vitamins can be broken down into two groups: fat soluble and water soluble. The fat soluble vitamins (A, D,E and K) are stored in the body and need not be replenished as often as the water soluble vitamins. Since the fat soluble vitamins are stored in the body it is possible to have an overdose. The water solubles (C, B-1, B-2, B-6, B-12 etc.) are found most often in vegetables; especially leafy vegetables and grains.

THE U.S. RECOMMENDED DAILY ALLOWANCES (RDA)

Protein—65 grams
Vitamin A—5000 units
Vitamin C—60 mg.
Vitamin B-1 Thiamin—1.5 mg.
Vitamin B-2 Riboflavin—1.7 mg.
Vitamin B-6 Pyridoxine—2.00
Vitamin B-12 Cobalamin—6 mcg
Vitamin D—400 units
Vitamin E—30 units

Freezers

Unless you live in a remote area or on a farm, the supposed savings of buying bulk and storing in a freezer will most often get eaten up in the cost of purchasing the freezer, the cost of operating the freezer (especially with electric bills climbing), and waste. Freezer plans that include the purchase of the side of beef are often aimed at the ignorant consumer with claims that the "saving from bulk buying will pay for the freezer." Often these plans are offered with low-down financing and high interest rates. Don't get caught in that game, rip-offs occur and if it was really such a deal everybody would have one. Fraud and deceptive practices abound in the beef-freezer business.

Liquor

Beer, wine and liquors can be a source of considerable savings. Below is a list of the way to save:

Find a good "house brand." You can always pour from a decanter.

Buy in bulk or large containers.

Limit drinking especially outside the house where you may have to drive.

Buy on sale.

Measure your drinks.

With mixed drinks you can usually get away without a name brand.

Price liquor by the ounce.

Clothing

Buying clothes is like buying anything else today, in order to get the best value for your dollar you must follow the fundamentals.

1. Follow your budget.

2. Make the decision to buy at home—don't buy on impulse.

3. Shop carefully and thoroughly until you know the merchandise.

4. Make the purchase on the best terms for you.

Clothes buying is a specialized process though, and the following guidelines and methods will make your clothing budget work efficiently.

1. Allocate a certain amount to each person in the family rather than an overall figure. Women and girls typically spend more for clothes.

2. Plan your wardrobe. The best way to begin your plan is to take an inventory of what you presently have.

3. Buy your seasonal clothing well in advance. Winter clothing should be purchased in early fall and summer clothes in early spring.

4. Underclothes, socks, stockings, etc. are best bought on sale.

5. A few high quality clothes are better and will be a better

value than lots of cheap clothes in general. High quality does not necessarily mean the most expensive. Check the seams, buttons, button holes, type of material and zippers.

6. Buy a wardrobe that is color coordinated. Stick to the more standard type and avoid fad clothing.

7. Rapidly growing children should pass their clothes on to smaller children. Friends and relatives with children may be a good source of clothing.

8. Adults know your sizes. Write your size down and keep it with your records. Always try on clothes to make sure they fit properly. Different styles and brands do vary.

Clothes Care Costs

Proper maintenance of your wardrobe will keep your clothing its best for the longest time. Cutting costs of cleaning as well as preserving longevity can be effected by purchase of easy care clothing and quality clothing. Here are some tips for care of clothing.

1. Permanent press fibers are the easiest to care for. To get the most out of these fabrics, wash in small loads; immediately put them in the dryer at the low temperature setting and when they are dry immediately put them on a hanger. Buttoning the top two buttons will keep shirt collars from wrinkling. Pants should be hung up by their full length.

2. Most clothes that recommend dry cleaning can be hand washed.

3. Dry cleaning bills can be reduced by dry cleaning at coin

operated dry cleaners.

When using stain removers always read the directions and test the product in an inconspicuous place on the garment. Let it dry to be sure that the stain remover does not also remove the fabric!

Appliances

Appliances are another set of nifty items that require care before selection. Almost all appliances are labor saving devices except TV's and stereos. To be sure you are getting a labor saving device, check carefully the quality of the appliance. Check with others to find out their experiences with a potential purchase. The best place to check is the Consumer's Union rating service. This is a periodical with monthly issues and special annual reports on products. The service reports the brand name and model number for a wide range of appliances test results. With this service you can call a number of stores with the brand and model number you found best in your price range and request a price. So simply by checking at the local library in the Consumer's Union report and a number of phone calls you are fully prepared to enter an appliance store or department and make your judgments about the appliance based on a demonstration. If everything checks out you can buy confidently, knowing that you have done a good job of shopping.

Try to buy appliances on sale where discounts of 10-30% are significant dollar amounts $5 to $60 and more, can be saved. But beware of sales or discounts at stores that perpetually discount items. Again, if you have checked around sufficiently, you will know if an item is a bargain. Model clearance sales usually are genuine sales. Floor models should be adequately discounted. Ask how long its been on the floor. Discounts should be at least 10% if you cannot see anything wrong and more if there is some damage. Used appliances can be a rip-off if you do not buy from a reputable dealer who will warrant the product. As-is deals are strictly luck if you get a good deal. Also used items should be substantially discounted from the new price. Paying more than ½ or ⅓ of the new price should be a maximum.

T.V.'s

I have provided some guidelines to be used in the purchase of a television.

1. Make your decision regarding whether or not you need a new TV and if it will fit the budget at this time.

2. Become familiar with the various models and features and their prices. Use a note pad to take notes for comparison.

3. Find out about the warranty.

4. Check the picture for clarity and distortion.

5. Determine what type of antenna you will need. Color TV sets require larger antennas.

6. Make sure the brand you buy has adequate service in your region or the region you may be moving to. If you don't have an authorized service center in your area, repairs will be costly and time-consuming.

7. Here are some further considerations to cope with after you get to this point:

— Buy solid state circuitry.

— Check the specifications for the numbers of IF stages—it should have 3.

— Make sure the set will fit in with your decor at your home.

— Do not lease or rent a TV, the rates are usually equal the payments you would make if you had bought it new. If you need a TV temporarily you can usually find a used one that works in the paper or at the store for about $30. Unless you need your TV for less than 3 months it will probably be cheaper to buy a used set.

Stereo

Stereophonic equipment sales is a highly competitive field so you should be extra careful to shop around for a set that will suit your requirements. Stereo equipment is offered in AM and FM radios, record players, tape players, eight track, and cassette players, portable models and combinations of the above. In short, you name it in stereo and you can buy it.

To get an idea about what you want, first go to several stores and try out some of the equipment and compare some prices. When you have decided on what quality of sound you want—go to the library and check the Consumer's Union Reports. Then compare prices and look for sales till you feel ready to make the purchase.

Remember —

—Records are cheaper than tapes.

— The cassette is considered to be trouble-free compared to the 8 track.

43

— The system will be as strong as its weakest component.

— Service can be very important.

— Turn the sound up to check distortion in the system and speakers.

Repairs

The first thing to do is check in your records for the warranty to see what the warranty covers. This, of course, assumes that your appliance really needs repair. To be sure it does need repair, go through this checklist to save time and money:

— Plug — is it plugged in?

— Check the fuses in machine (after you unplug it) and in the circuit.

— Ask someone with a mechanical aptitude to look at it to see what can be done.

If the above fails to produce the desired results, contact a few reliable repair people and ask them what they think it is, what it will cost to fix, and what the part costs and what their hourly rates are. How far you get with these questions and what you are able to compare will tell you who to take the appliance to. Always bring the appliance in if possible, it's cheaper.

Get an estimate from the repair people before they start work. You are entitled to such an estimate. Or ask them to call you if repairs are more than $5 or $10. If the estimate is too high, you will definitely want to get another opinion because it may be cheaper in the long run to buy a new appliance.

Utilities And Energy

Your utility bills have undoubtedly increased in the last few years and the energy crunch only promises higher fuel electricity bills in the future. A geometric increase in worldwide energy use, and limited technology, indicate that the future holds shortages and increased prices for you in the years to come.

To hedge against such an eventuality and current bill, there are several things you can do to save. Incidently, if you own your own home, making such improvements as outlined here will increase the value of your home and make it more comfortable to live in.

1. Install storm windows to cut heat loss, through glass windows, one of the worst offenders in heat loss. Also buy heavy drapes and close them at night.

2. Insulate your attic. You can do this yourself or hire a contractor. Many utility companies have programs for financing and contracting the insulation of your attic. Saving may run as much as 25% per year. Be wary of private contractors and as in any contract get the correct specifications and put it all down in the contract estimate. Get several estimates and pick the one that gives you the most value for your money. Insulation varies in quality from R-22 that should be a minimum of 10" thick to R-11 which should be at least 5" thick. Make your contractor prove that he is bonded and that his workers are covered for disability—if he is not covered, you may be liable for damages and/or injuries.

3. Use weatherstripping or caulking around doors and windows to prevent drafts and heat loss.

4. Let the sun shine on your house. If folliage, trees and awnings are blocking the sun from hitting your house, you will profit by trimming and removing these things that block the sun from warming your house.

5. If you have a swimming pool, get a cover for it to save 30% of heating cost. Turn the heater off in winter months and "spot" heat if you plan to use it one weekend. The optimum pool temperature is 78 degrees, according to the American Red Cross, but you can reduce your pool heating costs 25% by keeping the temperature at 75 degrees. Use an immersion bulb thermometer to measure in your pool. Better than all the above is to invest in a reliable solar heater for your pool. Do be thorough in your investigation of solar heaters as there are many that do not measure up to reasonable standards. Also, do not store pool chemicals in the same structure as your heater as these chemicals are highly corrosive and combustible.

The Phone Bill

People complain most often about the amount of their phone bill, yet by following a few simple rules your bill can be substantially reduced.

— Dial long distance yourself. Collect, person to person, etc. are sometimes double or more of regular rates.

— Take advantage of the lower rates advertised in the evenings and early morning hours.

— Organize what you are saying.

— Write a letter if this is practical.

— Get credit for reaching a wrong number on long distance calls. Just tell the operator.

—Use your home phone instead of expensive pay phones.

Safety

Exercising safety measures will prevent accidents that can be costly not only in terms of dollars and time, but most important to your health. Taking the time to go through the following lists may be one of the most important steps in your lifetime. Your health is the most important thing. So do it now while you are reading.

Fire Protection

Smoking, matches, wiring, appliances, heating equipment, and chimneys are the leading causes of fires in the United States today. Check your personal habits to see if you are playing with fire. As a means to cut back on smoking some of my friends have decided not to smoke in the bedroom.

— Is your house or apartment equipped with enough ashtrays or do you leave your cigarette sitting on the counter where it can be inadvertently knocked on the floor to star a fire?

— Make sure appliances are working properly and that wires and plugs are not frayed, dried or cracked.

— Service your furnace or heating system once a year per service instructions and clean the filter monthly.

— Keep a fully charged fire extinguisher available and make sure everyone can use it.

— Check with the local fire department to determine the best extinguisher type for you. Do not use water type on electric fires; you could be shocked.

— Keep your chimney clear and get an approved fire screen.

— Do not put a heavier fuse in your electric box unless you check it out with a qualified electrician. Fuses are put there to stop overloads; Don't defeat this safety feature.

— Fuses or circuit breakers continually go out or appliances do not operate properly. Make an appointment to have an electrician check out your system for your safety and peace of mind.

— Use non-flammable cleaning agents.

— Remove old newspapers and oily rags that may begin burning on their own.

— Get a smoke detector that is approved by UL, and your local fire department.

Household Safeguards

Thousands die each year from accidents around the house including falls down the stairs, from the roof, off ladders, in the shower, through glass doors and on loose rugs. Use caution in these matters by providing adequate lighting on stairs.

Put a non-slip pad in the shower. Check out glass doors for safety and if necessary put decals, available in variety stores, on the glass doors. Secure rugs to the floor.

Children are often the victims of other's neglect for safety. Haul off old refrigerators, take the door off or wire it shut. Keep cleaning liquids, medicines, garden chemicals, soaps and the like out of reach and locked up from children.

Pests can be a real problem in the house and garden if they are not taken care of. It is possible to control some insects without the heavy toxic pesticides.

Aphids—Lady bugs eat aphids as well as mites. Lacewings also eat aphids and mites and moth eggs. Preying Mantises will eat any insect smaller than itself.

Cockroaches—Sprinkle boric acid powder in the infected area or put the powder in crumbs in area.

Flys—Fly swatter, fly paper are effective. Make fly paper with molasses spread on paper.

Fleas—Try a flea collar made of eucalyptus seed.

Many carcinogens remain on the market despite tests proving their cancer-causing characteristics. Some are still on the market because the tests have been contradicted by other tests. And others are generally accepted as being carcinogenic in high doses, yet remain on the market. For instance, the government allows Red dye No. 4 in Maraschino cherries because they figure that the average person will not consume too many cherries, 4 a day!! To reduce your chance of cancer avoid or do the following:

— Drink purified water.

— Avoid excessive use of cosmetic and skin preparations that are suspected of being carcinogenic.

— Avoid use of poisonous and carcinogenic chemicals.

— Do not smoke any substance.

— Do not eat bacon or meats like hot dogs containing sodium nitrate.

— Clean vegetables thoroughly.

— Do not eat beef liver where DES accumulates. Women should not take DES.

— Do not sit closer than 6 feet from a color TV set and check with the US Consumer Product Safety Commission to see if your old set emits too much radiation.

— Avoid x-rays if possible and have a lead shield placed on you to protect your organs. Radiation has a cumulative effect. Make sure your microwave oven does not leak radiation.

— Wear an approved filter breathing mask when working in a dusty area or where the air is clogged with heavy particles.

Burglary

Burglaries have always been a serious problem so take preventive measures to increase your chances against being a victim of burglary!

Be especially careful during the holiday when burglaries increase. Use a dead bolt on all wood doors and get a "pin" to lock sliding glass doors.

If you go on vacation use a timed light to turn on lights and a radio in the evening, have a neighbor pick up the mail and papers, and notify the police of your departure and expected time of return.

Have a peephole put in your door to see who is there. Participate in Operation Identification and put a sticker in your window.

Consider a burglar alarm system and dobermans (dogs), if you keep valuable artwork and jewelry at home.

Check the reputation of those working around your home (remember casual labor should be insured.)

Sending Packages

Freight rates vary considerably depending on the carrier, speed of delivery you desire, and convenience. Be sure your package is well wrapped preferably in cardboard with heavy paper and twine. Write the address with a felt pen and put a return address and point of origin on the package. Insure fragile or valuable contents.

Check with the various services available to see what the particulars are for what you are sending and where you are sending it.

Bus

Bus service involves taking your package to the bus station and having the recipient pick it up. The most efficient bus service is between large cities at a short distance. If you are sending across long distances, the bus services will take more time as the package will have to be transfered.

Parcel Delivery Services

The large carriers provide door to door delivery and have numerous services beside the standard delivery. All are relatively efficient and fast. If the recipient is not at the address when the service attempts a delivery, then a note will be left and several more attempts made. Finally if the service cannot deliver to the recipient or a neighbor, the recipient may have to pick it up.

U.S. Postal Service

Parcel post is the cheapest and therefore slowest service offered by the Post Office. However, if you have planned ahead far enough, this economical service will provide entirely adequate service.

Priority mail is processed by hand as compared to machine with parcel post and is therefore faster and more expensive.

Express mail service will guarantee delivery in about a day and one-half or give a full refund. This is the U.S. Post Office's fastest service and is expensive. However, the difference between 50 miles and 2,000 miles is only a couple of dollars.

To Your Health

High medical prices have been the subject of much discussion and complaining, yet, you the consumer are one of the primary causes. You demand excellent care and if something goes wrong are quick to serve a "Notice you have been sued!" paper on your physician. Generally physicians are very well trained and ethical people—most suits don't pay off. However, this barrage of suits has increased your health bill with higher malpractice insurance premiums and extensive double checking on diagnoses. High quality care means increased accuracy in diagnoses and shorter stays in the hospital with a better chance of living a normal life in the event of a serious illness. If hospitals are now $100/day and you stay two days, that's better than $50/day and a four day stay.

The average person visits the doctor about 5 times a year for various reasons and the dentist once or twice a year. You should budget yourself and family members for this amount and have a sufficient amount in your emergency fund to cover medical emergencies that are not covered under your insurance plan.

There are ways to reduce the amount spent on medical services if not the services. Find a doctor who is competent and reputable. If you are new in town and cannot get recommendations from satisfied patients whom you know, then check with the local medical society for a doctor who is listed on the staff of a good hospital or clinic (not necessarily large). Having your own doctor is most important in saving money as only your doctor knows your history. Often minor complaints can be handled over the phone without having to make a visit.

Do not ask for house visits unless absolutely necessary. Let the doctor determine this. House calls are expensive. Physicians fees should be discussed so that you know what the charge will be, and if you know what the charge will be, and if you have some difficulty in paying, arrangements can sometimes be made for a reduction in fee or terms cut, check this out first. It will put you in a better position.

Get an annual physical exam especially if your family or you have had a history of serious illnesses. The essentials of a physical will include:

Blood pressure, breast examination, Pap smear, eye examination, urinalysis, stool analysis and blood test.

Shop for a hospital to find one that provides the most services for the least charge. Unfortunately doctors do not associate with all hospitals and limit their associations. Check with your doctor to see which hospitals he is associated with so you can compare services. A university teaching hospital will generally have a more sophisticated staff. If you have to use an emergency room or an ambulance your choice will depend on the amount of service provided and the rates. Some are going to provide the same services for less.

Surgery is a major expense and though most of us are covered by insurance, it is not the sort of thing you just say OK to. Major abuses have occured in the recommendation of surgeries as indicated by differences in rates of surgery for different states—some have over 1000% differences in the rates of surgery. If surgery is recommended to you, get an independent opinion. Find a specialist on your own and tell him you want an opinion only, that he definitely will not be performing the surgery if it is indicated.

Many people are having cosmetic surgery in this modern age. If you are vain enough to proceed with such an operation be sure that you get a thoroughly reputable physician who specializes in the particular surgery of your desire. Check with your regular physician for a recommendation and be sure to see if the doctor is board certified and call the County Clerk to see if he is named in any malpractice suits.

Drugs

You can save considerably on prescription drugs by 1. shopping for a pharmacy and 2. asking your doctor to use generic names for prescriptions. Generic named drugs are up to 500% cheaper than brand named drugs. The chemical composition is the same only the name has been changed because the drug is marketed by a different company. Pregnant women should be very cautious about taking drugs of any kind. Evidence has linked the use of drugs, alcohol, nicotine and aspirin to abnormal babies. Give the kid a chance to decide for himself what drugs he wants. Drugs are most dangerous in the first three months of pregnancy.

Most over the counter drugs are used to aid healing or ease pain. Always read the precautions on the label. Simply put: some work and some don't. Aspirin is the most effective for many ailments. Antacids will do the job. Acne preparations main job is to cleanse the skin and this can be done effectively with an antibacterial soap. First aid ointments containing Bacitracira, Polymixin B sulfate with a complementary drug and tetracycline are effective. Antiperspirant manufacturers were sweating in 1973 when problems with sirconium surfaced. The common cold has no cure and mustard oil, oil of turpentine, expectorant ingredients, anticholinergics ingredients are considered not safe and effective. Diet aids are considered not safe and effective. Hearing aids should be recommended by a doctor. Most sleeping pills are not very effective and should not be taken often.

BIRTH CONTROL

If you do not practice the most effective form of birth control (no intercourse) and yet do feel responsible for any life that may be forth coming there are several methods to exercise control.

Oral contraceptives are the most effective means of control and they are relatively inexpensive but there are drawbacks such as increases in the chances of serious illness such as stroke and heart problems.

After oral contraceptives and ranking very close, IUD's (intrauterine devices) are the next most effective means of contraception and after that in order are prophylactic devices, diaphragms with cream or jelly alone. The risk of death from childbirth is less in all contraceptives above except with oral contraceptives for women over 40 years old.

Vasectomy, hysterectomy, and other contraceptive operations are also an alternative and in the case of a vasectomy may be cheaper in the long run. Operations are generally permanent.

BUYING A CAR

The purchase of an automobile represents a substantial investment for most families and should therefore be the object of intense scrutiny. Knowing what you can afford, shopping the market place, and negotiating the sale are the basic components of a successful purchase. Since buying a car is a large purchase, large savings can be had or large losses can be the result of being had.

Decide whether you want a new car or a used car first. New cars represent the best automobile; trouble free driving and the most modern comfort and safety—new cars also cost the most. The variety of used cars is endless. For the same price as a new compact you can get an older large car. Used cars are cheaper than new cars but a used car is a used car, i.e. it has been driven X miles, has X dents, and has X miles left to drive. The easiest way to decide if you want a new or a used car is to decide the type of car large-small, sport-sedan, etc. When you put type and price together it will be evident whether a new or used is the way to go. If you need help deciding what you can afford in the way of monthly payments call or drop by your bank and tell your loan officer what you are considering in the way of dollars in payments then ask what you can qualify for. The bank loan officer will need to know if you are considering a new or used car so be prepared. Often the bank will make a tentative commitment for a loan of x dollars or x percentage of value at specified rate usually 11 to 15% APA at x $$ per month for x months.

Go to the library and look up the Consumer's Union reports. Also check the other auto magazines for their reports on new cars.

Now you are ready to seriously look at and test drive the makes you have decided on for a closer inspection. Take your paper with you and fill out your information for each make. You will have to get the salesman's help with the final price-out the door. Don't be afraid to show him your sheet. If anything the sheet will indicate that you are a serious buyer who is knowledgeable so you will get better service. If you don't get good sales help and the salesman tries to discount your comparison approach, there is a good probability that he knows his make will not compare favorably. This may not always be the case but it is something to look out for, because an experienced salesman will know if his car is the deal in a particular class. However, do not be so naive as to believe it if he tells you he has the best deal. Just get a complete written price: tax, license, preparation, extras, as you want, and take a test drive. Thank the man as you note the results.

Getting a bargain price on a new car can be an exhilarating experience. The bargain price you might have guessed, is somewhat lower than the sticker or suggested retail price. Dealers mark up small cars about 15%, intermediate and standard about 20% and luxury about 25%. Accessories are marked up about 50%. To figure what you should pay, add

— Base price (Intermediate)	6,000
20% Mark up	—1,200
	4,800
Accessories total	+1,000
— 50% of 1,000	5,800
	—500
Dealer's Approx. cost	5,300
Dealer's Profit (5-15%)	+600
	5,900
Dealer Preparation & Freight	+300
	Price you want to pay 6,200
(Plus tax & License)	Sticker Price 7,300

You may not always get such a discount but if you shop during the slack months, during a blizzard, during an advertised special you should be able to get a good price.

TRADE INS

If you have the time and are willing to sell your own car, it is possible to make money by selling your car yourself rather than trading it in. But make these considerations first:

—What can you sell the car for?

— What will advertising cost? Try free papers and word of mouth.

— How much time will it take?

— What will a dealer give me for it? (In some states trade ins reduce the price of the car and the amount of sales tax paid. Hence, if you were to get $2000 plus 6% or $2,120 selling it yourself plus advertising and your time.)

58

— Maybe you can get more selling it yourself.

USED CARS

When purchasing a used automobile one of the most important questions to answer is who am I dealing with? You can buy a used car either from a dealer or a private party. With either one you will have to be cautious and keep a wary eye for fast talk. Check with the Better Business Bureau for complaints about your prospective dealer. Usually the used car lots that are part of a major dealership will be the most reputable and have the best cars.

Since most of the depreciation in a car happens in the first year or two it makes sense that a two year old, well maintained automobile may be a good place to start looking at used cars.

Know the value of your prospective car. Your bank will show you the range of values in a book of used car price averages. Look at several, at least 4, of the type of car which you want to compare prices and conditions.

	#1	#2	#3	#4
Where Seen				
Year and Model				
Miles				
Price				
Tires				
Battery				
Brakes				
Interior				
Paint/Body				
Clutch/Transmission				
Testdrive/Engine				

Invest in a mechanic's opinion before closing the deal. A mechanic can not only tell you how your prospective car is running but how much the car is worth to some degree. Always read your purchase agreement thoroughly. Warrantees are something you ask for after you get a written price because a dealer will otherwise boost the price to meet the cost of a warranty.

LEASING AN AUTO

There are two ways to lease an automobile basically, closed end and open end leases. The closed end lease is generally more expensive as the lessee makes a fixed monthly payment for the term of the lease, where in the less expensive open end lease the lessee carries some of the risk. The risk is carried by the lessee because under an open end lease the lessee agrees to a residual value for the car at the end of the lease. If the car cannot be sold for the residual value, then the lessee will have to pay the difference. On the other hand if the car is worth more than the residual value, the lessee will receive the difference.

To compare leases check these features in the agreement:

Maintenance
Insurance
Tire Replacement
Dents
Excess mileage
Lease cancellation
Initial costs
Monthly payment
Residual value (open end only)

Leasing can be cheaper if you buy a new car every year or

two and/or you use your car strictly for business. If you keep your car for three years or more it will generally be cheaper to buy. The advantages to leasing are no downpayment, and very little bargaining.

VACATION TIME

Take your time shopping for a vacation. It will not only save your money; it will be an enjoyable experience. Half the fun of taking a vacation is getting there and half the savings can be generated by knowing how to get the bargains in transportation. The other half of savings can be had in the form of savings on meals and lodging. The easiest and most convenient way to find out what is available is to find a good travel agent.

TRAVEL AGENTS

The best way to determine if you are working with a reliable agent is to check on the prices he quotes you. The best way to find a competent agent who is knowledgeable about all the tours is to compare responses of several agents to the same questions regarding a particular vacation you have planned.

If you decide a travel agent is not for you and you want to make all your own arrangements, you will find that it may be easier for weekend holidays to nearby locations you are familiar with. Far away locations particularly overseas destinations will require quite a bit of investigation and the agent can help you out considerably in this respect.

AIR

The largest savings can be effected by booking well in advance in economy class. First class can be ⅓ to ½ more expensive. Flying at night, during the week, and during off season can also save you money. There are a multitude of bargain air fares—your travel agent can point you in the right direction.

RAIL

Amtrack, this nation's passenger rail service, has modernized and upgraded train service throughout the country. Fares are competitive with air transportation. Check your local directory for the Toll free number.

If you plan to use a Eurailpass for traveling in Europe be sure to get it in the United States—it will be too late if you want to get that bargain transportation in Europe because its only available in the U.S. So buy before you go so that you will have it when you get there.

HOTELS AND MOTELS

Someone once said, "Parks are the cheapest hotels," but if you want more comfort or are staying in a large city, having a convenient, clean, and perhaps plush accomodations will make your stay nicer. To assure proper accomodations always 1) be familiar with the hotel and the area it's in and 2) make reservations and give yourself plenty of time to check in. The newest and most modern hotels will be the most expensive. If you're just driving through why not pick out the least expensive accomodations that will suit your taste.

P.T. Barnum said "there's a sucker born every minute"

and despite all the consumer protection information available, that statement is still as true today as it was when Mr. Barnum was alive.

There are no reliable statistics on consumer fraud. Like rape, a lot of consumer fraud goes unreported.

CAVEAT EMPTOR

Caveat Emptor — let the buyer beware, is the watch word of the day. Fraudulent schemers are always with us, in good or bad times. However, when the times get tough, there is usually a substantial increase in unethical and downright illegal activity.

Millions of consumers are cheated out of billions of dollars each year by con artists. Far too often it is our own greed that lures us into the hands of a swindler. Often we are terribly gullible, sometimes just plain careless.

It has been estimated that over 90 percent of the victims are not aware they have been cheated until it's far too late to do anything about it. Those that may be aware of having been defrauded are reluctant to report it to the police, either out of embarrassment or out of belief that the police won't do anything about it. And that's often the case — not because the police don't want to, but because their available manpower is allocated toward more serious matters. Thus, with few exceptions, promoters and swindlers run free throughout our society, taking advantage of our weaknesses, our greed, our gullibility, and our basically trusting nature.

This chapter will explore some of the more common types of consumer fraud. Every type of fraud has endless variations, so don't for a moment think that the schemes described here are the only ones that you might fall victim to. In any kind of transaction you must be aware of certain basic patterns, which can indicate that you might be involved in a fraudulent setup. The basic patterns appear in the following situations:

You're led to believe that you're getting something for nothing or are offered a deal that sounds too good to be true. There is no such thing as "something for nothing" and any deal that sounds too good to be true is usually neither good nor true.

A salesperson (or even a stranger) tries to sell you something with such vigor or with such cleverness that you find yourself on the verge of spending money for something that you might otherwise have ignored. In such cases you must immediately ask yourself, "if this thing he's selling is so good and so beneficial, then why is he willing to sell it to me? Could it be that he'll get more benefit out of it by selling it to me than I can by buying it from him?"

The advertiser or the salesperson tells you that you can obtain something that is not otherwise available through normal channels. This may be a miracle cure for some ailment, a chance to get rich quick, or a chance to become famous. These offerings will do nothing but deplete your bank account.

One final warning before we embark on tales of the wild and wooly world of consumer fraud: While most advertising media (newspapers, magazines, radio, television) attempt to police the advertising that they present to the public, there are definitely flaws in the system. Some policing efforts are not adequate, and misleading advertising can slip past the censor's scrutiny. Further, misleading advertising that appears in an otherwise legitimate medium takes on an aura of legitimacy. "It must be so if it appeared in the daily paper. If it weren't legitimate, the newspaper wouldn't run it." Being constantly alert is no guarantee that you'll never get stung. But lack of constant alertness will almost guarantee that you will get stung.

BAIT AND SWITCH RACKETS

The oldest con game of them all. First the sharpie offers a "fantastic value" to put you in a very receptive frame of mind. The switch occurs when you are in the store ready, willing and anxious to buy. The clever salesperson diverts you from the bait item and switches you to another item that offers him a higher profit. The switch can happen in many ways, and even otherwise legitimate merchants often find themselves slipping into this form of deception.

For instance, you're sitting up with insomnia watching late late show on television, and here comes good old Gideon Gotcha "out here in automobile land ready to sell you folks some real zing-doozies of some beautiful cars of all makes and models. Here's a 1980 Cadillac with only 1600 miles on it, in perfect condition, with brand new radial-ply-biased-steel-double-whitewall-hand-autographed tires, and a built-in Hammond organ in the back seat! About $15,000? Maybe at some other place, but not at Gideon Gotcha's! Would you believe only $3995!"

Right then you rush down to Gideon Gotcha's where, of course, you find that the lot is closed for the night! You camp on the doorstep until morning and when Gideon comes in to open up the shop, you hand him an envelope full of cash and tell him you want to buy the $3995 Cadillac you saw on television just a few hours ago.

"Oh, I'm really sorry," says Gideon, "but we sold it during the night. I got a call at my house from an old customer out in the country who insisted on having that very car, and he sent a courier at 4:00 a.m. with the cash. But now that you're here, maybe I can interest you in a brand new

Cadillac whose classic beauty will withstand the years better than the Mona Lisa. And since you came down so early in the morning, I could make a special deal for you.

While auto dealers may be the number one traditional culprits in bait and switch rackets, any merchant (furniture stores, video and stereo shops, carpet dealers, and hundreds of other companies) can play this insideous game.

Bait and switch tactics are outlawed by the Federal Trade Commission as well as by many state and local laws. But they still occur in abundance, and your best protection against getting involved is your own careful scrutiny of the advertising, your willingness to shop around for similar products, and your ability to resist the temptation in the first place.

Distinction should be made between bait and switch on the one hand and "loss leaders" on the other. A loss leader is a product offered by a merchant at a lower-than-normal price to entice you into the store where, it's hoped, you'll buy other merchandise as well as the loss leader. Supermarkets and discount stores use loss leaders all the time, and there's nothing wrong with this practice if you are getting the goods as represented and not a cheap replacement.

Where loss-leader advertising is employed, legitimate merchants will note in their advertising any catches in their offering, such as a limited supply, or will make clear that the offer is good only at certain stores or at certain hours. The Federal Trade Commission says that if a loss leader or other kind of promotional product is offered, the merchant is expected to have a sufficient amount on hand to meet what he reasonably expects to be the demand. Many merchants, realizing the value of pleasing their customers, will offer rainchecks if they run out of the supply of a loss leader. It might be worth inquiring of the merchant whether rainchecks will be given out should you get to the store and find that the loss-leader items are sold out.

If you detect a bait and switch operation in action in your community, alert the newspapers (or radio or TV station) where the advertising was placed. You may also want to notify the local Better Business Bureau.

YOUR VANITY CAN BE YOUR DOWNFALL

An ego out of control is the delight of a vanity racketeer. The vanity rackets prey on the common desire in so many people to be recognized. Ads offer to publish your book, your song, your poem, even your baby's picture in a directory sent to television products.

Anyone who has ever tried to have a song or book published through normal channels knows how frustrating it can be; rejection slips pour in, and it seems as though there's no way ever to achieve success. How wondrous it is, then, when you see an ad by a publisher soliciting your work. "Authors wanted" — "Songwriters wanted." Technically the ads may not be illegal — they promise nothing specifically, but the high hopes of the victim-to-be lead him to believe that fame and fortune are just around the corner.

In the legitimate publishing world, most books and songs are created by established artists under contract to the publisher. In those rare instances when a publisher will acquire your work, he will pay you for the rights to publish.

In the vanity publishing world, the publishers will publish virtually anything, provided you pay them enough money. They may actually deliver printed copies of your book manuscript or produce recordings of your song, but the veiled promises of fame and fortune will never materialize. You will have paid a high price to have your ego massaged.

In his book *PUBLISHING FOR PROFIT,* author Russ von Hoelscher had this to say about vanity-type publishers . . . "The Vanity-style publishers who also use other names (subsidy, cooperative, etc.) are another means to "break into print." They may or may not be book printers (many are not, but they use various printers and act as printing jobbers). It is my opinion that this type of "publishing" operation is the most deceptive operation any would-be author can find himself in association with. Picture yourself swimming in the beautiful blue Pacific Ocean on a warm summer day. You glance over your shoulder and stare at a twenty-five-foot Great White Shark looking suspiciously like the monster in the film "Jaws" rushing toward you. His fierce teeth are bared and you're feeling more than a little uneasy. You then notice a waving sign tied to his dorsal fin that says, "Hi there, new author. I'm ready to help you. Let's cooperate." Somehow, you don't really believe it, and if you're smart, you desperately swim toward shore. Get the picture? Perhaps I've been overly dramatic in this illustration, but frankly, I consider these literary con artists to be sharks. They might not eat humans, but they do feed on an author's money and efforts!

In the late seventies and early eighties the words "Vanity" or "Subsidy" publishing has become so unpopular that many in this type of operation went searching for a new banner. "Co-op publishing" or "Co-op publishing and distributing" are now popular slogans being used by former "Vanity"-type houses. Regardless of the names used, the results are usually the same. The "publisher" implies that he will share the expenses with the author. He almost always is "thrilled" after reading the author's manuscript and strongly suggests the author sign his contract and "get published" at once. Usually he states that many copies can be sold so that the author can not only get back his original investment but also receive a "nice profit."

In recent years competition has become so fierce between these operators that their sophisticated sales literature began making more and more irrational statements, all promising authors great rewards for signing on the dotted line. So many complaints were filed with various government agencies that the Federal Trade Commission (FTC) finally was forced into action. They issued "cease and desist" orders against many Vanity and Co-operative publishing companies. Many of those still in business have suits filed against them, but still continue to operate while fighting legal battles.

LAZY WAYS TO GET RICH QUICK

Like Ivory soap, the mails may be 99.4% pure, but look out for that 0.56%!

Get rich quick schemes abound from silly, unworkable home-work plans, often a few sloppy printed pages, sold for ten dollars or more a pop, to "sucker" lotteries and chain-letter rackets that almost always disappoint participants.

When economic times get tough, get-rich schemes and chain-letter con artists come out of their holes in record numbers.

Keep in mind there are many legitimate multi-level products and services sold locally by many names, but don't confuse these with worthless chain letter operations. How do you know the difference? One sure-fire method is to evaluate the product or service. Does it offer some kind of value? Or are you being asked to send money to people you don't know in hopes that "thousands" of other strangers will soon be sending you money? Common sense will usually allow you to separate the guys wearing the white Stetsons as opposed to those wearing the black hats.

Another "get-rich" scheme that will profit no one except an unscrupulous promoter, is one of the "addressing envelopes" home-work schemes. The person answering the home-work ad may have visions of earning some extra money stuffing envelopes. More often than not, they will be asked to pay for a kit of envelopes, circulars, etc., that gives them the privilege to mail out commission circulars advertising the company's services or products. Any orders received will pay the homeowner a commission. However, nine times out of ten, he or she won't even get back mailing expenses. How does the company make out? A whole lot better! First they have hundreds of homeworkers paying for the printed ads, catalogs or circulars they produce and secondly, their hapless clients pay the postage to mail them to potential buyers. Thirdly, they receive at least half of all money generated to fill the orders. With enough homeworkers they can prosper while their "partners" slowly (but not too slowly) lose any money they invest in the bogus "home-work" operation.

SNAKE OIL SHAMS

"Lose Twenty Pounds in a Week," ... "Live to be 120" .... "Cure Baldness Overnight' ... "Dramatically increase your Bust Line" ... "Instantly Cure What Ails You" ... "Become a Sex Dynamo" ... These type of ads, offering instant benefits, are reminders of a colorful character of America's past, known as "Snake Oil Sam" who sold caramel-flavored alcohol to the gullible from his traveling sideshow wagon. In some of his stops he used a bible-pounding preacher to attract a crowd, in others a couple of dancing girls and a magician accomplished the same task.

Let your common sense direct you. If it sounds too good to be true, it probably is. What makes these types of shams extremely dangerous is that the gullible can lose more than their money, their health could be endangered by some of the highly questionable products often sold by these quacks.

HOME IMPROVEMENT SCHEMES

You don't always have to go out looking for con artists. Sometimes they'll come to you, either knocking on your door or calling on the telephone. As with street schemes, the element of surprise works in favor of the con man. He's prepared to sell you something, and you're totally unprepared for his pitch. And since he's coming to you rather than you going to his place of business, you have no way of knowing if you can ever find him again if things go wrong.

Demand credentials from anyone offering home improvements (that includes yard work, masonry, air-conditioning or heating, tree trimming, etc..) Ask them to give you references, do not sign any contract unless you are 100 percent satisfied that your interests are fully protected. Also, never pay in advance.

CAREFULLY READ — THEN REREAD
ANY CONTRACT

The quick-talking salesman knocked at the door and told the gullible young couple that their house had been chosen as part of an advertising program. They would receive a "free" aluminum siding job on the house. All they had to do was tell their friends and neighbors and any passerby who had done this magnificent work. Thereby, the home improvement company would receive many referrals and everybody would be happy. The young couple couldn't sign the contract fast enough.

The work was done, and a month later, to the couple's amazement, they received a bill from a finance company for the first installment on a very expensive contract. Then - too late - they read the contract in detail. It stated quite clearly that they were obliging themselves to pay for the entire siding

71

installation, but that they would receive a discount for every referral they made that resulted in another installation for the company. If they made enough referrals that resulted in enough contracts, then presumably their own job would have cost them nothing.

Is this a fraud or not? The contract was explicit but the young couple failed to read it or understand it. It could be said that this was a fair business deal and if the couple didn't understand the terms, they should legally bear the consequences. However, after the end of the second month, the siding began to peel and their "model home" began to look a shambles. They called the improvement company to repair the shoddy work, but the company's phone had been disconnected and they were nowhere to be found. The finance company that had purchased their contract was demanding payment. The couple had to hire a lawyer at considerable cost to attempt to void the allegedly fraudulent contract. They were successful, but they were still out of pocket many hundreds of dollars and had to repair the house at their own expense.

In addition to the "too good to be true" and "something for nothing" appeals of the home improvement pitchman, there are some other aspects of the sales presentation that should cause you to be wary.

GUARANTEES AND DELIVERABILITY

The materials and their installation might be accompanied by an "unconditional lifetime money-back" guarantee. The guarantee is only as good as its written statements and only as good as the ability of the guarantor to perform. If there is to be a guarantee, it should be spelled out in explicit detail and you should understand exactly what is and is not guaranteed. Even though the guarantee might appear to be iron-clad, how about the ability of the firm to honor it? If they're not in business a month or a year after your job is completed, the best guarantee in the world is meaningless.

There may be representations that the work will save you many hundreds of dollars over that it would cost through other contractors. You can never know this for sure unless you have properly drawn plans and specifications and obtained bids from reputable local contractors. Until you have done that, the salesperson's words are nothing more than puffery.

The salesman may make representations that the materials such as aluminum siding, are "maintenance free forever." No substance yet discovered by science and affordable to the average homeowner is maintenance free forever.

The salesman will be very anxious to get you to sign a contract right away. He knows that if you don't, and if you have time to think about the deal, he may lose you. This is where the pressure will begin. He may try to convice you that getting other prices will be a waste of your time; that his price is certainly the lowest; and that if you don't sign right now, his low price won't be available later. This "Now or never" kind of pressure may sound convincing. Note well: when you're dealing with legitimate contractors, there's no job that can't be contracted for a day or so later as well as it can at that moment. If you feel that by not signing right away you're losing out on something special, you had best begin preparing yourself for the worst.

BRAND NAMES

Another ploy used by home improvement rackets to gain respectability involves the use of major brand names by the promoters. There have been hundreds of cases in recent years involving improvement swindlers using the names of national firms to convince customers that they themselves are legitimate.

73

The impression given is that the promoter is in direct alliance with the manufacturer, with the implication being that such national firms certainly wouldn't condone anything but the highest quality workmanship with regard to their products, and thus the salesman must be of the highest repute.

In fact, anyone can go out and buy most of these name brand products. Many homeowners have been bilked, believing that the contractor will use such brand name products, only to find when the job is done that inferior brands have been used.

PONZI SCHEMES

Charles Ponzi was a hustler who plied his skills in Boston during the 1920's. He so popularized an ancient scheme that it has carried his name ever since - the Ponzi scheme. It was simple, straightforward, and attracted victims like a magnet. It worked like this:

Ponzi told victims, "You give me $100 today and in 30 days I'll give you back $120." Thirty days later he did just that. His own initial investment of $20 paid off, since now he had avid believers who would do exactly what he said. "Want to try it again for another 30 days?" The first wave of investors took the plunge again. Ponzi had no trouble soliciting a second wave of investors and he used their money to pay off the first wave. He would solicit a third wave and use their money to pay off the second wave, and so on, until one day Ponzi simply took the money and ran.

A Ponzi scheme, then, is in essence a plan whereby new investors are constantly solicited and their money is used to pay off older investors. Keeping the initial investors happy keeps the money pouring in, but at some time the promoter will skip, and the last group in never gets out - at least not with their money.

Closely related to the Ponzi scheme is the pyramid scheme, which often is the basis for chain letters. The pyramid scheme also involves using new investors to pay off old ones. The promoters who start pyramid schemes can make money, but at the risk of jail sentences, for the schemes are illegal and in many states a criminal offense.

A pyramid involves giving money to someone whose name is at the top of a list, then erasing that name and inserting your own name at the bottom of the list. You then give the list to as many people as there are names on the list. As your name hits the top of the list, you'll supposedly collect money from everyone who is involved in the pyramid. Example: a list of 10 names will be sent to 10 people. Each of them are told to send it to 10 people, so now there are 100 people involved. Each of the 100 will send the list to 10 people, so now there are 1000 involved. If this is carried out to the tenth level, you will note that 10 billion people will be involved in the pyramid. That's more than double the population of the entire earth. And that is where the pyramids eventually collapse. They simply run out of people who are willing to participate and the victims find that their names never move up the list beyond one of two notches.

The Ponzi and pyramid concepts are at work in most types of investment schemes. If the boiler room operator selling shares in the linoleum mine wants to keep his investors happy and spreading the good word, he may pay them a token dividend a few weeks after they invest. This not only reassures them that the promised wealth is on its way but it also gives them a false sense of security and inhibits them from alerting the authorities to the scheme. Naturally, in such an event, the money to pay the dividend to the initial investors comes from the second wave of investors. And so it goes.

LAND FRAUDS

Will Rogers once said "Buy land, they ain't making any more of it." The real estate industry has greatly profited selling that concept. Unfortunately, land fraud sharks have also bilked the public by selling them on the idea that any land bought represented a good buy - even if it was underwater in Florida.

Land fraud schemes flourished in the 1970's and then slowed down as the impact of a newly created federal agency - the Office of Interstate Land Sales Regulation - began to be felt. Unscrupulous salesmen sold unwitting victims worthless swampland in Florida and barren desert in Arizona under the guise of "future retirement communities," "vacation rancheros," and just plain double-your-money-in-a-hurry investment opportunities.

But swindlers are not to be outdone by the creation of a mere federal agency. They simply went into hiding, to emerge again in another guise. In the field of time-sharing resorts, many of the same patterns have emerged that were prevalent with the land sales: high pressure "opportunity meetings." "if you don't buy now, the price will go up tomorrow" tactics, and the like. While many time-sharing opportunities may be valid, there will also be many situations in which the facilities don't exist, or in which the buyer is sold far more than what is delivered.

TIME SHARING

The redhot, but not always good, real estate investment of the 1980's is called *Time Sharing*. The concept is good. Several people will pool their money and become co-owners of a home or condo in a very desirable vacation spot. A co-owner is then able to select one or more weeks (determined when the time-share was purchased) at this oasis, each year. Many promoters also allow co-owners to "trade" their time, during any given year, for equal time at some other spot in the country or abroad.

Hucksters often hike "maintenance fees" to unbelievable levels to fleece the co-owners. Also promises of the right to "trade" vacation time for time at some other tropical paradise is often a sham or at least greatly overstated. One woman in Portland, Oregon, purchased a one week time share in Palm Springs, California. She was verbally told she could take her vacation any time she wished, and only needed to give 30 days prior notice. She was shocked to discover that the fine print stated she had to vacation during July, August, or September, the months when it's very nice in Portland, and very, very hot (almost always well over 100 degrees) in Palm Springs. When she decided to trade her time in the desert for a log cabin near a Michigan lake, she was told that was just fine as long as someone else would agree to switch places with her. None were! A good attorney broke the contract for her, but the experience was dismal and she was an overall loser when the attorney fees were tabulated.

Some people have had pleasant time sharing experiences, others have been taken. The concept looks good on paper, but too often you are asked to pay far too much for what you receive, and many time people don't receive the benefits they expected.

A time sharing contract is only as good as the people who sell it and stand behind it. If you are thinking about entering into this kind of purchase, you are strongly advised to check the credentials of the promoters thoroughly.

FIGHTING BACK!

Rip-off prevention is far better than any action taken after you have become a scam victim. Retrieving lost money is not easy. Con artists are infamous for their fly-by-night tactics, and often they do really fly away, seeking new sites and new suckers.

Even though the chances of getting your money back may be slim, you still should take action if you believe you've been defrauded. If nothing else, your action may help put a stop to certain fraudulent practices, thus benefitting your fellow citizens. And if they do the same, their actions will benefit you. Here are the main sources of possible help:

FTC

The Federal Trade Commission (FTC) is a governmental agency charged with many areas of responsibility including deceptive business practices. The FTC is based in Washington and has regional branches in Atlanta, Boston, Chicago, Cleveland, Dallas, Kansas City, Los Angeles, New Orleans, New York, San Francisco, and Seattle. FTC officials emphasize, however, that they are not in a position to represent individial consumers.

Information regarding possible deceptive practices can come to the attention of the FTC in a number of ways. Complaints from individual consumers are probably the predominant way. In addition, newpaper clippings and complaints from other businessmen also supply information.

The FTC does not have the staff or the funds to investigate every complaint that comes to its attention. When there is enough frequency of a certain type of complaint against a given company, the investigative staff may look into it. If, after due investigation, the FTC has reason to believe that a deceptive practive has occured, the agency will call this to the attention of the alleged offender and attempt to work out what is called a "consent order." A consent order is a rather curious document in which the alleged offender promises not to do what he has been accused of doing, but does not admit that he was guilty of doing it. In other words, in effect, he's not guilty, but he promises he won't do it again. If he does violate the consent order, serious punishment can follow. If the offender does not feel he has done anything wrong and does not want to sign a consent order, the matter must proceed to the law courts.

From the time that consumer complaints start trickling in until the time a consent order or court determination is obtained, many months can elapse. If an out-and-out fraudulent activity has been underway, the perpetrator may have long since vanished by the time the consent order is issued.

Why doesn't the FTC alert the public when first receiving complaints? Wouldn't this help tip off the public at the earliest stages of the game? While such warning bulletins might be of some value to some people, there are dangers inherent in such a course. Many innocent parties could suffer if announcements were made by the FTC on the basis of mere suspicion of a violation of the law. It is possible for a jealous or angry competitor to set up a malicious campaign against a perfectly innocent businessman. Investigation is necessary before any allegations of law-breaking can be justified. Further,if the FTC were to tip its hand too early, doing so might harm the agency's ability to obtain justice later on in the courts. Thus, there is a need for some degree of secrecy until the basic investigative work has been completed and a complaint is issued.

The Federal Trade Commission does not have immediate injunctive powers; it cannot come swooping down on an alleged deceptive business practice and order it to cease and desist on the spot. The agency must go through the consent order ritual which, as noted, can take months.

If the FTC is limited in its powers, it is even more limited by a closed-mouthed public. This federal agency can function only if it gets the input from the public. Lacking that input, it has nothing to go on. While it may serve little purpose in your own situation to alert the FTC to a deceptive business practice, doing so could aid the agency on the broader scale of bringing such practices to an end.

THE POST OFFICE SERVICE

Contact the Mail Fraud Division of the U.S. Postal Service, if you suspect that the U.S. mails have been used to perpetrate a fraud. As with the FTC, the postal service is limited in the available money and manpower to track down every complaint, but it does what it can. The more complaints there are on a given matter, the better the chance the Postal Service has of obtaining a satisfactory conclusion.

STATE AND LOCAL GOVERNMENT AGENCIES

All 50 states have some form of consumer-protection office. Frequently it's associated with the Attorney General's office. Many large cities also have consumer-protection agencies. As with the aforementioned federal agencies, lack of money and manpower deter these agencies from being able to assist you in getting satisfaction in a fraudulent situation, but they should be contacted anyway, immediately, and with all pertinent details. If there seems to be any hope at all of apprehending the promoters, your local police or sheriff's office should also be contacted.

In addition to governmental agencies, there are a number of nongovernmental sources of possible assistance.

YOUR LOCAL MEDIA

TV and radio stations, and your local newspaper are probably interested in consumer protection. Newspaper people and broadcasters have been doing an ever-expanding job of surveillance and reporting on consumer fraud. These columns and reports are provided at considerable expense by the media as a public service. Very often they're able to resolve matters right on the spot.

Con artists fear exposure, and they know a local paper or station can give them negative publicity overnight.

BETTER BUSINESS BUREAU

Better Business Bureaus can be helpful before the fact; a call to your local BBB prior to entering into a transaction might disclose whether or not the person you're dealing with has a record of complaints with the bureau. BBB personnel might also be able to give you general guidelines on what action is available if you have unsatisfactory dealings with any firm. Understand that if a business has a clean record with the BBB, it does not necessarily mean that all is on the up and up. The clever con man will know how to keep his BBB record clear and will also time his activities cleverly enough so that he can be out of town before the complaints begin hitting the BBB office.

FINANCIAL INSTITUTIONS

Banks, savings and loan associations, credit unions, and consumer finance companies are all actively involved on a day-to-day basis with the flow of IOU's generated from all kinds of business activity. If a deceptive practice is under way, an alert to these institutions could help bring an end to the activity. Such institutions might be involved in buying fraudently induced IOU's and tens of thousands of dollars' worth of paper can be generated before anyone is aware that a fraud is in the works. The sooner the institutions know of it, the sooner they can stop buying the IOU's and that can be the death knell for the fraudulent endeavor.

Your financial institution can also be of help to you if you consult them regarding your own financial situation before you get involved in signing any contracts. The astute loan officer might spot trouble in a situation that you might not otherwise be aware of.

SMALL CLAIMS COURT

Your local Small Claims Court can be of assistance in settling a claim of fraudulent or improper business practices, if you can locate the party who has wronged you. Small Claims Courts differ from place to place, but in general you do not need a lawyer to represent you. If the amount of money involved in a claim exceeds a certain limit (perhaps $750 or $1000, depending on the court), the Small Claims Court will not hear your case. Contact your local court to determine their rules and procedures.

ATTORNEYS

If you sincerely believe you have been ripped off and the sum involved is substantial, you probably need professional legal help. However, with lawyers charging between $50 and $150 per hour, you can't afford an attorney unless the grievance is great.

All attorneys are not equal. Ask friends and relatives for the names of attorneys that they have had satisfactory dealings with. Call your local Bar Association for a referral. Select your counselor with care and by all means select a specialist, if the matter in question requires special expertise.

CHAPTER THREE

YOU NEED A BUDGET

Just what is a personal budget? In simple terms, it is a plan to manage your finances. A plan to deal with anticipated revenue. A method to practice personal financial planning.

If you do not have a plan you may suffer. Money problems are one of the leading sources of marital discord and other personal problems. If you are spending your paycheck without a plan, then it will - unless you have a very large paycheck - be hard for you to achieve financial goals that will provide the things you wanted but thought you could not afford. A budget will get you many things you may have thought were impossible to get. It should also tell you what is not possible. In any event it is only fair to yourself to take the time to plan out what you would like to do with your money.

It's very important that you anticipate expenditure in various categories - food, housing, travel, medical care, vacations, etc... The objective is to control these expenditures so that you can keep them within the limits of your income and, if all works out according to plan, even have a little left over to put into a savings account each month.

Many people who overspend have a good idea of where they should cut back, but they lack the self-discipline to do so. Budgeting, by forcing them to take a hard look at their spending habits, can help provide the needed incentive.

There is one question in particular that often comes up about budgeting: Just how much money, many people ask, must a typical family earn to be able to live reasonably well in American today? In truth, the question isn't meaningful. Chances are that, for the near future at least, you are stuck with what you already make. The immediate problem - and one that a budget is designed to deal with - is to fit your expenses into your income, not to build your income to match your expenses.

Budgeting, then, enables you to plan what you will do with your limited resources. But that's the easy part.

Some surveys have shown that fewer than half of all budgeters actually end up spending within the limits of their plan. This, then, becomes the real challenge of budgeting.

A formal budget is by no means essential. Some people seem to have a knack for handling their day-to-day expenditures with ease. They always have a good approximate sense of where their money is going, and seldom, if ever, find themselves unexpectedly short of cash. For them a formal budget may be more fuss that it is worth.

Others, by budgeting, learn to control their expenses. Eventually they outgrow their need for this type of disciplinary mechanism.

But what about the rest of us? We're the people who never are fully in control of our financial affairs, and for whom dollars seem to disappear right out of our pockets through a mysterious process that, in our view, only a certified public accountant could understand. Sound familiar? Then some sort of simple budget is called for.

Noticed that we said "simple" budget. A common mistake is to make the family budget into such a big and complex deal that there is no way it will ever work. Figuring each category down to the exact penny of shifting cash from envelope to envelope usually is self-defeating.

What you should be after is a budget that is effective, yet easy to operate—one that doesn't become more of a burden than it is worth. For simplicity's sake, all figures should be rounded off to the nearest dollar.

Start off by listing your "fixed" expenses on a sheet of paper - that is, expenses over which you have relatively little control. These include such items as mortgage payments or rent, insurance premiums, transportation, utilities, installment payments and taxes. You may be amazed to discover how large a portion of your expenditures, perhaps well over half, fits into this category.

It may be tougher, on the other hand, to find out just how much you are spending for other, more flexible items - food, luxuries, repairs, personal care, entertainment, etc. One approach is to keep track for two or three months in order to come up with average monthly figures.

Once you know where and how much you already are spending you are in a position to draw up a realistic budget.

You may find that you are consistently spending more than you earn. In that case you are just going to have to make some have choices in terms of where to cut back. Choosing where to cut back is never easy, but it cannot be avoided if you are going to live within your means and avoid eventual financial disaster.

Perhaps deep cuts can be made in personal luxuries. Some examples: an evening cocktail hour may be costing you $600 a year; a $5 *businessman's lunch* each working day adds up to more than $1,200 annually; two packs of cigarettes every day comes to over $800 a year.

Do you shop around for the best prices as diligently as possible? Food purchases, in particular, are an area where careful shopping and selection can result in real savings. The nutritional quality of what we eat, experts point out, has little to do with the price we pay.

A few hints: always check the displays for special prices; buy food in season, when it tends to be plentiful and less expensive; always look at unit prices when they are shown on the shelf strip; buy the most economical size for your needs; avoid prepackaged "convenience" foods, which usually are expensive.

87

Do you avoid unnecessary use of credit? The widespread availability of consumer loans has made the "easy" purchase of luxury items too darn tempting for many people to resist. To their sorrow they soon discover that they have "overloaded" themselves with unmanageable debt that throws their budget out of kilter. One of the worst possible moves of all is to take out a loan to meet current expenditures. The result is that you simply end up even deeper in the hole.

If you are in particularly bad financial shape, you might consider selling some of your assets. An expensive car or home may not be essential; you may even find that the large commitments such an item entails are actually at the heart of your financial problems.

In the final analysis, however, you may decide that you just cannot cut back and that the only answer is to take an extra job. That's fine, if you think it is the best course and are willing to put in the additional hours.

Although there is no "typical" way in which you should spend your money, the U.S. Bureau of Labor Statistics does keep track of the broad spending patterns of families throughout the country. A look at these patterns may give you some insights into how you should allot your own hard-earned cash.

For instance, the table shows how the average urban family of four, with an "intermediate" level of income, spends its money. The theoretical family cited by the Bureau in this example consists of a husband aged 38, a wife not employed outside the home, a 13-year-old boy and an 8 year-old girl. Figures are based on estimated spending levels in late 1976. No provision is made for savings—a category you will want to add to your own budget.

These figures, as we mentioned, should not be followed rigidly. Your own particular circumstances and needs should be taken into full account. This includes an awareness of your

88

Monthly Income	10 Years	20 Years	30 Years	40 Years
$ 500	$ 60,000	$120,000	$ 180,000	$ 240,000
600	72,000	144,000	216,000	288,000
800	96,000	192,000	288,000	384,000
1,000	120,000	240,000	360,000	480,000
1,500	180,000	360,000	540,000	720,000
2,000	240,000	480,000	720,000	960,000
2,500	300,000	600,000	900,000	1,200,000
3,000	360,000	720,000	1,080,000	1,440,000

As you can see from the above chart, there is no question that a lot of money will come your way. What's the problem? It's how to keep some of it from passing through your fingers, isn't is?

life-style and its financial implications. Some people choose to entertain frequently and lavishly, and to skimp on savings. Others choose to save, and to forgo entertaining. One individual isn't right and the other wrong. Both are right so long as they are satisfied with their life-style and can make ends meet.

In terms of the mechanics of maintaining a budget, there are a number of systems. One is to make entries on some sort of ledger sheet, just as a businessman would do to keep track of his firms's income and expenditures.

A better approach might be to keep your budget in a standard ring-bound notebook, with a separate page devoted to each spending category. At the top of each page you can list the total amount you have budgeted for that category. Then, as the month goes by, you can keep running track of actual expenditures by listing them on the page.

If you find you are consistently overspending in a particular category, you should seriously consider the possibility of increasing your allocation there. In that case, of course, you will have to take away from another, less important category to keep the overall budget in balance.

A budget must be a living document that changes as your spending needs and your income change.

WHERE YOU LIVE DOES
MAKE A DIFFERENCE

A 1977 national survey by the Department of Labor found that there was a substantial difference in how much money people needed to maintain the same life styles in various cities in America.

For example, a family of four in Anchorage, Alaska, would need $23,071 to maintain the same life style as a family of four in Austin, Texas who made only $14,209. Baltimore, Maryland and Seattle, Washington both checked in with the national average of $16,236. Please keep in mind, this survey is several years old and the national average income is believed to be approximately $24,500 now (1984 estimate).

I present this 1977 survey only because it was the last one available at the time we went to press and because it does illustrate relative costs.

Although some changes (living costs have increased) have occured over the past few years since this survey was taken, it is probable that no major changes in how these various cities compare to the national average have occured.

	Annual cost	Percent of total budget
Food *(including meals out)*	$ 3,859	23.8%
Housing *(including heat, utilities, operating expenses, furnishings)*	3,843	23.7
Transportation	1,403	8.6
Clothing	1,141	7.0
Personal care	355	2.2
Medical care *(including health insurance)*	900	5.5
Other consumption *(recreation, education, reading, etc.)*	869	5.4
Income taxes	2,236	13.8
Social security and disability insurance	898	5.5
Miscellaneous	731	4.5
Total "intermediate" budget	$16,236	100.0%

WHERE YOU LIVE DOES MAKE A BIG DIFFERENCE

The "intermediate" budget of $16,236 a year for a family of four is the national urban average. However, living expenses can vary substantially from region to region and city to city.

For instance, the cost of living in Anchorage, Alaska, is nearly 70% higher than in the rural South. Similarly, living in New York City is about 30 percent more expensive than in Dallas.

In addition to its "intermediate" budget, the Department of Labor estimates "lower" and "higher" budgets for the same theoretical family of four. The lower budget, in the most recent study, was $10,041 and the higher budget $23,759.

Annual "intermediate" budget for a family of four	Relative cost in relation to the U.S. average
Urban U.S. average	$16,236	100%

NORTHEAST

Boston	$19,384	119
Buffalo	17,175	106
Hartford, Conn.	17,238	106
Lancaster, PA	15,685	97
New York	18,866	116
Philadelphia	16,836	104
Pittsburgh	15,515	96
Portland, Maine	16,633	102
Nonmetropolitan areas	16,040	99

NORTH CENTRAL

Cedar Rapids, Iowa	$15,976	98
Champaign-Urbana, IL	16,578	102
Chicago	16,561	102
Cincinnati	15,708	97
Cleveland	16,412	101
Dayton, Ohio	15,101	93
Detroit	16,514	102
Green Bay, Wis.	16,008	99
Indianapolis	15,911	98
Kansas City	15,628	96
Milwaukee	17,307	107
Minneapolis-St. Paul	16,810	104
St. Louis	15,623	96
Wichita, Kansas	15,102	93
Nonmetropolitan areas	14,926	92

SOUTH

Altanta	$14,830	92
Austin, Texas	14,209	88
Baltimore	16,195	100
Baton Rouge, LA	14,472	89
Dallas	14,699	91
Durham, NC	15,525	96
Houston	14,978	92
Nashville, Tenn.	14,821	91
Orlando, Fla.	14,378	89
Washington, D.C.	16,950	104
Nonmetropolitan areas	13,855	85

WEST

Anchorage, Alaska	$23,071	142
Bakersfield, Calif.	15,004	92
Denver	15,906	98
Honolulu	19,633	121
Los Angeles	16,016	99
San Diego	15,989	98
San Francisco	17,200	106
Seattle	16,204	100
Nonmetropolitan areas	14,627	90

KNOW YOUR NET WORTH

It is always prudent to know just what your *NET WORTH* is. This will be invaluable information in your financial planning and absolutley required information if you want to apply for a loan from a traditional source.

HOW TO CALCULATE NET WORTH

On the plus side of your net worth ledger are such items as cash (including monies in a checking account), savings, value of your house and furnishings, today's market value of your car (not the amount you originally paid for it), investments, cash value of any life insurance, pension-plan holdings and anything else of value that you own. On the negative side you must list such items as your home mortgage, unpaid bills, installment payment and any other debts.

A typical net worth report may look something like this:

ASSETS

Cash	$ 1,100
Savings	7,000
Investments	15,000
Value of home	75,000
Home furnishings	5,000
Automobile	3,800
Cash value of insurance	1,280
Pension holdings	12,000
Misc. belongings	1,000
TOTAL ASSETS	121,800

LIABILITIES

Mortgage	57,250
Car payments	1,850
Other debt	2,220
Unpaid bills	1,050
TOTAL LIABILITIES	62,370

NET WORTH ($121,180 minus $62,370) equals *$58,810*.

Knowing your net worth will keep you in touch with your "personal financial status." I hope you will be seeing it grow by leaps and bounds every year. I recommend an annual *NET WORTH REPORT,* and the end of each year is usually a good time to file this report. Put these reports in a folder and place in a safe place where you can always find them. As the years pass, they'll tell you the direction you are heading in.

POSITIVE AND NEGATIVE CASH FLOW

The following charts may be helpful to you in planning your budget.

Planning for Income

	Jan.	Feb.	Mar.	Apr.	May	June	July	Aug.	Sept.	Oct.	Nov.	Dec.	TOTALS
Husband's income (net)													
Wife's income (net)													
Dividends													
Interest													
Profit from sales													
Rental (net) income													
Bonuses													
Alimony													
Child Support													
Other													
TOTALS													

	Jan.	Feb.	Mar.	Apr.	May	June	July	Aug.	Sept.	Oct.	Nov.	Dec.	TOTALS
Rent or Mortgage payment													
Utilities: Gas													
Electric													
Fuel													
Water													
Phone													
Charge Accounts													
Loans: Personal													
Home Improve.													
Auto													
Education													
Insurance Homeowners or Apt.													
Health													
Life													
Auto													
Medical & Dental													
Savings & Investments													
Taxes Property tax if not in monthly mortgage payment													
Income tax due or refund.													
Goals: Monthly													
5 Years													
Lifetime													
TOTAL													

The above list should then be estimated for each month, similar to the income chart. Figure out what your payments will be for each month in each of the categories. Medical and dental should be an average of the past few year's bills with 10% to 15% more for inflation or extra visits. If your property taxes are due in one large payment at the beginning of your budget or before you have accumulated enough money from monthly allocations to cover the amount due, then simply draw into your savings for the amount and **don't** forget to replace the withdrawal with monthly allocations to the savings.

	Jan.	Feb.	Mar.	Apr.	May	June	July	Aug.	Sept.	Oct.	Nov.	Dec.	TOTALS
Food: At home													
Restaurants													
Clothing: Husband													
Wife													
Children													
Transportation: Gas													
Maintenance													
Furniture													
Education													
Vacations													
Holidays													
Gifts													
Allowances: Husband													
Wife													
Children													
Miscellaneous: Maintenance													
Cleaning													
Repairs and Replacements													
Other:													
Contributions													
Total Adjustable Expenses													

	Jan.	Feb.	Mar.	Apr.	May	June	July	Aug.	Sept.	Oct.	Nov.	Dec.	TOTALS
INCOME Use Average Per Month													
Carryover Plus or Minus													
Minus Basic Expenses													
Minus Adjustable Expenses													
Equals Carryover													

Just by filling out the above, you will be able to see easily where you spend your money and if there may be areas where improvement may be easily accomplished.

CHAPTER FOUR

MONEY MATTERS

In recent years, saving money at traditional saving account institutions (banks, savings and loans, credit unions, etc..) has lost most of its appeal. Many other investment vehicles offer far greater potential than the 5½ compounded interest paid by most banks and *S&L*'s. Few, if any, however, offer as much safety.

While I do not recommend that the bulk of your money sit in a bank, safe and secure, but multiplying at a very slow rate, we do believe a portion should be put in a savings institution.

Building a "ready-money" account of $5,000 to $10,000 should be a matter of high priority. The term "savings," as we use it here, means any risk-free mechanism for setting aside cash at a reasonable rate of return.

It is important to note right at the start that savings accounts are the most useful when you discipline yourself to deposit specified amounts - perhaps $25, $50 or $100 a month - on a regular basis. This can be accomplished through payroll deductions at work, automatic transfers from your checking account, or regular deposits on your own. You will be able to build a substantial savings reserve in just a few years this way.

A savings and loan association or a conservative money market fund (now available through most *S&L*'s and banks) does not offer you the greatest return on your money, but they do provide the highest degree of security and instant liquidity (of course you can lose substantial interest on any fund that you raid prior to maturity).

The typical 5 or 6 percent interest rate on a regular savings accout may be a negative rate of return.

Let's explain that point. Everybody is aware of how badly their puchasing power has been undermined by inflation in recent years. In fact, the prices you pay for food, clothing, medical care and other products and services have been rising at a rate of nealy 8 percent annually. Just to keep even with this price inflation, so that your dollars will be able to buy the same amount of goods in the future that they buy today, you would have to earn 7 percent annually,   after taxes, on your savings account. And what did we say? Five and a half percent is actually a fairly typical rate of return on savings. And that 5½ percent is before the Internal Revenue Service takes its bite of your interest income each April 15, not after.

The result: You are falling behind if you only earn 5 to 6 percent. In subsequent chapters, we discuss ways to try to beat inflation by earning more from your cash. Our message here is that you should have adequate savings primarily because of the safety and because of the convenience of withdrawal and a conservative money market fund is usually your best investment for liquidity and return.

Once you have established an adequate money reserve, you are ready to start putting your additional excess cash into forms of investment that are potentially more rewarding.

PREPARING A BUSINESS PLAN
TO ATTRACT VENTURE CAPITAL

You need a comprehensive plan in order to operate any business. Also, if you ever wish to approach private investors or traditional lending sources, a business plan is a prerequisite. It is almost impossible to obtain any kind of loan without preparing a document that sets forth your qualifications and objectives.

A comprehensive business plan is a report that summarizes your business activities, the importance of your products/ services, and the qualifications of the owner and/or manager, projected sales volume over a one year period and any other "factors of importance." It should be concise and "tightly" written. Not more than five or six pages in length is usually best. A title page with a table of content will give it a professional touch. A one page introduction should summarize the rest of the document.

The product (or service), potential market, and the special skills (if required) by the owner or manager are of paramount importance. To obtain venture capital you must paint a rosy picture, and yet refrain from making statements that take your proposal out of the frame of reality.

Projected sales volume for a year from the date of the report and also five years into the future is important and major consideration of any potential lender. You may even be asked for ten year projection although one and five year projections are standard when less than two hundred thousand dollars is required.

A "*Research & Development*" section should briefly outline any improvements you expect to make with your product or service that will give you a competitive edge.

The final section of the report can be entitled "Capital Use," and should clearly spell out exactly how you intend to use borrowed monies. The appendice can be used to include your resume, a cash-flow projection, a current balance sheet, and any and all supplies and equipment you have on hand.

Excerpts from letter praising your product or services, with name and addresses, can also be very helpful. Add to your presentation folio copies of your ads, editorial mentions, circulars, and sales letters.

INVESTING IN INFLATION

There are three major reasons why you must learn to be an enlightened investor and money manager:

(1) To increase your income.
(2) To reduce your tax liabilities.
(3) To make your money multiply.

INVESTING WITH INFLATION
FOREVER IN MIND

Our recent economic past is our guide to the future. We are living in an age of inflation. Accept this fact of life and prepare accordingly and you can survive financially. Disregard this fact and you face financial destruction. Oh, I'm aware we just came out of a financial recession and other recessions will be forthcoming. Nevertheless, the overall trend for the 1980's and 1990's is inflationary.

Inflation does not destroy wealth. Inflation redistributes wealth. It robs those who do not understand how it works and gives to those who do. Inflation enriches the well-informed and impoverishes the ignorant.

WHO'S TO BLAME?

Although politicians would like you to believe otherwise, they are the problem. Your government is the primary cause of inflation. They do this in the name of benefits and in hope of wooing your vote. They know the majority of citizens want ever-increasing help - such as guaranteed employment, health insurance, and 1001 different entitlement programs. Many politicians equate "entitlement" to being entitled to support from birth to death. And with "good reason", they know millions of our citizens feel this is their right. Not a very realistic financial attitude, but none the less, a popular one today.

Politicians have also discovered inflation makes it a lot easier to meet government financial obligations. When companies or cities are facing financial destruction, *Uncle* is available with a quick Fix. For example, witness what has recently happened to Lockheed (millions in loans), Chrysler Corporation (many more millions) and New York City (a bond guarantee). Also, if you're a researcher who just happens to be interested in the mating habits of the California fruit fly, you may well qualify for a couple of million for this "Vital research" and, of course, if you're a big banker who has poured billions into low-interest foreign loans (while at the same time making it next to impossible for your fellow citizens to get a few thousand), don't fret, your government will raise taxes and underwrite your bad judgement.

When we penalize the best among us to reward the worst, we help fuel the raging furnace that is inflation. In recent years, the Reagan administration cooled down the inflationary furnace, but the problem has not disappeared, and today is making another comeback.

PRINTING PRESS MONEY

Inflation increases the money supply while decreasing the purchasing power of your dollars. As congress votes to increase currency and credit to bail out the housing industry, the auto industry, or any other industry, your dollar shrinks in value—and the next time a bleeding heart liberal campaigns for more welfare benefits, remember he's reaching into your wallet. When a politician says, "the government can afford to do this or that," he's really saying that you and I can afford to pay.

103

The more dollars that are chasing goods and services, the higher the cost of those goods and services. These are the facts of life, financially speaking.

A SLICE OF BREAD

In 1930 you could go to your grocery store and buy eleven loaves of bread for one dollar. In 1940 your dollar bought ten loaves, by 1950 you could only buy six loaves; by 1960 only four; by 1970 only three; by 1980 only one. At this rate, one dollar will get you half a loaf in 1990, and perhaps one slice by the year 2000.

Another way to comprehend your diminishing purchasing power is to consider these facts: If you earned $18,000 in 1960, you needed $25,000 in 1970 and $59,000 in 1980, just to stay even. By 1990, if inflation in the 80's matches inflation in the 70's, you'll need $188,000 in order to enjoy the same lifestyle that $18,000 provided in 1960.

The puritan work ethic has always taught us to work hard and not to borrow. Although working hard - and smart - is still a desirable trait, (albeit shunned by many millions of our citizens), no borrowing is bad advice today. At least, as it relates to investing. The dollars you borrow for sound investments today can be repaid with "cheaper" dollars later, provided that you are not forced to pay exorbitant interest rates.

Never borrow to cover ordinary living expenses or for pleasure. Throw away your Visa and Mastercard unless you know how to use them wisely (most folks don't!). Borrow only for long-term, relatively safe investments - never to go on a spending spree!

THE GREAT INJUSTICE

I am both saddened and angered when I see so many of our

people, especially the elderly, stripped of their purchasing power, and floundering on the battlefield of inflation. The great injustice is that millions of these good people worked hard all their lives and made many sacrifices to save what little money they could. Faithfully, on the advice of their parents and their friendly banker, they have invested in ultra-conservative "Safe" savings accounts, only to see their purchasing power evaporate, while their dignity was being compromised. For these people to end up no better than the drones of society, is a damn shame.

You either win or lose the war against inflation. There are no non-combatants. There is no middle-ground. To win, you must build an inflation proof investment portfolio. Your investment portfolio must maximize your after-tax income, and still be reasonably safe. At least safe enough to allow you to sleep well most nights. There is no such thing as a "risk-free" investment. All investments are either low, medium, or high-risk, or something close, such as "pretty-safe" or "pretty risky."

To win the battle against inflation, you must have the right mix of investments, and your portfolio must always be in tune to prevailing economic conditions, the realities of today! This means that nothing you have can be tucked away in an old shoe box or safe-deposit box and forgotten. In investing and personal money management, victory belongs to the flexible, aware and alert.

Inflation is not going to go away, at least not in the forseeable future. Love it or hate it, you must live with it. If you ignore it, or say it will soon vanish, you are flirting with disaster. You must, instead, use inflation to multiply your wealth. You must allow it to push you towards your financial goals, much the same way a raft is pushed down a floating river. The river sets the direction, the raft goes with the flow, not against it.

CHAPTER FIVE

DOUBLE THE DOW

In my opinion, we will be in an overall bull market that should last through the 1980's. I would not be surprised to see the *Dow* at or near 2,500 by 1988. That would be approximately double its current level (Fall, 1983.) American industry has suffered many setbacks in recent years, but new technology is keeping it headed in an upwards direction.

WHAT IS STOCK?

When you buy stocks, you become a "partner" in that business, however limited your involvement.

Corporations issue stock to raise money for company operations. A stockholder receives a stock certificate which shows his ownership of a portion of the corporation.

If the company earns money, the Board of Directors may decide to give cash dividends to the stockholders, or they may decide to plow the earnings back into the company as "retained earnings." Subtracting all the debts from the assets leaves the "equity" owned by the stockholders. Dividing the equity by the number of stock shares outstanding equals the "book value" - this is the amount each stockholder would receive if the company went bankrupt today.

In terms of investing, the book value is unimportant compared to the earning power and the growth potential the company has. A share of stock is usually worth what someone in the market wants to pay. And stocks usually sell far over their book value. Stock will increase in price if new buyers think it will go higher in price - the demand is higher than the supply.

THE FOUR TYPES OF SECURITIES

There are four basic types of securities. They are:

(1) Common stock
(2) Preferred stock
(3) Options
(4) Bonds

COMMON STOCK

All corporations have common stock. In some (commonly called closed corporation) one person, one family, or a small group of investors may own all the shares. In many others, "ownership" through the issuing of stocks is divided among several hundreds or many thousands of individuals who are called "shareholders of common stock."

PREFERRED STOCK

Preferred stock is a stock on which a fixed dividend must be paid before the common stock holders are entitled to their dividends. The preferred stockholder usually gets a higher dividend. Also, if it is a cumulative preferred stock, any dividends in the past that have been omitted, must be paid before common stockholders are entitled to their dividends.

OPTIONS

Options are a purchased right to buy (known as a "call" option) or sell (known as a "put" option) stock at a fixed price.
Many investors like options because they offer an opportunity to make a large profit on any move of a given stock

while limiting the amount of possible loss. For example, you may feel that the XYZ Corporation, selling at $20 today is going to soar to $40 very soon. It would cost you $2,000 plus commissions to buy 100 shares. However, if an option was available, it could be only $200 for 100 shares. If the stock made a big move, let's say it went up to $35 within the option period, by exercising the option and buying the 100 shares at $20 each, and then turning around to sell at $35 per share, the option holder would receive $3,500. From this amount he must deduct the $2,000 he paid to exercise his option, plus the $200 paid to buy the option in the first place. This would leave $1,300 less brokerage commissions.

If, on the other hand, the stock in the XYZ Corporation had gone into a big tailspin, losing half its value soon after the option was purchased, what would the investor do? Answer: Nothing! He simply lets the option expire. His loss is thereby limited to his $200 option investment and he can thank his lucky stars that he did not buy common shares.

A "Call" option is the purchased right that allows the buyer of that option to buy a particular stock at a specific price during a defined period of time, regardless of the market value of that stock. A covered call option is an option written by a seller who owns the underlying security. When an individual writes a covered call option, they receive an option premium and also continue to benefit any dividends that will be paid on the stock.

The combination of the income from the option premium plus the dividends from the owned stock may be two or three times the amount of the dividend income alone. Option writing can substantially increase your income from the stock without a commensurate increase in risk. You may also lock in profit. If you bought a block of stock with the objective of taking $6 per share profit and sell an option at $6, you lock in that profit. The overall strategy when you sell call options is to produce more current income and reduce risks in down markets.

When buying a "call" option (sold in lots of 100 shares) the fixed period of time usually runs nine months and ten days (for tax reasons) but can be for 30 days, 60 days, or any other length of time. The price you pay for an option is generally 10 to 15 percent of the value of the stock.

With a "put" option you have the privilege of selling shares of the stock at a set price within the option period, as opposed to the "call" option which allows you to buy.

BONDS

When you buy stock in a company you become an "owner" in that firm, when you buy bonds, you are only a lender.

Stocks do not pay their holders a fixed annual rate of return, nor do they have a fixed length of life. Bonds do.

High-grade, 30 year corporate bonds, for instance, have been paying annual rates of return of about 10 percent in recent years, attracting many investors who used only to buy stocks.

As with a stock, you can always resell a bond through a broker. This means you don't necessarily have to keep a bond for its full life. But if you do resell in advance of the scheduled "maturity" (the date at which the issuer has promised to repay the full "face value" of the bond,) you may or may not get back your full investment. This is because prices of bonds move up and down in the market-like stocks, but generally not to the same sharp degree.

Most bonds are issued in minimum denominations of $1,000. (however, brokers generally do not like to handle orders smaller than $5,000 or $10,000). Interest payments to bond-holders generally are made semi-annually.

U.S. government bonds are the safest. In mid-1978, long-term government bonds were paying yields of approximately 8¼ percent.

Some corporate bonds are very safe, others very speculative. A key to buying corporate bonds is to know the "rating." This is a guide to the relative quality of the bond. AAA is the highest rating, followed by AA and A; any bond in those three top categories can be considered reasonably safe. Novice bond investors are best off avoiding lower-rated bonds—those with a B, C or D in their ratings.

Tax-exempt municipals are a third major category. These bonds are issued by state and local governments throughout the U.S. By law, interest income from these bonds is exempt from federal income tax. And if you purchase a municipal bond issued by a government or governmental agency within your own state, interest probably will also be exempt from state and local income tax. As with corporate bonds, it is best to stick to quality issues—those rated AAA, AA or A.

Are bonds for you? Bonds are a good investment if you want to earn a substantial cash income, as opposed to seeking capital gains through price appreciation; can afford to take some risk of fluctuating bond prices, as opposed to the absolute security of a money account; and have a minimum of $5,000 to $10,000 to invest. There is less risk (and correspondingly, less potential profit) investing in bonds that investing in stock.

Let's consider these major differences:

STOCKS

(A) No guarantee as to principal
(B) No guarantee regarding the rate of return
(C) Guarantee to participate in the destiny of the corporation

(1) "Guaranteed" as to principal if assets are available at maturity
(2) "Guaranteed" regarding rate-of-return if funds are available
(3) No guaranteed growth, even if profits of corporation increase

CONVERTIBLE BONDS

A convertible bond is a bond that almost always carries a lower rate of interest than a regular corporate bond, but is convertible into common at a specified ratio.

For example, if a convertible is bought at par, which in a bond is usually $1,000 and is convertible into 100 shares of common at the holder's option and the common is selling at $10, there would be no incentive to exchange, for the bond will usually carry a higher yield than the common. However, if the market price of the common should increase to $15, you would now have a bond with a value of $1,500. If on the other hand, the common goes below $10 you still own your bond with its higher yield acting as a cushion underneath the bond.

The trouble with convertibles is, in bear markets they fall along with common stock, and in a bull market their profitability is not dramatic. The opportunities for great gains (or loss) lies with stocks.

HOW WALL STREET WAS NAMED

When one thinks of Wall Street in New York, one thinks of the world of high finance and fortune-building. It may interest you to know that this famous street had much humbler beginnings.

The *Dutch* were first to settle on Manhattan Island. Their favorite meat was pork, so they brought hogs from the Netherlands. To confine their hogs they built a large wall to make a pig pen - from whence came the name Wall Street. There are still many investors who get piggish. They almost always lose like the old saying goes, "on Wall Street, the bulls sometimes make it and the bears sometimes make it, but the hogs never do."

THE STOCK EXCHANGES

The New York Stock Exchange (NYSE), also called "the big board," is the oldest and largest. It began soon after the birth of our nation. America's first Secretary of the *Treasury* realized that we needed to set up a monetary system. Banks had to be established. To establish a bank system, stockholders were needed to invest money. A means to sell shares in the new banking system was required. To make a market for these bank stocks and other issues, a group of eleven businessmen used to meet under an old buttonwood tree at the foot of Wall Street and trade among themselves and as representatives for their clients. Eventually they moved inside a building on Wall Street. From this spartan beginning grew the mightiest financial center on earth.

NEW YORK STOCK EXCHANGE & AMERICAN STOCK EXHANGE INDEXES

Each of the two major stock exchanges compute an average market value index "base value" of all of the stocks traded on that exchange.

On December 31, 1965, the New York Exchange set a base value of 50. A higher or lower figure today indicates how

113

much that exchange's average stock price has increased or decreased since 1965.

The American Exhanges set a base value of 100 on August 31, 1973.

These "base value" indexes are different from the "Daily net changes in average price" that are often quoted on television. Those daily net changes cover only one day and are not related to a years-ago base value.

THE DOW JONES INDEX

Although the Dow Jones measures only 30 stocks out of approximately 1700 on the New York Stock Exhange, those Dow Jones Companies represent about 30% of all the New York Stock Exchange companies total asset value. These are the giant corporations such as General Motors, U.S. Steel, Goodyear, Kodak, DuPont, IBM, etc..

The Dow Jones is "price weighted" so that changes in the price of larger Dow Jones companies have more of an effect than changes in the price of smaller Dow Jones companies. Because the Dow Jones Index is composed of large conservative companies, it is a non-volatile index - it rises and falls more slowly that the market as a whole.

In 1974 the Dow and American Stock Exchange Index were in nearly a 10 to 1 proportion. By adding a zero to the American Stock Exhange Index (AMEX) you can easily compare how well the 30 Dow stocks have done in relation to the AMEX as a whole since 1974.

How is the Dow Jones Index average of 30 stocks relevant to the thousands of other stocks traded, or even to the future prospects of one stock you may own? It isn't. But newspapers and television can say things like: "The Dow rose 20 points today" or "the Dow is down 15 points today." This creates the infectious buying or selling mass psychology that causes average people to buy or sell, and may eventually cause other stock to rise or fall.

As we have previously said, the Dow Jones, the Standard and Poors, and to some extent the NYSE, indexes are price and size weighted.

To avoid the distortions caused by giving price and size weight to an Index calculation, the Value Line Company publishes an unweighted average called the Value Line Composite Index. This includes New York Exchange stocks, some American Exchange stocks, and even some Over The Counter stocks. Unweighted means that each stock has an equal influence on the Index. Experts consider the Value Line Index much more representative of real stock market performance than the Dow and Other weighted indexes.

SPECIAL INDEXES

The National Association of Securities Dealers publishes an index of the 2500 most popularly traded Over The Counter stocks. Also Standard & Poors and the Dow Jones have special indexes of solely utility stocks, or solely transportations stocks, etc.

Some brokerage houses keep their own indexes of "glamour" stocks (for example, Harris, Upham, and Company.) These are usually popular, fast growth potential, speculative stocks.

FINAL THOUGHTS ON INDEXES

Though all these indexes seem confusing, they simply mean that you can't base your opinion of the stock market on just one index. Indexes of glamour stocks or Over The Counter stocks may rise while other indexes fall and vice versa.

Stock indexes tell you about long-range price movements in the entire stock market. Individual stocks may boom or fall, irrespective of whether the stock market is up or down; but it is easier to make money in a rising overall market than a falling one.

Remember that indexes show only price movements. They do not show whether dividends are increasing.

UNLISTED OVER-THE-COUNTER

Another large part of the overall stock market is the "unlisted market" or over-the-counter- (OTC) market. There is "no counter" or meeting place.

The OTC market is a huge negotiated market. For many years there was no central marketplace for these stocks. Various brokerage houses would "make a market" in a particular stock. This means that they would inventory the stock they bought and sold. There are now over 50,000 stocks traded in the over-the-counter market through a network of telephone and teletype wires linking the various brokerage houses.

There is a daily "pink sheet" giving "bid" and "asked" quotations of the market makers from the previous day reporting to the National Daily Quotation Service. ("Bid" means what someone is willing to pay for the stock "Asked" is the amount that someone is willing to pay for the stock. "Asked" is the amount for which someone is willing to sell, subject to confirmation or change in price.) When you see a market report on a listed stock in the paper, you know that a trade actually took place at that price. In the over-the-counter market, you could have a quote with no trade taking place.

There is a wide range of quality in the stocks traded in the over-the-counter market. Traditionally, bank and insurance company stocks have been traded there, even though they have substantial assets. On the opposite end are "penny stocks"(those that sell for a nominal amount per share),

116

which also trade there.

Sometimes a stock will trade for many years on the OTC market, build a sound foundation and then apply for and receive a listing on one of the major exhanges.

For a long time the OTC was considered an "insiders" market and somewhat of a crap shoot for outsiders. The establishment of the National Association of Security Dealers Advanced Quotations (NASDAQ) has had a very positive and stabilizing effect on this market.

NASDAQ

Early in the 1970's NASDAQ appeared on the scene. Various market makers of OTC stocks feed in the changes in their markets to Bunker-Ramo Central Control, which updates the "bid" and "asked" offers available.

NASDAQ has had a beneficial effect on the OTC market, making current markets available to all parts of the country at the same time and enabling dealers to give prompt and accurate service.

YOUR ACCOUNT

How do you use this mass network of facilities? How do you open an account with a stockbroker? It's just as easy as opening a charge account. As a matter of fact, your prospective broker will probably ask fewer questions than the department store where you applied for your last charge account. He will need to know your address, home and office telephone numbers, occupation and company for which you work, spouse's name (if married), social security number, and bank reference; and he will also want to know if you are over 21, if you are a U.S. citizen, and how you want your stocks registered.

A good financial planner will ask much more information

about your assets, your age, your tax bracket, your financial objective, and your temperament. (A financial planner is a stockbroker, but a stockbroker is not necessarily a financial planner — unless he or she is trained to assist you with your complete financial planning needs.) If in doubt, you may want to choose one who is a member of the International Association of Financial Planners and perhaps has earned the certified financial planner designation.

When you make a purchase or sale, it is a firm commitment, regardless of whether the stock goes up or down. A confirmation is mailed to you showing the number of shares of stock purchased or sold, price, commission and fees, net amount due, and settlement date. Within five business days from the trade date, you must pay for stocks you have bought. If you sold a stock, you must deliver your stock certificate within the same period of time, and receive payment.

STOCK COMMISSIONS

Compared with other investments, stocks carry very low rates of commissions. If you sell a piece of real estate, you probably will pay a commission of 6 percent to the realtor, plus another 4 percent or more for all the various closing costs. That reduces your money by at least 10 percent. Buying or selling an investment grade diamond or other type of precious stone can easily cost you 20 percent or more in commissions. Selling 100 shares of a $35 listed stock will usually mean a commission of only 2 percent or less.

Discount brokers are recommended for the investor who wants to save even more and who does not want or need advice from a stock broker.

EXECUTING YOUR ORDER

Once you have opened your account, you may place orders by phone with your broker, asking him to buy or sell stocks for you. For example, let's assume that you place an order to buy 100 shares of West Virginia Widgets (WVW) "at the market." Your broker then gives the order to his company's trader. The trader immediately contacts its floor broker on the floor of the exchange, who quickly walks (its against the rules to run) to the post where West Virginia Widgets is traded. Since you want to buy, the floor broker tries to buy at the lowest price.

At the same time, there may be a computer programmer in Minnesota who wants funds for his daughter's college education. He contacts his broker, his broker contacts his floor broker, and the two of them meet. The exchange is an auction market, and bids and offers are made vocally. This is why the floor of the exchange is so noisy. Your stock broker's company floor broker will be trying to buy for you at, let's say $39. The computer programmer's broker will be trying to sell at $39½. After a brief period of time, your broker decides he can't buy at $39, and the Minnesota man's broker realizes he can't sell at $39½, so a price of $39¼ is agreed upon.

A record of the trade is then written on a slip of paper and handed to a "runner" who places the slip in a pneumatic cylinder that carries it to the tape operator. Within minutes the trade is recorded on the "ticker tape" and the transaction is confirmed.

YIELDS AND RATIOS

Ratios can be confusing to a new stock market investor. To illustrate how they are figured, lets take a look at two

119

companies, A and B. Let's say that they both make computer hardware and that their products are much in demand. For comparison, let's assume that the stock in both companies sell for $20 per share and that both earn $2 per share.

Stock A pays a $1 dividend and stock B pays a 20¢ dividend. Now let's find the yield of each and the price earning ratio.

STOCK	MARKET PRICE	EARNINGS PER SHARE	DIVIDEND	YIELD	PRICE EARNINGS RATIO
A	$20	$2	$1	5%	10:1
B	$20	$2	20¢	1%	10:1

Yield is always the relationship of the dividend to the market price. Therefore, a $1 yield on a $20 stock must be 5 percent per annum. A 20¢ dividend on a $20 stock is a 1 percent yield.

The price-earnings ratio, often referred to as the P/E is the relationship of the market price to the earnings. This can range from three or four to one, up to 100 to 1 or more. It indicates how much investors are willing to pay for $1 of earnings. In this example, both stocks had the same market price,$10 and the same earnings. Thus both have P/E ratios of 10:1.

If you are wondering which stock is best, think about this: one pays more income now, the other should be willing to pay more later (assuming they are both equally sound, well-run companies.)

Do you need income now, or will you need income later? What tax bracket are you now in? These and other important financial questions is what makes all investments dependent on each investor's individual requirements and personal temperament.

If company A pays $1 to you and you are in the 30 percent

tax bracket, you lose 15¢ to the friendly folks at the IRS. If you are in a 50 percent tax bracket, your *Uncle Sam* will demand 25¢. If you are not pressed for income now, you could be better off in the long run with company B, who will be able to reinvest the money they "saved" by not paying a high dividend, developing new products, enlarging plants, etc. . . .and thereby increasing company worth and eventually stock value.

Sometimes it's better to take the money and run; other times it's wise to sit tight and wait for long-range capital gains.

THE INVESTING TRIANGLE

At the top of the investing triangle is *Growth,* at the right *"Safety,"* and at the left is *Income.*

Growth

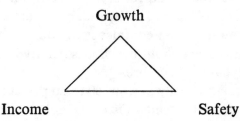

Income   Safety

Always remember, the farther you move away from safety, put simply, the farther your outreach for large potential profits, the greater your risk. If you move too far from your own "safety zone," you may find getting a good night's rest becomes increasingly difficult, and a good night's rest is also a wise investment.

While no investment is 100 percent safe, savings accounts and conservative money market funds come pretty close. Not surprising, they also yield a smaller rate of return for your dollars. Owning blue-chip stock, also may be considered relatively safe. When you venture into growth stock, oil, gas, precious stones, precious metals, etc . . . the potential return on your invested dollars shoots upward, but so does your risk.

INCOME STOCKS

When you invest your money for income you want stocks that have a good record of paying high dividends. But don't get piggish (remember the hog story!). Stability is important, you want your money invested with a company that has planned well for the future. And, one that won't completely fall out of bed when the market, as it's prone to from time to time, turns downward.

A redeeming characteristic of solid income stock is a good measure of resistance against cyclical swings in the economy. The economy should produce products or services that can be expected to be in demand for at least the foreseeable future.

When choosing stocks for dependable income, you want a seasoned veteran with a confidence-building long successful track record. Forget about new issues here, you want an old pro who still has a rosy future.

Income stocks usually pay out 60 to 80 percent of their net earnings in cash dividends. Once a regular dividend rate is established, it is extremely unlikely that this dividend will be reduced even if the company has one full year of reduced earnings or and/or falling market price. In the short run, earnings and market price will have little bearing on dividends paid by an income stock. In the long run they do have a profound impact.

In case you were wondering "who decides how big my dividend will be?", let me explain; the decision as to whether a dividend should be paid in the first place, and if so, how much it should be, is made by the board of directors of the corporation. The amount of money that will be paid in dividends must come from money remaining after the firm pays all expenses and taxes.

YOUR PURCHASE PRICE DETERMINES YOUR YIELD

As you learned earlier, yield is the relationship of the dividend to the market price. Although all shareholders are entitled to an equal dividend per share owned, the price they paid for their shares will vary substantially. If you paid $25 for a share of stock and the dividend is $2 your yield on your invesment is 8 percent. If you paid only $12.50 for a share of this same stock, your yield becomes a very respectable 16 percent. I hasten to add yields over 10 percent are quite rare with solid income stocks.

INCOME STOCK STRATEGY

If you are not pressed for income now, consider companies with slightly lower yields. Often these companies are plowing back a larger portion of their earnings into expanded facilities that should in time yield higher earnings that would allow them to pay out higher dividends. Over a ten to fifteen-year period, many growth stocks have actually had a larger cash pay-out than income stock. Two percent on $10,000 is only $200. But let's assume the growth stock continues to grow and reaches a value of $100,000. Two percent on $100,000 is $2,000 or 20 percent on your original investment.

A booklet that you may find of help if you are interested in selecting stocks for income is one published by the New York Stock Exchange, entitled "Investment Facts Cash Dividends Every Three Months from 25 to 100 years." The booklet points out that the widespread ownership of stocks listed on the New York Stock Exchange is due in large part to a growing awareness that surplus dollars can be put to work in investments that can help bring dignity to a person's future

123

leisure years.

The ability of common stocks to mirror these developments constitutes their greatest attribute. Of course, it is also their greatest risk. On the plus side is the fact that over the years the yields from good common stocks have helped their owners owners keep in step with living costs. There is no such phenomenon as a "sure thing," and past performance does not guarantee the future. But the financial facts of the past may serve as a guide to the future. If so, this booklet may be invaluable to you. It lists recent stock prices, along with their dividend and yield records. If you decide to invest in income stocks, you want a company with a proven past and a bright future. Interestingly, of the many income-oriented common stocks listed in this booklet, 100 have paid a dividend for every quarter for 50 or more years, and several of these have not missed paying a dividend for over 100 of these years.

PREFERRED STOCKS

Equities that are senior to common stock, but a step down to indebtedness of the issue are called preferred stocks. Eighty-five percent of the dividends from an American corporation is exempt from taxation when received by another American corporation. This tends to raise the market price of the high yielding preferreds, making them less attractive to you. You will normally receive a higher rate of return from a high-quality corporate bond than from a preferred stock.

WHAT COLOR ARE YOUR STOCKS?

Many stable income stocks would generally be called blue chips. What is a "blue chip" stock? First, the name can be traced to the game of poker, in which there are three colors of chips: blue for the highest value, red for the next in rank, and white for the lowest value stock.

In the past many of our parents and certainly our grandparents, who did invest in blue-chip companies, bought stocks in major corporations, tossed them into an old cigar box, and forgot about them. This used to work fairly well back then, but that was another era. Today this approach is extremely risky. The blue-chips of today can become the red-chips, white-chips or fresh-out-of chips of tomorrow. To profit in today's market, it's essential that you watch your investments carefully, always ready to adapt to ever changing economic condition.

In all fairness, there are some characteristics of the so-called blue-chips that are worthy of your consideration. They are:

1. A long history of cash dividend payments in bad times and good.
2. A long history of solid earnings in both bull and bear markets.
3. Leadership in an established industry.

INCOME OR GROWTH?

The stock market offers a wide buffet of investment alternatives. When you invest in growth companies, you pay a price in terms of P/E relationship, and, therefore, recieve a smaller amount of current income. Growth companies traditionally reinvest the larger part of their income. This means very little is available for payout ratios.

Simply stated, the high-yielding common stocks have lower expectations of future growth, and therefore lower P/E's than their growth oriented brethen.

If you do not expect growth from a company, you should

ask yourself why the price is so low, making the yields so high. Is the company in serious financial straits? Is the company likely to cut its dividends? Is the regulatory environment likely to be adverse so that the company may have to reduce its dividend to conserve its cash for working capital needs? What is the outlook for the industry? Will this investment keep me ahead of inflation?

It is clear that investing for income is not without risk. If you had bought certain steel company issues a few years ago for income, you would have had your dividends reduced and in some instances eliminated. Not only did the income go down, but the principal loss was also substantial. It is also clear, however, that investing for high income can have its rewards. In periods of high merger activity some cash-rich income stock companies became the targets of acquiring companies. Some of those acquired had spectacular rises in their prices, and if you had sold your shares at the proper time, you would have realized excellent capital gain.

In summary, if you demand income:

1. Look for companies that have a long unbroken dividend record.
2. Don't reach too far for yield and jeopardize principal.
3. Remember that too high a yield can be dangerous and indicates trouble ahead.
4. Favor companies producing consumer goods and services.
5. Select sound companies that continue to increase their dividends.

Income stocks are not too difficult to select after you've conscientiously done your homework. However, selecting growth stocks can be one of the greatest challenges you have ever undertaken, and one of the most rewarding if you can select just a few big winners.

GROWTH STOCKS

Growth is a magic word on Wall Street. A growth company is one that is rapidly increasing its sales and earnings at a much faster rate than the growth of the national population, business, and the economy in general.

Most growth companies are producing products or services in revolutionary new or expanding industries. The 1940's saw oil, television, shelter-related, and pharmaceutical stocks soar. In the 1950's cameras, airplanes, missiles, and electronics got hot. The 1960's saw the computer-oriented stocks begin to move, along with renewed interest in all forms of insurance, drugs, retail stores, soft drinks and many other leisure-time industries. The market suffered a major correction during the early 1970's, taking a major nose-dive in 1973-1974. Nevertheless, several new high-technology companies enjoyed a banner decade as did many consumer-oriented companies.

High tech is still the magic word of the mid-1980's but you can expect big winners from many various industries. How can you spot the smashing success stories of the 1980's and 1990's? Know what to look for!

WHAT TO LOOK FOR
IN SELECTING A GROWTH STOCK

To become a growth stock whiz, you must stay up-to-date on current events - supply, demand, new trends, new technology, psychology, politics, and the overall money markets. Nothing remains static, change is an intricate and undeniable fact of life. Change may not always be for the best, but it is a reality. No one can make long-range profits in securities unless he is willing to accept this fact.

If you're looking for the "right" growth stock, it's a case of timing. Being in the right industry at the right time! It's also crucial that you buy a little ahead of big demand. If you can predict a trend before it makes its big move and sell before the trend expires, you will greatly prosper. Acquire as much knowledge of technological changes and new technology as possible. Stay in touch with public opinion, for it is the people, with their wants and needs, that make forward movement possible.

Beware of "good ideas" that are not yet a developed, proven reality. Just because somebody has come up with a brilliant idea for a product or service, doesn't mean they can turn it into a profitable venture. Will they have adequate financing? Will management be strong? Is their timing good? Can they obtain the necessary permits and licenses? These and other questions may render a great new idea, less than feasible.

WHO RUNS THE COMPANY?

Any company, large or small, is a group of people. Product is very important, as is adequate capitalization, but the bottom line must be, how good is management. There is no substitute for creative, energetic, dedicated and enthusiastic leadership. They should be a profit-minded team that is deeply concerned with raising stock market value. An excellent management team with a good product will almost always out-perform a mediocre management team with a great product. The dynamic duo, of course, is great management and a superior product.

CONSISTENT GROWTH OF EARNINGS

A growth stock is not just a stock that increases in price. You want stocks that have shown a consistent, year-after-year superior growth in earnings even in the face of business reverses and that have a consistent year-in, year-out market for their products or services.

You will want to discover the companies that dominate their markets or are leaders in fast-growing fields. These can be companies in emerging fields or companies that have developed new ideas in established fields.

Most short-termed speculators use the so-called "cyclical" stocks. These stocks are found in those industries most sensitive to swings in the business cycle. They include the heavily capitalized industries such as steel and heavy machinery. These areas are traditionally strongest in periods of prosperity and at a low ebb in times of recession. The trick is to buy cyclical stocks in the early stages of a business upturn and sell them as near as possible to their top. Everything in life seems to be cyclical, and so it is with the stock market.

STAR PERFORMERS

Another trading technique is to move along with the "star performing" stocks of the moment. You can make as much money, short term, on what others think a stock is worth, as on what it is really worth. In the long term we have returned to basics. Star performers only maintain their glitter so long.

Following the stars in finance is hazardous. However, if by using good logic you are convinced that a new industry is about to boom, then cautious selections of a stock in that industry may prove rewarding. The trick is to buy early and then, when everyone is clamoring for shares in that industry, sell! Often the stock market stars are at the height of their popularity, will sell above sensible valuations. It's easy to become "star-struck" but don't "let star gazing" blot out the realities of sound investing.

INVESTING OR SPECULATING?

We have looked at some of the basic characteristics that you must consider in becoming an investor for growth. Should you ever speculate in the stock market? Are there differences between being an investor and being a rank speculator?

THE TRADER

In even the most worthy growth stock selection, there is a time to buy and a time to sell. However, there is another area of the stock market that I would like to classify between the growth stock investor and the shoot-from-the-hip speculator. It is that of the trader.

There appear to be a least three classes of people who fit this category. If you do not have ample capital, I hope you will resist the temptation to join their ranks, as most out-and-out traders lose money. These three classes are:

(A) The constitutional speculators: not necessarily gamblers, but people willing to "Take a chance - to take big risks in hope of big profits.

(B) People who think they can increase their income by moderate trading.

(C) Folks with huge amounts of income to whom fully taxable income is uninviting, who instead desire long-term capital gains.

CUT LOSSES QUICKLY

Many, perhaps most, people who get involved with the stock market, become good buyers and poor sellers. This is to say that they have more trouble deciding to sell a stock than to buy one. This usually spells trouble! Don't try to squeeze that last point out of your stock. Don't be a hog! Successful traders set objectives and they buy and sell accordingly. Also, nothing is more important than to cut losses quickly. If you have made a mistake, admit it. Don't hang on to a loser to find out just how bad your judgement was. A 20 percent drop in value is a darn good "sell" signal." If you bought at $30 a share, and your stock soon falls to $23 or $24 per share, chances are good that it's time to unload.

DON'T FALL IN LOVE WITH YOUR INVESTMENTS!

In trading, it is absolutely necessary to cut your losses quickly. If you've made an error in judgement, don't wait around to find out just how wrong you really were. You can't afford an ego trip. If a 20 percent drop occurs, go back and review your homework and be sure you have all the information you need. It may be that the market is just wrong or it may be that you've made an error in your calculations.

Some of my clients act as if the stock knew they owned it or what they paid for it. The stock doesn't even know that your cousin, once removed, works for the company.

Don't think about an impending dividend, or that you have a loss in the stock, or that you just bought it. Also, don't hesitate to buy it back, even at a high price, if you made a mistake in selling. Above all, don't get married to a stock. Be objective. Be flexible. Don't be guilty of prejudices in stock. We all have them occasionally, but the sooner you recognize them and shed stocks that hinder your investment judgement, the better investor you'll be and the bigger and better your portfolio will be.

Clear, concise thinking is your greatest ally. You probably will not be able to produce a superior investment performance all of the time. Some of the most respected professionals do not, and they occasionally lag behind the averages. First of all, you'll want to search for bargains. If you can buy stocks at a fraction of what you think they are worth, in the long run most of them should turn out better than if you had paid all you thought they were worth.

CHAPTER SIX

MUTUAL FUNDS

Many individuals find letting the professionals do their investing a difficult arrangement to accept. The admission that someone else can handle our finances better than we can is intolerable to many of us. The same doctor, dentist, engineer, pro-football player, or automobile mechanic who is a specialist in his or her field, is often reluctant to take advice in the arena of financial planning and investing.

It is true that some women and men take to investing much like a duck takes to water, nevertheless, the full time pros usually outperform the part time pros.

If you are willing to let a full time professional help, here are some of your options:

PERSONAL PROFESSIONALS

If you are blessed with a large amount of money to invest, you may qualify for private professional management through an investment advisory service. There are some that will accept as small an account as $50,000 for a fee of 1 percent of the net assets per annum. Most of the top services will not accept an account of less than $250,000. Some services will not accept a private account of less than $20 million. Management charges run from ½ to 1 or 2 percent, usually depending on the size of the account.

Let's assume that you have sufficient funds to qualify for private professional management. What should you do? Study!

First, do an in-depth study of the professional teams available. Become acquainted with their personnel, and take a good hard look at their past performance. After all, you are buying brains. You might as well get the best "brains" you can for the money you are paying.

Second, you will sign an agreement allowing the management service discretionary power to buy and sell for your account. This can be cancelled or amended at your discretion. In the agreement you should designate the stockbroker of your choice.

Third, you will need to transfer the agreed amount of money or stocks to the bank or broker that is to act as the custodian of the assets in the account. They will then make the proper delivery of stocks and money at the discretion of the advisors.

After these necessary steps have been taken, you will begin to receive confirmations from your broker on each buy and sell. Your service will also make a monthly or quarterly report to you, giving you a resume of all transactions, a report on gains and losses, and often a comparison of your portfolio's performance against that of the popular averages. You may withdraw the account at any time.

PUBLIC PROFESSIONAL MANAGEMENT

If the amount you have for investment in equities is less than $250,000, as is the case with most people, you should consider using public professional management, through the investment medium of the investment company trusts, commonly called mutual funds. Even if you had a quarter of a million or more to invest, it's hard to beat the returns of a good mutual fund.

"Mutual" means you may mutually benefit from pooling your resources with others. For example, let's say you have $1,000. Alone you could not obtain diversification or professional management. But let's assume there are 999 others who each have $1,000 and have the same financial objective that you do. If all of you pooled your funds, you would have a million dollars. With a million dollars, you would have sufficient money to spread your risk among a number of different industries. You would also have enough money to hire some top professional money managers to select and constantly supervise your holdings. A mutual fund, then, should do for you what you would do for yourself if you had sufficient time, the proper training, the right temperament, and sufficient money to diversify. It offers the same advantages to the small investor that the wealthy have always had. The wealthy have enough money to diversify and enough money to hire the pros.

There are now 20 million shareholders investing 300 billion in mutual funds. They are the fourth largest type of financial institution in the United States and they are growing.

The Investment Company Act of 1940 provides that a mutual fund may not have more than 5 percent of its assets in any one company nor own more than 10 percent of the outstanding shares of any one company. Because of this regulation, if you own a mutual fund you know that you will always have at least twenty stocks in your fund's portfolio, and also that any one of the twenty will not represent more than 10 percent of the outstanding shares of that company. This in itself ensures a fair degree of diversification.

Diversification such as this can permit you to own your slice of the U.S. economy by becoming a part owner of the major companies whose products and services you use regularly. It's often not a bad idea to own a piece of the company where you buy goods and services.

SELECTION AND SUPERVISION

The thoroughness and training of many mutual fund specialists fulfill two other vital requirements of successful investing - proper selection and constant supervision.

In addition to these requirements of successful investing, the properly selected mutual fund can provide other valuable benefits. These benefits include:

1. Convenience
2. Dollar-cost averaging
3. Easy record keeping
4. Matching your personal financial goals
5. Passing on professional management
6. Ease of estate settlement
7. Lower costs
8. Quantity discounts and rights of accumulation
9. Exchange privilege
10. Timing
11. Performance
12. A check a month

Convenience, an Essential Ingredient. The first is convenience. We all do what is convenient for us. Mutual funds can offer this convenience with a plan that will fit almost any pocketbook. You may start an investment program in a mutual fund with a relatively small amount of money; in fact, some funds have no minimum initial investment. Others will accept as small an amount as $100. You may then add funds in any amount which may be as low as $25. In addition, you have the privilege of automatically reinvesting both your dividends and your capital gains, usually without commission. Some funds charge to reinvest dividends. None charge to reinvest capital gains. If you were to receive these same dividends from individual stock in your private portfolio and you realized capital gains from your buys and sells and wanted to re-invest, you would be charged a commission. Since a mutual fund permits immediate reinvestment of small or large amounts of money, it gives you an opportunity to speed up your compounding potential.

Dollar-Cost-Averaging As You Earn. The second item in the list of twelve additional advantages that a mutual fund may offer is that you can truly dollar-cost average. This means putting the same amount of money into the same security at the same interval. One certainty of the stock market is that it will fluctuate. So put this characteristic to work for you instead of worrying so much about it. Choose an amount you can comfortably invest each month (not too comfortably or you may not save anything) and invest that amount on the same day each month.

Many funds provide a bank draft authorization so that the bank can automatically draft your account each month. I find this to be a satisfactory arrangement. Banks never forget! People do.

The mutual funds will carry your share purchase out to the third decimal point, which allows you to truly dollar-cost-average. This makes this investment medium a good one to use for this purpose.

Recordkeeping Made Easy. Another characteristic of the mutual fund is that you have professionals doing your recordkeeping. You will have five choices when you open an account. Regardless of which choice you make, the fund will provide you a historical record of your account.

1. Reinvest all distributions.

2. Reinvest all distributions, and you may add amounts systematically or when you desire.

3. Receive dividends in cash and reinvest capital gains.

4. Receive dividends and capital gains in cash.

5. Receive a check every month.

All you need to do is keep the last confirmation you receive that year, and you will have a complete record of your account. The mutual fund also will send you (and IRS) a Form 1099, showing the dividends and capital gains paid to you for the year. This you will want to keep and attach to your federal income tax return.

You will receive a confirmation statement every time there is any activity in your account. You do not need to worry about the safety of your share certificates. They will be held for you by the fund's transfer agent, or sent to you if you wish.

YOUR FINANCIAL GOALS. A mutual fund must state in its prospectus its financial objective. This financial objective is not subject to change without stockholder consent. The fund rarely changes its objective. If it is at present an income fund and management also desires to manage a growth fund, they will establish a new fund and add it to their family of funds.

TYPES OF MUTUAL FUNDS

There are approximately eleven types of mutual funds: growth (aggressive, quality with income), income, tax-advantages trusts, corporate bond, balanced, convertible bond, speciality funds, option, municipal bond, and money market funds.

GROWTH FUNDS

Under the growth designation you could have four sub-headings: "go-go," very aggressive growth, quality growth,

138

and income producing growth.

If you invest in a quality growth fund, you will be placing your dollar in long term growth because its objective is long term growth. Intermittent volatility should not be of great concern. Nor should you be interested in dividends. As a matter of fact, if it were possible for the fund managers to select stocks that paid no dividends and just grew in value, with no need to buy and sell and realize capital gains, this would be ideal for you. What you really want is for $1 to grow to at least $3 in ten years. You would prefer not to have any tax liability in the meantime if this can be arranged.

COMMON STOCK FUNDS

Those funds which seek growth with income are the backbone of the mutual fund industry. It is the place where most investors feel the most comfortable.

When deciding where you should be on the triangle, you should remember that your temperament is important in your investment program. I find in my counseling that once I have sufficient information about a person's time schedule, assets, and tax bracket, it is not difficult to find the investment that would fulfill his needs financially, but it may not fit his temperament. Regardless of how much I think he should invest for maximum growth, if I detect that volatility would disturb his peace of mind, then the best investment for him will probably be in the middle. Peace of mind is a good investment.

"Get rich quick" seldom (but sometimes) works. Most of us have been reared to believe that we must work hard for everything we get. A common stock, growth with income mutual fund, fills the bill as a "working hard and getting rich slowly investment."

139

INCOME FUNDS

There are a number of good, sound, income funds. Their portfolio managers choose stocks that have paid good dividends, and have a reasonable expectation of continuing good dividends and market stability of their shares. If your need is for income now, rather than later, this is the type of fund you may want to own.

BOND FUNDS

When you invest in a bond fund, you are placing your dollar in the lower right-hand side of the triangle (D). Bond funds have been around for many years; however, during the growth craze of the 1960's, they attracted very little attention. With the severe corrections in the stock market in the 1970's they became popular again.

Bond funds invest most of their funds in debt-type securities. These are corporate bonds and debentures, perhaps a few convertible bonds, treasuries, or commercial paper. Instead of taking an equity position in the market, you become a lender of money when you choose these funds.

When you invest in a bond fund, do not think that the price of the shares will remain fixed. It will not. It will fluctuate with interest rates.

If your fund is composed of bonds with an average yield of 12 percent and the going interest rate is 14 percent, then the fund will not be able to sell its bonds at par; therefore, the price of your shares will decline. On the other hand, if the going rate drops to 10 percent, the fund probably can sell the bonds at a premium (above par) and the price of your shares will increase. If a bond was purchases at par (usually $1,000) and carries a rate of 9 percent, and if it matures January 1, 2000, this does not mean that the fund must hold the bond

140

until the year 2000 to turn it into cash. It means that on January 1, 2000, the person holding the bond is guaranteed $1,000. Between now and that date, the value will usually fluctuate with the country's going interest rate. If you have owned a bond fund over the past few years, you have a loss in it today. I would suggest, if it is part of a family of bonds, that you exchange it for one of the more growth-oriented funds and charge the loss off on your tax return.

BALANCED FUNDS

Balanced funds are funds that invest approximately 60 percent of their funds in high-quality bonds and the remainder in high-quality, income-producing "blue-chip" stocks. In periods of market decline, if that decline has not been caused by extraordinarily high interest rates, they could experience less volatility than the growth funds. Conversely, in a rising market they usually bring up the rear, losing ground in relationship to other investments.

SPECIAL FUNDS

Special funds may concentrate on insurance, bank, utilities, or gold stock. I have not placed them on the triangle because their characteristics are not easily categorized. Utility shares may be popular from time to time for those who want income. Gold stocks can be a very good investment. Their overall trend appears upscale and they often skyrocketed in times of worldwide conflict or economic instability.

CONVERTIBLE BOND FUNDS

In an effort to obtain the best of two worlds, some management groups a few years ago established convertible bond funds. These funds were designed to have a relatively good yield and some potential for growth. As discussed earlier, convertible bonds are supposed to offer you the best of two worlds: the guarantees of principal and rate of return of a bond, and the potential for growth of common stock.

The theory runs that, even though you may be placing a bit of a damper on maximum growth potential, there is downside protection, for the convertible bond should drop in price only to a level where it will take on the characteristics of a bond yielding the current interest level. Unfortunately, we've had wildly gyrating and unusually escalating interest rates that have made these funds more volatile.

The limited number of quality convertible bonds available in the marketplace has tended to make for a thin market (not enough traders to make it competitive). Also, many of the firms who offered convertible bonds in the past were not the blue-chip companies. They had to offer convertibles to "sweeten the kitty" to sell their bonds. Because the convertible bonds have been tied to less stable securities, they have been more volatile than some shareholders have been willing to accept.

TAX-MANAGED TRUSTS

Recently a new type of fund that has attracted some attention is one that elects to be taxed as a corporation rather than act as a conduit, as a regular mutual fund does. You are not given a choice of whether or not you will receive your dividends in cash. They are reinvested for you. The fund pays the tax if any is due. Usually the fund can avoid the tax by conscientious portfolio management. If you've held your shares for over a year and want some cash distribution, just liquidate some shares. The gain will be treated as a capital gain for tax purposes.

One of these funds will let you exchange publicly traded securities you may hold, both stocks and bonds, for shares of the trust, and thereby you will avoid the commission on their sale.

FLEXIBLE FUNDS

There is another category of funds that is difficult to place in any one position. Their chief characteristic is that they are allowed by charter to invest all or a portion of their funds outside the United States. This can be a valuable feature because there are times when there are good buys in other countries and not here. The majority of the few funds following this approach have done very well.

MUNICIPAL BOND FUNDS

These are covered in more detail in a later chapter. They provide tax-free income, permit additions in small amounts, and provide reinvestment privileges to allow you to compound tax-free. If you have had the misfortune to have invested in any bond fund over the past several years, you probably have a rather substantial loss. Should you establish your loss by selling your municipal bond fund? The answer is probably yes.

MONEY MARKET MUTUAL FUNDS

In my opinion, there are only two places to have guaranteed liquid dollars: in a checking account or a money market mutual fund. You need funds in a checking account for convenience. Money market mutual funds have made passbook savings accounts and certificates of deposit obsolete.

Money market mutual funds came about during the mid-

1970s when high interest rates became available to those who had $100,000 to put into savings. You probably remember seeing ads back in 1974 offering 12 percent on $100,000 certificates of deposit. Well, some people didn't have $100,000, so some of the funds established money market funds whereby investors with as little as $1,000 could take advantage of these higher rates by pooling their money with others in the fund.

When you deposit money into one of these accounts, there is no cost to put it in and no cost to take it out, it compounds daily, your rate will usually be comparable to that on a million-dollar certificate of deposit, you can write a check for $500 or more, and you can even draw interest while it is clearing. If you don't think your check will be processed for a few days, you should certainly use your money market mutual fund check-writing privilege. Money has tremendous earning power and you'll always want it working for you rather than someone else.

Your regular money market fund will be invested in large-denomination, short-term money market instruments issued by the Treasury, government agencies, banks, and corporations.

There are also money market mutual funds that must have 100 percent of their assets invested in either Treasury, federal agency obligations, or deposits backed by them. Their yield is generally ½ to 1 percent less, and some of them are exempt from state and local taxes.

A few years ago Americans who did not have large amounts of savings had to accept the small percentage that was available on savings accounts because of Regulation Q. It was great for the banking industry but deprived many a depositor of a decent return on his money. The money market funds came to the rescue of the small saver.

I can see six advantages to money market mutual funds

144

(don't confuse these with the so-called money market certificates issued by some savings and loans). They are: (1) higher yields; (2) instant liquidity; (3) check-writing privileges; (4) funds draw interest until a check is cleared; (5) more safety; and (6) more privacy.

The "more safety" I've mentioned above may have surprised you. I know the argument that deposits in banks are protected by the FDIC (up to $100,000) while there is technically no insurance for money market funds. However, if there should be a run on the banks, the $100,000 would be hard to deliver. If that should occur, only about 2 percent of all bank deposits could probably be paid off under the guarantee.

On the other hand, if you want added safety, you may use the funds that only invest in U.S. government paper, which is backed by the people who print the money.

A LOW COST INVESTMENT

Mutual funds do not make a good "trading vehicle" (as noted earlier, I am not an advocate of lots of trading anyway). Although, overall a low cost investment, commission can be higher to buy than for individual stocks. However, there is no commission to sell regardless of how much the shares may have grown in value. Also, most funds do not have a commission to reinvest dividends or capital gains.

A study conducted by the National Association of Security Dealers indicated that an investment of $5,000 in sixteen individual issues, which is what they deem necessary for adequate diversification, would cost 7 percent in commissions, assuming an "in and out" transaction in listed securities. If you conclude that dividend reinvestment at asset value is worth 1 percent to the average investor, that rights of accumulation are worth 0.5 percent, and that the exchange privilege is worth 0.4 percent, the commission on individual stocks would be 8.9 percent. This study also found that the average charge on fund sales is only 4.4 percent because of the discounts obtained on purchases of over $10,000 and cumulative discounts.

On the basis of prevailing commission rates, $5,000 invested into twenty different stocks at $25 per share would pay commissions around $474 each time, or 9.5 percent of the amount involved. The average fund has over 100 stocks, or five times this diversification, plus a team of professionals selecting the stocks.

For example, a $50,000 investment in a fund with 100 stocks in its portfolio would carry a 4½ percent cost in and no cost to come out. compared to purchasing and selling 100 shares of a $20 stock, the commission would be around $75 or a little over 3%. That's for just one trip and one stock. It's difficult to trade for as low a cost. The funds also pay commissions, but with negotiated rates you would find it difficult to match their lower costs.

HOW MUCH DOES IT EARN?

So many investors get hung up on what it costs to invest. there seems to be some degree of concern and resentment on how much commissions a broker will make.

The bottom line is earnings! Not cost!

Also, while I may choose a no-load mutual fund over a load fund, if everything else is equal, history clearly shows many of the load funds have performed as well as the no-loads.

146

ACQUISITION COSTS

Not unlike most of life's acquisitions, the investor with larger amounts of capital will obtain quantity discounts in obtaining mutual funds. Here are some typical acquisition fees.:

Amount of Purchase	Total Acuqisition Cost
Under $10,000	8.50%
$ 10,000 but less than $ 25,000	7.50%
$ 25,000 but less than $ 50,000	6.00%
$ 50,000 but less than $ 100,000	4.50%
$ 100,000 but less than $ 250,000	3.50%
$ 250,000 but less than $ 500,000	2.50%
$ 500,000 but less than $1,000,000	2.00%
$1,000,000 but less than $2,000,000	1.50%
$2,000,000 and more	1.00%

THE EXCHANGE PRIVILEGE

An important characteristic of most mutual funds is that they offer you the privilege of exchanging one of their funds for another one of their funds. There would be no commission and there would either be no charge or a $5 exchange fee that would go to the transfer agent for his expense in doing this for you. This privilege could be of interest to you if your financial objective has changed.

For instance, if your financial objective has been growth but you are retiring, you may now be more interested in income. You have the privilege of changing from one fund to the other without a sales charge. You should be aware, however, that if you realize a gain on your shares, the IRS consid-

147

ers this a sale, and you'll have to pay a capital gains tax on your profit. A better way may be for you to just begin receiving your check a month from your growth fund, hoping that appreciation will replace the value of the shares redeemed.

You may also establish a loss for tax purposes using the exchange privilege. Let's assume that the market has dropped below your cost. You are still confident of the investment ability of the management team and believe that temporary market conditions have adversely affected anticipated performance. You are nearing the end of the year and have some capital gains already established for the year through the sale of some property. You may want to exchange the fund that you own for one of their other funds, thereby establishing a loss for tax purposes. Even without a capital gain, you could establish a $6,000 loss to be used against $3,000 of ordinary income. If you do not use all of the loss in that year, you may carry it forward indefinitely until you have used all of it.

You would need to wait at least thirty-one days before moving back to your original fund, or the IRS would disallow the deduction, calling it a "wash sale." Again, there is no commission to exchange it back to your original position.

LETTER OF INTENT

Perhaps you do not have a sufficiently large sum today to cross one of the discounts, but you will during the next thirteen months. Then you may want to consider buying under a letter of intent. The letter of intent is not a commitment to buy, but a privilege to buy at a discount during the thirteen-month period. For example, let's assume that you have $10,000 to invest today, but anticipate having an additional $15,000 to invest during the coming thirteen months. You would then invest under a $25,000 letter of intent. When you do that, you receive the same discount on your $10,000 purchase as if you had invested $25,000. The custodian bank then escrows some of your shares. When the additional $15,000 is added, the custodian releases your shares. If you decide you do not want to add the remaining $15,000, that is your privilege. If the thirteen months pass and you have not completed your letter, you have two choices: return the discount, which you would not have received anyway without the letter, or the custodian bank will sell enough of your escrowed shares to return to the fund the second discount you received and will send you the remaining shares. Your discount would be adjusted back to the $10,000 level. Therefore, the letter of intent never costs you more and can save you money. You are not required to return the dividends and capital gains on the extra shares you received during the period they were in escrow.

ADDING MORE AT A DISCOUNT

Under what is called "rights of accumulation," you may also qualify for additional discounts. Let's assume that you own shares that have a value of $20,000 and that you have $5,000 you would like to add to your account. You may do so under the "rights of accumulation" at the $25,000 discount level. As your account grows, you may continue to add at progressively smaller opportunity fees as you cross each discount. Pension and profit-sharing plans use mutual funds shares because of their lower cost of acquisition, diversification, ease of record keeping, and because they meet the "prudent man" rule and fiduciary requirements.

TIMING

The greatest advantage to the exchange privilege is that it gives you the opportunity to move in and out of the market

149

without a commission. If the Federal Reserve is severely tightening the money supply, which looks as if it will choke the market, and your fund is part of a family of funds that has a money market fund, you may want to move over to this safer harbor, ride out the storm, and draw a tidy interest in the meantime.

You may be wondering why the fund managers do not take this action for you. They do move into as defensive a position as they can under the regulations by which they must abide. However, to qualify as a regulated investment company, which is important to you in terms of your taxes, less than 30 percent of their gross income in any fiscal year can be derived from holding securities less than three months. This regulation may inhibit moving from stock to cash on a short-term basis, which for your purposes may be the most prudent action to take. The exchange privilege gives you the opportunity to take advantage of the strengths of top professional management while avoiding the weakness caused by these regulations. This can make it possible for you to exploit their offensive ability by holding their funds during rising markets and avoiding what may be short-term weakness by moving out of the funds entirely during down markets.

TIMING SERVICES

You can attempt to time your own moves in and out of the market or you can use a timing service to do this for you. Timing services have become very viable considerations during the past few years, because the Federal Reserve has been "manipulating" the money supply and causing great volatility in interest rates and available capital.

MUTUAL FUNDS AND YOUR IRA

Mutual funds make a great investment for many IRA accounts. You may contribute 100 percent of your earned income up to a maximum of $2,000 and deduct it from your taxable income. You can also let the earnings compound tax-deferred. If you have a non-working spouse, $2,250 can be put in an IRA. If both husband and wife work, $4,000 may be contributed.

The contribution can be made any time prior to filing your income tax return and will be credited for the year you are filing for.

If you invested $2,000, $2,250, or $4,000 per year and averaged a 15 percent return on investment (ROR) you would have the following assets in your *Individual Retirement Account* (IRA):

Years	Amount
$2,000 per year	
10	$ 46,699.00
20	235,620.00
30	999,914.00
40	4,091,908.00
$2,250 per year	
10	52,536.00
20	265,072.00
30	1,124,903.00
40	4,603,396.00
$4,000 per year	
10	93,398.00
20	471,240.00
30	1,999,828.00
40	8,183,816.00

Your regular investing (even if modest) in a good vehicle, plus time, plus American capitalism growth equals a big pay-off. Think of it, a young couple, 25 years of age, who invested $4,000 per year for 40 years, can retire at age 65 with eight-million-one-hundred-eighty-three-thousand-eight-hundred-sixteen dollars. Wow! Over 40 years they would have contributed $160,000 for their retirement. Our capitalistic system would have given them the rest - over eight million dollars! I realize putting four thousand aside each year may be no easy task for a young married couple. But if they can swing it, perhaps by accepting a lower standard of living and a few less "fun things" during the first few years, even if inflation reduces the value of a dollar several times during those 40 years, they still should be able to retire very rich.

CHAPTER SEVEN

NO-LOAD MUTUAL FUNDS

Although the investor of the mid to late 1980's is being offered a vast mix of financial opportunities, few, if any, offer greater advantages than investing in No-Load Mutual Funds. The Profit Ideas financial team and I are so high on this form of investment that this special chapter has been included in this book.

NO-LOAD FUNDS...
WHAT THEY ARE AND HOW THEY WORK

What exactly is a mutual fund?

A mutual fund is a company that uses professional management to invest your money. Depending on the type of fund, investments can be in stocks, bonds, money market instruments, or a combination of these. Investors with similar financial objectives—such as growth of capital, income, safety of principal, or tax-exempt income—pool their assets to obtain both the management and the portfolio diversification they probably could not obtain if investing individually. Investors purchase shares of the fund and participate in the income, gains and/or losses.

What's the Difference Between a No-Load and a Load Fund?

"Load" is the technical word for *sales charge.* A no-load fund does not carry a sales charge; a load fund does. For no-loads, shares are purchased directly from the fund rather than from a broker, so that *100%* of the money invested goes to work for *you.*

153

Load funds charge a commission which often works out to be more than 9% of your investment. If you have $10,000 to invest, for example, less than $9,100 actually goes into your account; the remainder goes to pay a broker.

Without a Broker, Isn't it Difficult to Deal with a Fund?

Over the past several years, no-load mutual funds have made it easier and easier for investors to deal with them directly, eliminating the need for a broker. In many cases a fund transaction can be completed simply by dialing a toll-free number. Today, the vast majority of all mutual fund shareholders are no-load investors. That's millions of people taking advantage of the ease and profitability of no-load investing.

OK. No-Load Funds Don't Have a Sales Charge. But They Must Charge Something for Their Management.

All mutual funds, load and no-load, charge a management fee—usually between ½ of 1% and 1% of monies invested. Considering all the advantages of mutual fund investing, that's quite a bargain.

HOW TO INVEST IN NO-LOADS

1. Determine your own investment goals.

You must first take the time to identify your investment objectives or goals—safety of principal, high current income, long term growth, tax-free income, etc. Often you will have more than one investment goal, or your goal may change over time. The following table will assist you in this determination.

2. To determine which fund or funds to contact, refer to the section of this chapter that best matches your goals.

3. Act today!

Your next step is simply to call the fund directly or complete and mail one of the forms in the back requesting literature be sent to you. Before you invest, read the material carefully, and if you have any questions, call the fund for assistance.

EXPLANATION OF THE LISTINGS

The Sections

At the beginning of each heading on the following pages is a general description of the funds in each category giving their general objectives, nature of investments, and any features unique to that type of fund.

The Column Headings: Fund Name

Adviser/Management Company in italics
fund's address
telephones: toll free 800 number if available; local number

Investment Objective and Policy

A capsule description of the fund's objectives, and the investment policies practiced by the adviser to achieve that goal.

Year first offered

Year shares first sold to public.

Assets (Mil.) 12/82

The fund's size in millions of dollars.

Purchase Requirements

Dollar Amounts indicate minimum investments.

General Characteristics of this Group of Funds

If your basic objective is	You will want the following type of fund	Listed under	Investment Policy	Potential Capital Appreciation	Stability of Income	Stability of Principal
Current income PLUS capital protection	Money Market	Money Market Funds	money market instruments	None	Low	Very High
Tax-free income PLUS capital protection	Tax-Exempt Money Market	Tax-Exempt Money Market Funds	short-term municipal bonds	None	Stable	High
Tax-exempt income	Municipal Bond	Tax-Exempt Income Funds	municipal bonds	Moderate	Stable	Low to moderate
Current income	Fixed Income of Bond Funds	Income Funds	bonds; preferred stocks	Moderate	Stable	Low to moderate
Current income	Option income	dividend paying	Moderate common stock on which call options are traded	Stable	Moderate	
Current income and conservation of capital	Balanced	Balanced Funds	stocks and bonds	Moderate	Grows modestly	Moderate
Capital appreciation	Growth	Growth Funds	stocks	High	Moderate to low	Low
Income and capital growth	Growth and Income		stocks	High	Possible growth	Low to moderate
Aggressive growth	Aggressive Growth		stocks	Very High	Low	Very Low

156

Tel.—telephone orders accepted.

Wire—Bank wire.

If no other instructions are indicated, initial purchase must be in writing accompanied by fund's application and a check or money order. Subsequent purchases must be accompanied by account identification and a check or money order.

Redemption Procedures:

Tel.—Telephone.

Wire—Bank Wire.

Ck. Wrtg.—You write a check on checks provided by fund; clearing of check at Fund's bank causes automatic liquidation of shares to cover amount.

EFT—Electronic Funds Transfer—a method to move money by telephone between your fund and your bank account.

NOTE: ABOVE PROCEDURES ARE PREDICATED UPON AUTHORIZATION FORMS COMPLETED AND ON FILE WITH THE FUND IN ADVANCE.

Writ.—request must be in writing.

Sig. Guar.—written request must have a signature guarantee stamped by a bank or broker.

Services: Dividends:

Auto.—Your income or capital gains divided may be automatically reinvested into additional fund shares.

A—annual.

S/A—semi-annual.   indicated frequency

Q—quarterly.   of fund's dividend

M—monthly.

Retirement Plans:

Master or prototype plans made available by funds for tax-deductible contributions for qualified investors. A Master plan is administered by the fund itself; a prototype plan is not. See "Retirement" section for explanations of each type of plan.

Keo.—Keogh.

IRA—Individual Retirement Account.

Corp.—Corporate pension or profit sharing plans.

SEP—Simplified Employee Pension.

Muni—Deferred Compensation Plan.

401(k).

403(b).

Other:

Syst. With—a pre-arranged systematic withdrawal system whereby the fund automatically liquidates sufficient shares to pay the investor a specific amount of money at certain intervals, e.g., monthly.

Auto. Pur.—automatic periodic, pre-authorized purchase of Fund shares through payroll deductions, automatic monthly or quarterly bank drafts against your checking account, or social security or military pay checks deposited directly into your fund account.

Exch. Writ. or Tel.—switch investments from one fund to another, usually within one fund complex, or with an outside fund under mutual agreement between funds; some funds permit this by writing only, some by preauthorized telephone instructions.

Grp. Acct.—services offered by some funds to maintain individual account records for large groups—such as corporate or municipal employee benefit plans.

Var.Ann.—an annuity using mutual fund shares as investments with distributions accumulating tax-deferred.

EFT—Electronic Funds Transfer (See "Redemption Procedures").

PLEASE NOTE THAT THIS IS A GENERAL DE-
SCRIPTION OF THE SERVICES OFFERED TODAY BY
NO-LOAD MUTUAL FUNDS. BE SURE TO CONSULT A
FUND'S PROSPECTUS FOR COMPLETE DETAILS OF
THE SERVICES OFFERED BY THAT PARTICULAR
FUND, AND INSTRUCTIONS ON EXACTLY HOW TO
USE THESE SERVICES.

MONEY MARKET FUNDS...
FOR SAFETY OF PRINCIPAL, HIGH CURRENT INCOME, INSTANT LIQUIDITY

GENERALLY USED BY:

Individuals, corporate, institutional and association cash
managers, and bank trust departments to maximize their return while maintaining safety of principal.

WHAT THEY BUY:

Short-term (less than one year maturities) money market
instruments such as U.S. Government obligations, certificates of deposit, corporate commercial paper, etc.

HOW THEY DIFFER:

Primarily on the length of maturity of the portfolio. Also,
some funds may specialize in or emphasize a particular type
of money market instrument.

UNIQUE FEATURES:

Interest is accrued on a daily basis, paid monthly or quarterly, or can be reinvested for automatic compounding; has
instant liquidity, often via telephone, wire or by writing a personal check on the account.

Fund Name (Advisor) Address and Telephone Number	Investment Objective and Policy	Year First Offered	Assets Mil. 12/31/82	Purchase Requirements Initial	Subsq.	Redemption Procedures	Services
ADVISORS CASH RESERVE FUND, INC. *(American Investment Mgrs., Inc.)* 11400 Rockville Pike, Ste. 300 Rockville, MD 20852 301-770-1600	**Maximum current income consistent with preservation of principal and maintenance of liquidity by investing in high quality money market instruments.**	1982	$ 4	$1000	$100	Tel.; Wire; Ck. Writ.; Writ. with Sig. Guar.	*Dividends:* Auto.; M. *Ret. Plans:* IRA, Keo. *Other:* Syst. With.
AMERICAN EXPRESS GOVERNMENT MONEY FUND *(The Boston Company Advisors Inc.)* One Boston Place Boston, MA 02106 617-956-9748	High current income, stability of principal and liquidity investing in obligations issued, insured or collateralized by U.S. Gov't.	1982	14	1000	100	Tel.; Wire; Tel. exchange Ck. Writ.; Writ. with Sig. Guar.	*Dividends:* M. *Ret. Plans:* IRA *Other:* no wire red. fee
AMERICAN EXPRESS MONEY FUND *(The Boston Company Advisors Inc.)* One Boston Place Boston, MA 02106 617-956-9748	Seeks to achieve high current income, stability, or principal and liquidity by investing in high grade money market instruments.	1982	24	1000	100	Tel.; Wire Tel. exch.; Ck writ.; Writ with Sig. Guar.	*Dividends:*M. *Ret. Plan:* IRA no wire red. fee
AMERICAN INVESTORS MONEY FUND, INC. *(American Investors Corp.)* P.O. Box 2500 Greenwich, CT 06836 800-243-5353/203-622-1600	Highest income from quality, short-term securities of U.S. Corp. and certificates of deposit of U.S. banks; no foreign investments.	1982	.1	2500 400-Ret. plans	100 Mail 1000 Wire 20 Ret. plans	Mail, check tel, wire sign. over $5M guar.	*Div.:* Auto.. M&Q *Ret. Plans:* IRA Keo., Corp. *Other:* Exch. priv. Tel., wire, mail
BOSTON COMPANY CASH MGMT. FUND *(The Boston Advisors, Inc.)* One Boston Place Boston, MA 02106 800-343-6324/617-956-9740	As high a rate of current income as is consistent with the preservation of capital and liquidity by using money market instruments.	1979	324	1000	0	Tel.; Wire.; Ck. Writ.; Writ. with Sig. Guar. Tel. Exch.	*Dividends:* Auto.; M. *Ret. Plans:* Keo., IRA, Corp. *Other:* Syst. With.; Auto No wire fee
BOSTON COMPANY GOVERNMENT MONEY FUND *(The Boston Company Advisors Inc.)* One Boston Place Boston, MA 02106 800-343-6324/617-956-9740	High current income, safety of principal and daily liquidity; invests excl. in oblig. backed by full faith and credit of U.S. Gov't.	1982	28	1000	0	Tel.; Wire.; Ck. Writing writ. with sig. guar. Tel. Exch.	*Div.:* declared daily. M. *Ret. Plan:* Keo., IRA, Corp. *Other:* no wire fee

Fund	Objective	Year	Assets	Min. Initial	Min. Subsequent	Redemption	Dividends/Ret. Plans/Other
CAPITAL PRESERVATION FUND, INC. (*Benham Management Corp.*) 755 Page Mill Rd. Palo Alto, CA 94304 800-4-SAFETY/800-848-0002 (AK and HI only)	Safety; U.S. Treasury securities backed by the direct full faith and credit of the U.S. Government and maturing within 1 year.	1972	2115	1000	100 Wire	Tel.; Ck. Writ.; Wire; Writ. with Sig. Guar.	*Dividends:* Auto.; Q. *Ret. Plans:* Keo.; IRA *Other:* Exch.-Writ.
CAPITAL PRESERVATION FUND II (*Benham Management Corp.*) 755 Page Mill Rd. Palo Alto, CA 94304 800-4-SAFETY/800-848-0002 (AK and HI only)	U.S. Treas. Sec. backed by the full faith and credit pledge of U.S. Gov't held under repurchase ag't avg. mat. 7 days or less.	1980	878	5000	100 Wire	Tel.; Ck. Writ.; Wire; Writ. with Sig. Guar.	*Dividends:* Auto.; Q. *Other:* Exch.-Writ.
DOLLAR RESERVES (*Bull & Bear Group*) 11 Hanover Square New York, NY 10005 800-431-6060/800-942-6911 (NY only)	Maximum current income consistent with preservation of capital and maintenance of liquidity; invests in high quality money mkt. inst.	1980	116	1000	100	Writ.; Tel.; Wire; Ck. Writ.	*Dividends:* Auto.; M. *Ret. Plans:* Keo., IRA, 403(b) *Other:* Syst. With.; Auto. Pur.; Exch. Tel.
FIDELITY CASH RESERVES (*Fidelity Group*) 82 Devonshire St. Boston, MA 02109 800-225-6190/617-523-1919	Current income consistent with stability and liquidity. Invests in high grade money market instruments (including Euro CD's).	1979	4039	1000	250	Tel.; Wire; Ck. Writ.; Writ. with Sig. Guar.	*Dividends:* Auto.; Q. *Ret. Plans:* Keo., IRA, Corp. 403(b) *Other:* Syst. With.; EFT; Exch.-Tel.
FIDELITY DAILY INCOME TRUST (*Fidelity Group*) 82 Devonshire St. Boston, MA 02109 800-225-6190/617-523-1919	Income: invests only in high grade money market instr., U.S. Gov. obligations, prime 1 comm. paper and short term corp. notes rated AA or better.	1974	$ 3473	$10M	$ 500	Tel.; Wire; Ck. Writ.; Writ. with Sig. Guar.	*Dividends:* Auto.; M. *Ret. Plans:* Keo., IRA, Corp., 403(b) *Other:* Syst. With.; EFT; Exch.-Tel.
FIDELITY MONEY MARKET TRUST (*Fidelity Group*) 82 Devonshire St. Boston, MA 02109 800-225-6190/617-523-1919	Current income — choice of three portfolios of money market securities for the large institutional, corporate and individual investor.	1979	2745	250M Wire only	0 Wire only	Wire Only	*Dividends:* Auto.; M. *Other:* Sub. Acct.; permanent acct. representative.
FIDELITY U.S. GOVERNMENT RESERVES (*Fidelity Group*) 82 Devonshire St. Boston, MA 02109 800-225-6190/617-523-1919	Current income consistent with stability and liquidity from portfolio of securities issued and guaranteed by U.S. Government and its agencies.	1981	409	1000	250	Tel.; Wire; EFT; Ck. Writ. Writ. with Sig. Guar.	*Dividends:* Auto.; Q. *Ret. Plans:* Keo., IRA, Corp. 403(b) *Other:* Syst. With.; Exch.-Tel.
FINANCIAL DAILY INCOME SHS. (*Financial Programs, Inc.*) P.O. Box 2040 Denver, CO 80201 800-525-9831/303-779-1233	As high a level of current income as is consistent with liquidity and safety of capital.	1975	252	1000	100	Tel.; Wire; Ck. Writ.; Written	*Dividends:* Auto.; M. *Ret. Plans:* Keo., IRA, Corp. 403(b) *Other:* Auto. Pur.; Exch.-Tel.

161

Fund Name (Advisor) Address and Telephone Number	Investment Objective and Policy	Year First Offered	Assets Mil. 12/31/82	Purchase Requirements Initial	Subsq.	Redemption Procedures	Services
FIRST TRUST MONEY MARKET FUND/ GENERAL PURPOSE (*Principal Protection Advisory Services, Inc.*) 110 N. Franklin St. Chicago, IL 60601 312-781-9490/800-621-4770	High level of current income consistent with principal of preservation of capital and maintenance of liquidity.	1983	.1	0	0	Tel.; Wire; Ck. Wrtg. $100 min.	*Dividends:* Auto.; **M.** *Other:* Syst. With.
FIRST TRUST MONEY MARKET FUND/ GOVERNMENT PORTFOLIO (*Principal Protection Advisory Services, Inc.*) 110 N. Franklin St. Chicago, IL 60601 312-781-9490/800-621-4770	High level of current income consistent with preservation of capital and maintenance of liquidity.	1980	7	0	0	Tel.; Wire; Ck. Writ.; $100 min.	*Dividends:* Auto.; **M.** *Other:* Syst. With.
FIRST VARIABLE RATE FUND (*Government Securities Management Co.*) 1700 Pennsylvania Ave., NW Washington, DC 20006 800-368-2748/301-951-4820	High yield, stability, liquidity. Invests exclusively in short-term and variable rate obligations backed by the U.S. Government.	1977	1279	2000	250	Tel.; Wire; Ck. Writ; Writ. with Sig. Guar.	*Dividends:* Auto; Q. *Ret. Plans:* Keo., IRA, Corp. *Other:* Syst. With: Grp. Acct; Auto Pur; Exch. Tel. or Writ. EFT called Calvert Money Controller
FLA. U.S. GOVT. MONEY MARKET (*Fla. Mutual-Fund Group. Inc.*) 1 Financial Plaza Ft. Lauderdale, FL 33394 305-522-0200/800-432-1592 (FL only)	Fund seeks to obtain as high a level of current income as is consistent with the preservation of principal and liquidity.	1980	10	1000 Tel.; Wire	100 Tel.; Wire	Tel.; Wire; Ck. Writ.; Writ. with Sig. Guar.	*Dividends:* Auto.; M. *Other:* Syst. With; Exch.-Tel.
FOUNDERS MONEY MKT. FUND, INC. (*Founders Mutual Depositor Corp.*) 655 Broadway Denver, CO 80203 800-525-2440/303-595-3863	Current income consistent with preservation of capital and maintenance of liquidity.	1981	11	1000	100	Tel.; Writ. with Sig. Guar.; Ck. Writ.	*Dividends:* Auto.; M. *Ret. Plans:* Keo., IRA *Other:* Auto. Pur.; Syst. With.; Exch.-Tel.
GREAT LAKES MONEY FUND (*Unified Management Corp.*) 400 Renaissance Center, Ste. 265 Detroit, MI 48243 313-259-9900/800-428-4492	Current income from diversified money mkt. instruments; U.S. Gov., 150 largest U.S. banks, short-term corp. debt and repurchase agreements.	1982	8	1000	100	Tel.; Writ.; Ck. Writ.	*Dividends:* Auto.; M. or Q. *Ret. Plans:* Keo., IRA, Corp., 403(b) *Other:* Syst. With.; Auto. Pur.; Exch.-Tel.

162

Fund	Objective	Year	Assets	Min. Initial	Min. Subseq.	Services	Dividends / Ret. Plans / Other
GUARDIAN CASH MANAGEMENT TRUST *(Guardian Investor Services Corp.)* 201 Park Avenue South New York, N.Y. 10003 800-221-3253/800-522-7800 (NY only)	Maximize current income with liquidity and preservation of capital by investing in money market instruments.	1982	4	1000	100	Tel.; Ck. Writ.; VISA Debit card; VISA cks.; Wire; Phone; Writ. with Sig. Guar.	*Dividends:* Auto.; M. *Ret. Plans:* Keo.; IRA *Other:* Syst. With.
IDS CASH MANAGEMENT FUND, INC. *(Investors Diversified Services)* Box 369, IDS Tower Minneapolis, MN 55440 800-IDS-IDEA/800-437-4332	Maximum current income consistent with liquidity and conservation of capital by investing in money market securities.	1979	1206	2000	100	Wire; Ck. Writ.; Writ. with Sig. Guar.	*Dividends:* Auto., M. *Ret. Plans:* Keo.; IRA; Corp. *Other:* Syst. With.; Exch.-Writ.; Grp.-Acct.
IDS GOV'T SECURITIES MONEY FD. *(Investors Diversified Services)* Box 369, IDS Tower Minneapolis, MN 55440 800-IDS-IDEA/800-437-4332	Maximum current income consistent with safety of capital and liquidity. Invests in money market securities backed by U.S. Gov't.	1982	25	2000	100	Wire; Ck. Writ.; Writ. with Sig. Guar.	*Dividends:* Auto., M. *Ret. Plans:* Keo.; IRA, Corp. *Other:* Syst. With.; Exch.-Writ.; Grp.-Acct.
LEHMAN CASH MGMT. FUND *(Lehman Mgmt. Co., Inc.)* 55 Water Street New York, NY 10041 800-221-5350/212-558-3288	Current income consistent with preservation of capital and liquidity; invests in high-quality short-term money market instruments.	1981	750	2500	100	Tel.; Wire; Ck. Writ.; Writ. Sig. Guar. over $5M	*Dividends:* Auto.; M. *Ret. Plans:* Keo., IRA *Other:* Exch.-; Tel. or Grp.-Acct; Syst. With.
LEHMAN GOVERNMENT FUND *(Lehman Mgmt. Co., Inc.)* 55 Water Street New York, NY 10041 800-221-5350/212-558-3288	Safety; current income consistent with preservation of capital and liquidity; invests only in obligations issued or guaranteed by the U.S. Government.	1981	$149	$2500	$100	Tel.; Wire; Ck. Writ.; Writ with Sig. Guar. over $5M	*Dividends:* Auto.; M. *Ret. Plans:* Keo., IRA *Other:* Exch.-; Tel., Writ. Grp. Acct; Syst. With.
LEXINGTON GOV'T SEC./MONEY MARKET *(Lexington Management Corp.)* 580 Sylvan Ave., P.O. Box 1515 Englewood Cliffs, NJ 07632 800-526-4791/800-932-0838 (NJ only)	High current income consistent with preservation of capital & liquidity through investments in U.S. Government obligations.	1981	33	1000	50	Tel.; Ck. Writ.; Writ. with Sig. Guar. over $5M	*Dividends:* Auto.; M. *Ret. Plans:* Keo., IRA *Other:* Syst. With.; Auto. Pur. Exch.-Tel.; Grp. Acct.
LEXINGTON MONEY MARKET TRUST *(Lexington Management Corp.)* 580 Sylvan Ave., P.O. Box 1515 Englewood Cliffs, NJ 07632 800-526-4791/800-932-0838 (NJ only)	High current income consistent with preservation of capital & liquidity.	1979	315	1000	50	Tel.; Wire; Ck. Writ.; Writ. Sig. Guar. over $5M	*Dividends:* Auto.; M. *Ret. Plans:* Keo., IRA *Other:* Syst. With.; Auto. Pur. Exch.-Tel.; Grp. Acct.

Fund Name (Advisor) Address and Telephone Number	Investment Objective and Policy	Year First Offered	Assets Mil. 12/31/82	Purchase Requirements Initial	Purchase Requirements Subsq.	Redemption Procedures	Services
LIQUID GREEN TRUST *(Unified Management Corporation)* Guaranty Building Indianapolis, IN 46204 800-428-4492/317-634-3300	Current income from diversified money mkt. instruments; U.S. Gov., 150 largest U.S. banks, short term corp. debt and repurchase agreements.	1980	152	1000 Wire	100 Wire	Tel.; Writ.; Ck. Writ.	*Dividends:* Auto.: M or Q *Ret. Plans:* Keo., IRA, Corp. 403(b) *Other:* Syst. With.; Auto. Pur.; Exch.-Tel.; Owners' use of home computer terminals; Payroll deduction plan
NEWTON MONEY FUND *(Heritage Investment Advisors, Inc.)* 733 N. Van Buren St. Milwaukee. WI 53202 414-347-1141/800-242-7229 (WI only)	To provide stability of principal and as high a rate of current income consistent with preservation of capital and liquidity.	1981	13	1000	250	Tel.; Wire; Ck. Writ.; Writ.	*Dividends:* Auto.; M. *Ret. Plans:* Keo., IRA, 403(b) *Other:* Syst. With.
PLIMONEY FUND, INC. *(Tenneco Asset Management Company)* 777 Walker, 2 Shell Plza., #2000 Houston, TX 77002 713-757-5673/713-757-5679	Maximum current income to the extent consistent with stability of principal.	1980	73	1000	0	Wire; Free Ck. Writ.; Writ. with no Sig. Guar. if shares are in unissued form	*Dividends:* Auto.; M. *Ret. Plans:* Keo., IRA, 403(b) *Other:* Syst. With.; Auto., Exch-Wit.; Pur.; Var. Ann. (qual. plans only)
T. ROWE PRICE PRIME RESERVE *(T. Rowe Price Associates, Inc.)* 100 East Pratt St. Baltimore, MD 21202 800-638-5660/301-547-2308	Preservation of capital, liquidity, and high income through prime money market instruments.	1976	3222	2000 Wire	100 Wire	Tel., Wire.; Ck. Writ.; Writ. with Sig. Guar. over $10M	*Dividends:* Auto.; M. *Ret. Plans:* Keo., IRA, Corp., 403(b), Muni. *Other:* Syst. With.; Auto. Pur. Grp.-Acct.; Exch.-Tel.
T. ROWE PRICE U.S. TREASURY FUND *(T. Rowe Price Associates, Inc.)* 100 East Pratt St. Baltimore, MD 21202 800-638-5660/301-547-2308	Maximum safety of capital, liquidity, and highest income through investments primarily in U.S. Treasury securities.	1982	143	2000 Wire	100 Wire	Tel., Wire.; Ck. Writ.; Writ. with Sig. Guar. over $10M	*Dividends:* Auto.; M. *Ret. Plans:* Keo., IRA, Corp., 403(b), Muni. *Other:* Syst. With.; Auto. Pur. Grp.-Acct.; Exch.-Tel.
QUAKER CASH RESERVES, INC. *(Stratton Management Co.)* Butler & Skippack; Box 550 Blue Bell, PA 19422 215-542-8025	Seeks the highest possible current income consistent with the preservation of capital and liquidity.	1981	4	1000	100	Tel.; Ck. Writ.; Wire; Writ.	*Dividends:* Auto.; M. *Ret. Plans:* Keo., IRA, 403(b) *Other:* Syst. With.; Exch.-Tel.

Fund	Objective	Year	Assets	Min. Initial	Min. Subs.	Redemption	Services
RETIRE. PLAN. FDS. OF AMER/MONEY *(Chicago Title & Trust Co.)* 111 W. Washington Street Chicago, IL 60602 800-621-1110/312-630-2540	Income consistent with preservation of capital; available only to tax-qualified retirement plans.	1978	24	250	250	Written	*Dividends:* Auto.; Q. *Ret. Plans:* Keo., IRA, Corp., 403(b) *Other:* Exch.-Tel.
SAFECO MONEY MKT. MUTUAL FUND, INC. *(Safeco Asset Management Co.)* Safeco Plaza 115 NL Seattle, WA 98185 800-426-6730	As high a level of current income consistent with preservation of capital by investing in money market instruments.	1982	17	1000	100	Tel.; Wire; Ck. Writ.; Writ. with Sig. Guar.	*Dividends:* Auto.; M. *Ret. Plans:* Keo., IRA, Corp., 403(b) *Other:* Syst. With.; Auto. Pur.; Exch.-Tel.
SCUDDER CASH INVESTMENT TRUST *(Scudder, Stevens & Clark, Inv. Counsel)* 175 Federal St. Boston, MA 02110 800-225-2470/617-482-3990	Income: Invests in debt securities with maturities not more than one year. Constant net asset value.	1975	1197	1000	0	Tel.; Ck. Writ.; Writ. with Sig. Guar.	*Dividends:* Auto.; M. *Ret. Plans:* Keo., IRA, Corp. 403(b), 401(k) *Other:* Syst. With.; Exchange-Tel.; Grp.-Acct.
SCUDDER GOVERNMENT MONEY FUND *(Scudder, Stevens & Clark, Inv. Counsel)* 175 Federal St. Boston, MA 02110 800-225-2470/617-482-3990	Income: Invests in U.S. Government and U.S. Government guaranteed obligations with maturities not more than 120 days. Constant net asset value.	1981	176	1000	0	Tel.; Ck. Writ.; Writ. with Sig. Guar.	*Dividends:* Auto.; M. *Ret. Plans:* Keo., IRA, Corp. 403(b), 401(k) *Other:* Syst. With.; Exchange-Tel.; Grp.-Acct.
SELECTED MONEY MKT FUND, INC. *(Burton J. Vincent, Chesley & Co.)* 105 W. Adams St. Chicago, IL 60603 800-621-7321/800-972-1092 (IL only)	Maximize current income to the extent consistent with preservation of capital by investing in money market instruments.	1977	65	1000	100	Tel.; Wire; Ck. Writ.; Writ. with Sig. Guar.	*Dividends:* Auto.; M. *Ret. Plans:* Keo., IRA, Corp. *Other:* Syst. With.; Exch.-Writ. and Tel.
SELECTED MONEY MARKET FUND GOVERNMENT PORTFOLIO *(Burton J. Vincent, Chesley & Co.)* 105 W. Adams St. Chicago, IL 60603 800-621-7321/800-972-1092 (IL only)	Maximize current income with preservation of capital by investing in government securities and repos.	1982	$ 3	$ 1000	$ 100	Tel.; Wire; Ck. Writ.; Writ. with Sig. Guar.	*Dividends:* Auto.; M. *Ret. Plans:* Keo., IRA, Corp. *Other:* Syst. With.; Exch.-Writ. and Tel.
SELIGMAN CASH MGMT. FUND *(J. & W. Seligman and Co., Inc.)* One Bankers Trust Plaza New York, NY 10006 800-221-2450/800-522-6869 (NY only)/ 212-432-4100	2 sep. investment portfolios: prime high qual. money market instrum. and Gov't portfolio; invests only in short-term sec. issued or guar. by the U.S. Gov't.	1977	693	1000	0	Tel.; Wire; Ck. Writ.; Writ. with Sig. Guar.	*Dividends:* Auto.; M. *Ret. Plans:* Keo., IRA, Corp. 403 (b) *Other:* Syst. With.; Auto. Pur.; Exch.-Tel.
STEINROE CASH RESERVES, INC. *(Stein Roe & Farnham)* 150 S. Wacker Dr. Chicago, IL 60606 800-621-0320/312-368-7826	Maximum current income — invests in short-term money market instruments maturing in 1 year or less.	1976	856	2500	100 Wire	Wire; Ck. Writ.; Writ. with Sig. Guar.	*Dividends:* Auto.; M. *Ret. Plans:* Keo., IRA, Corp. *Other:* Syst. With.; Grp.-Acct.; Exch.-Writ/Tel.

Fund Name *(Advisor)* Address and Telephone Number	Investment Objective and Policy	Year First Offered	Assets Mil. 12/31/82	Purchase Requirements Initial	Purchase Requirements Subsq.	Redemption Procedures	Services
STEINROE GOVERNMENT RESERVES, INC. *(Stein Roe & Farnham)* 150 S. Wacker Dr. Chicago, IL 60606 800-621-0320/312-368-7826	Safety of capital and liquidity from securities issued and guaranteed by U.S. Gov't and repurchase agreements.	1982	12	2500	100	Wire.; Ck. Writ.; Writ. with Sig. Guar.	*Dividends:* Auto.; M. *Ret. Plans:* Keo., IRA *Other:* Syst. With.; Grp.-Acct.; Exch.-Writ.-Tel.
THE MONEY FD. OF U.S. TREAS. SEC. *(PRO Services, Inc.)* 1107 Bethlehem Pk., c/o PRO Services Flourtown, PA 19031 800-523-0864/215-836-1300	Highest rate of return available from short-term U.S. Treasury securities consistent with maximum safety and liquidity.	1982	6	2000	100	Tel.; Ck. Writ.; Wire; Writ. with Sig. Guar.	*Dividends:* Auto.; M. *Ret. Plans:* Keo.; IRA, Corp., 403(b) *Other:* Syst. With.; Auto. Pur.; Exch.-Tel.
USAA MUTUAL/FEDERAL SECURITIES MONEY MARKET FUND *(USAA Investment Mgmt. Co.)* P.O. Box 33277 San Antonio, TX 78233 800-531-8181/800-292-8181 (TX only)	High current income with liq. safety by invest'g in short-term sec. issued or guaranteed by U.S. Gov't and backed by full faith and credit of the U.S.	1983	.1	1000	25	Tel.; Wire; Ck. Writ.; Writ. with Sig. Guar.	*Dividends:* Auto., M. *Ret. Plans:* Keo., IRA, 403(b) *Other:* Syst. With.; Auto. Pur.; Exch.-Tel.
USAA MUTUAL MONEY MARKET *(USAA Investment Mgmt. Co.)* P.O. Box 33277 San Antonio, TX 78233 800-531-8181/800-292-8181 (TX only)	Seeks the highest income consistent with preservation of capital and maintenance of liquidity.	1981	152	1000	25	Tel.; Wire; Ck. Writ.; Writ. with Sig. Guar.	*Dividends:* Auto., M. *Ret. Plans:* Keo., IRA, 403(b) *Other:* Syst. With.; Auto. Pur.; Exch.-Tel.
U.S. TREASURY SECURITIES FUND *(Growth Research & Mgmt. Inc.)* 15748 IH 10 West San Antonio, TX 78249 800-531-5777/512-696-1234	Highest level of income with highest degree of safety; U.S. Gov't securities backed by the full faith and credit of the U.S. Treas. and maturity within 1 year. No repos.	1982	12	1500	50 Wire	Tel.; Wire; Ck. Writ.; Writ. with Sig. Guar.	*Dividends:* Auto.; Q. *Ret. Plans:* Keo., IRA, 403(b) *Other:* Syst. With.; Auto. Pur.; Exch.-Tel.
VALUE LINE CASH FUND, INC. *(Arnold Bernhard & Co., Inc.)* 711 Third Ave. New York, NY 10017 800-223-0818/800-522-5217 (NY only)	As high a level of current income as is consistent with liquidity and preservation of capital by investing in high grade money market insts.	1979	686	1000 Wire	100	Tel.; Wire; Ck. Writ.; Writ. with Sig. Guar.	*Dividends:* Auto.; M. or Q. *Ret. Plans:* Keo., IRA, 403(b) *Other:* Syst. With.; Exchange-Tel.

166

VANGUARD MONEY MKT. TR./FED. PORT.
(Vanguard Group)
The Vanguard Group/P.O. Box 2600
Valley Forge, PA 19482
800-523-7025/ 800-362-0530 (PA only)

High current income consistent with protection of capital. Invests only in securities guaranteed or backed by the U.S. Govt. or its agencies.

1981 · 519 · 1000 Wire · 100 Wire · Tel.; Wire; Ck. Writ.

Dividends: Auto.; M.
Ret. Plans: Keo., IRA, 403(b)
Other: Syst. With.; Auto. Pur.; Exch.-Tel.; Grp. Acct.

VANGUARD MONEY MKT. TR./PRIME
(Vanguard Group)
The Vanguard Group/P.O. Box 2600
Valley Forge, PA 19482
800-523-7025/800-362-0530 (PA only)

Current income, consistent with preservation of capital and liquidity. Invests in domestic money market instruments of the highest quality.

1975 · 1205 · 1000 Wire · 100 Wire · Tel.; Wire Ck. Writ.

Dividends: Auto.; M.
Ret. Plans: Keo., IRA, Corp. 403(b)
Other: Syst. With.; Auto. Pur.; Exch.-Writ.; Grp.-Acct.

167

TAX-EXEMPT MONEY MARKET FUNDS...
FOR SAFETY OF PRINCIPAL, TAX-EXEMPT
INCOME, INSTANT LQUIDITY

GENERALLY USED BY:
   High tax bracket individuals seeking safety of their capital and seeking to earn short-term, tax-exempt income while having maximum liquidity.

WHAT THEY BUY:
   Short-term municipal notes and bonds, tax anticipation notes, industrial development notes, etc.

HOW THEY DIFFER:
   By the type and rating of the short-term municipal bonds and notes, and the length of maturity they maintain in the portfolio.

UNIQUE FEATURES:
   Tax-free interest is accrued on a daily basis, provides instant liquidity; also the ability to participate in tax-free securities with smaller amounts to invest.

Fund Name (Advisor) Address and Telephone Number	Investment Objective and Policy	Year First Offered	Assets Mil. 12/31/82	Purchase Requirements Initial	Subsq.	Redemption Procedures	Services
FIDELITY TAX-EXEMPT MONEY MKT. TR. (*Fidelity Group*) 82 Devonshire Street Boston, MA 02109 800-225-6190/617-523-1919	Current tax-free inc. consistent with stability and liquidity. Invests in high qual. short-term municipals w/avg. mat. of 120 days or less; none over 1 yr.	1980	$1918	$10M	$1000	Wire; Writ. with Sig. Guar.; Ck. Writ.	*Dividends:* Auto.; M. *Other:* Exch.-Tel.; Sub. Acct.
IDS TAX FREE MONEY FUND, INC. (*Investors Diversified Services*) Box 369, IDS Tower Minneapolis, MN 55440 800-IDS-IDEA/800-437-4332	High current income exempt from Federal income tax consistent with liquidity and stability of principal.	1980	51	2000	100	Wire; Ck. Writ.; Writ. with Sig. Guar.	*Dividends:* Auto.; M. *Other:* Syst., With.; Exch.-Writ.; Grp. Acct.
LEHMAN TAX-FREE RESERVES (*Lehman Management Co., Inc.*) 55 Water St. New York, NY 10041 800-221-5350/212-558-3288	Current income exempt from Fed. income taxes with preservation of capital and liq.; invests in high qual-ity tax-exempt sec. with short-term maturity.	1982	43	2500	100	Tel. Wire, Ck. Writ.; Writ. Sig. Guar. over $5M	*Dividends:* Auto.; M. *Other:* Exch. Writ. & Tel.; Grp. Acct.; Syst. With.
LEXINGTON TAX FREE MONEY FUND (*Lexington Management Corp.*) Box 1515, 580 Sylvan Ave. Englewood Cliffs, NJ 07632 800-526-4791/800-932-0838 (NJ only)	Current income, exempt from Fed. income taxes while maintaining sta-bility of principal, liquidity and pres-ervation of capital.	1977	37	1000	50	Tel.; Ck. Writ.; Writ. with Sig. Guar. over $5M	*Dividends:* Auto.; M. *Other:* Syst. With.; Auto Pur.; Exch.-Tel.; Grp.-Acct.
T. ROWE PRICE TAX-EXEMPT MONEY FD. (*T. Rowe Price Assoc. Inc.*) 100 East Pratt St. Baltimore, MD 21202 800-638-5660/301-547-2308	Preservation of capital liquidity, high income exempt from Fed. income taxes through short-term municipal securities.	1981	421	1000 Wire	100 Wire	Tel.; Wire Ck. Writ.; Writ. Sig. Guar. over $10M	*Dividends:* Auto.; M. *Other:* Syst. With.; Auto. Pur.; Exch.-Tel. Grp.-Acct.
SCUDDER TAX FREE MONEY FUND (*Scudder, Stevens & Clark. Inv. Counsel*) 175 Federal St. Boston, MA 02110 800-225-2470/617-482-3990	Fed. income tax exempt. High grade portfolio of municipal notes and bonds with weighted maturity of not more than 1 yr.	1980	153	1000	0	Tel.; Writ. With Sig. Guar.; Ck. Writ.	*Dividends:* Auto.; M. *Other:* Syst. with.; Exch.-Tel.; Grp.-Acct.
STEINROE TAX-EXEMPT MONEY FUND, INC. (*Stein Roe & Farnham*) 150 S. Wacker Drive Chicago, IL 60606 800-621-0320/312-368-7826	Maximum current income exempt. from Fed. income tax by investing in short-term municipal securities. Also seeks stability and liquidity.	1983	.1	2500	100	Wire; Ck. Writ. with Sig. Guar.	*Dividends:* Auto.; M. *Other:* Syst. With.; Grp. Acct.; Exch-Writ.-Tel.
VANGUARD MUNI. MONEY MARKET (*Vanguard Group*) The Vanguard Group/P.O. Box 2600 Valley Forge, PA 19482 800-523-7025/800-362-0530 (PA only)	Tax-free income, primarily from high quality municipal bonds with an average maturity of 120 days or less.	1980	239	3000 Wire	50 Wire	Tel.; Wire; Ck. Writ.	*Dividends:* Auto.; M. *Other:* Syst. With.; Auto. Pur Exch.-Tel.; Grp.-Acct.

TAX-EXEMPT INCOME FUNDS...
FOR INCOME FREE OF FEDERAL INCOME TAXES

GENERALLY USED BY:

Individual investors in high income tax brackets seeking current income free of Federal income taxes.

WHAT THEY BUY:

Municipal bonds issued by state and local government agencies.

HOW THEY DIFFER:

Bonds in the portfolios may vary in quality and length of maturity (short, medium or long term), depending upon the investment outlook of each fund. Some funds may emphasize bonds of a particular state.

UNIQUE FEATURES:

Distributions reinvested in the funds compound the interest on a tax-free basis. Some funds offer check writing redemptions and withdrawals by telephone or bank wire.

Fund Name (Advisor) Address and Telephone Number	Investment Objective and Policy	Year First Offered	Assets Mil. 12/31/82	Purchase Requirements Initial	Purchase Requirements Subsq.	Redemption Procedures	Services
CALVERT TAX-FREE RESERVES (Calvert Municipal Management Co.) 1700 Pennsylvania Ave., N.W. Washington, D.C. 20006 800-368-2748/301-951-4820	High current interest income. A choice of two portfolios exempt from Federal taxes consistent with stability and preservation of capital.	1981	$ 104	$2000	$250	Tel.; Wire; Ck. Writ.; Writ. with Sig. Guar.	*Dividends:* Auto.; Daily *Other:* Syst. With.; Auto. Pur.; Exch.-Writ or Tel.; Electronic Funds transfer-Calvert Money Controller
FIDELITY HIGH YIELD MUNICIPALS (Fidelity Group) 82 Devonshire St. Boston, MA 02109 800-225-6190/617-523-1919	Tax-free income; Carefully selected long-term municipal bonds of medium quality.	1977	407	2500	250	Tel.; Writ. with Sig. Guar.	*Dividends:* Auto.; M. *Other:* Syst. With.; Exch.-Tel.
FIDELITY LTD. TERM MUNICIPALS (Fidelity Group) 82 Devonshire St. Boston, MA 02109 800-225-6190/617-523-1919	Tax-free income; high quality tax-exempt obligations maturing in 15 years or less, with average maturity of 12 years or less.	1977	99	2500	250	Writ. with Sig. Guar. Tel.; Ck.-Writ.	*Dividends:* Auto.; M. *Other:* Syst. With.; Exch.-Tel.
FIDELITY MUNICIPAL BOND FUND (Fidelity Group) 82 Devonshire St. Boston, MA 02109 800-225-6190/617-523-1919	Tax-free income; invests primarily in high grade or upper medium grade, long-term municipal bonds.	1976	632	2500	250	Tel.; Writ. with Sig. Guar.	*Dividends:* Auto.; M. *Other:* Syst. With.; Exch.-Tel.
FINANCIAL TAX-FREE INCOME SHARES (Financial Programs, Inc.) P.O. Box 2040 Denver, CO 80201 800-525-9831/303-779-1233	Seeking as high a level of interest income exempt from Federal income taxes as is consistent with preservation of capital.	1981	45	1000	100	Written	*Dividends:* Auto.; M. *Other:* Auto. Pur.; Exch.-Writ. or Tel.
T. ROWE PRICE TAX-FREE INCOME (T. Rowe Price Associates, Inc.) 100 East Pratt St. Baltimore, MD 21202 800-638-5660/301-547-2308	High income exempt from Federal income taxes through investment grade municipal bonds.	1976	673	2000 Wire	100 Wire	Tel.; Wire; Written; Sig. Guar. over $10M; Ck. Writ.	*Dividends:* Auto.; Q. *Other:* Syst. With.; Auto. Pur.; Exch.-Tel.; Grp.-Acct.
SAFECO MUNICIPAL BOND FUND, INC. (SAFECO Asset Management Co.) SAFECO Plaza T15 NL Seattle, WA 98185 800-426-6730	High interest income exempt from Federal incomes taxes. Invests primarily in high grade or upper medium grade municipal bonds.	1981	16	2500	250	Writ. with Sig. Guar.	*Dividends:* Auto.; M. *Other:* Syst. With ; Auto. Pur.; Exch.-Writ.

Fund Name (Advisor) Address and Telephone Number	Investment Objective and Policy	Year First Offered	Assets Mil. 12/31/82	Purchase Requirements Initial	Purchase Requirements Subsq.	Redemption Procedures	Services
SCUDDER MANAGED MUNI. BONDS *(Scudder, Stevens & Clark, Inv. Counsel)* 175 Federal St. Boston, MA 02110 800-225-2470/617-482-3990	Income tax exempt (Federal) invests in a high grade portfolio consisting primarily of municipal bonds.	1976	198	1000	0	Writ. with Sig. Guar.; Tel.	*Dividends:* Auto.; M. *Other:* Syst. With.; Exch.-Tel.; Grp.-Acct.
SELECTED TAX-EXEMPT BOND FUND *(Burton J. Vincent, Chesley & Co.)* 105 W. Adams St. Chicago, IL 60603 1-800-621-7321/1-800-972-1092 (IL only)	To earn current income exempt from Federal income tax. Invest primarily in a portfolio of "high grade" bonds and notes.	1977	4	1000	100	Writ. with Sig. Guar.	*Dividends:* Auto.; M. *Other:* Syst. With.; Exch.-Writ. and Tel.
STEINROE TAX-EXEMPT BOND FUND *(Stein Roe & Farnham)* 150 S. Wacker St. Chicago, IL 60606 800-621-0320/312-368-7826	High current income. Invests primarily in municipal bonds so that at least 80% of income is exempt from Federal income taxes.	1976	156	2500	100	Writ. with Sig. Guar.	*Dividends:* Auto.; Q. *Other:* Exch. Tel.; Syst. With.; Grp.-Acct.
USAA TAX EXEMPT/HIGH YIELD *(USAA Investment Mgmt. Co.)* P.O. Box 33277 San Antonio, TX 78233 800-531-8181/800-292-8181 (TX only)	Invests primarily in investment grade tax exempt sec.; no limit on maturity of these securities.	1982	$ 22	$ 3000	$100	Tel.; Wire; Writ. with Sig. Guar.	*Dividends:* Auto.; A *Other:* Exch.-Tel.; Syst. With.; Auto. Pur.
USAA TAX EXEMPT/INTERMEDIATE-TERM *(USAA Investment Mgmt. Co.)* P.O. Box 33277 San Antonio, TX 78233 800-531-8181/800-292-8181 (TX only)	Invests primarily in investment grade tax exempt securities having a maturity of no more than 12 years.	1982	20	3000	100	Tel.; Wire; Writ. with Sig. Guar.	*Dividends:* Auto.; A *Other:* Exch.-Tel; Syst. With.; Auto. Pur.
USAA TAX EXEMPT/SHORT-TERM *(USAA Investment Mgmt. Co.)* P.O. Box 33277 San Antonio, TX 78233 800-531-8181/800-292-8181 (TX only)	Invests primarily in investment grade tax exempt securities having a maturity of no more than 5 years.	1982	15	3000	100	Tel.; Wire; Writ. with Sig. Guar.; Ck. Writ.	*Dividends:* Auto.; A *Other:* Exch.-Tel; Syst. With.; Auto. Pur.

Fund	Objective	Year	No.	Min. Inv.	Min. Add.	Redemption	Services
VANGUARD HIGH-YIELD MUNI BOND *(Vanguard Group)* The Vanguard Group/P.O. Box 2600 Valley Forge, PA 19482 800-523-7025/800-362-0530 (PA only)	Tax free income, primarily from medium and lower quality municipal bonds with an average maturity of more than 25 years.	1978	101	3000 Wire	50 Wire	Tel.; Wire; Ck. Writ.	*Dividends:* Auto.; M *Other:* Syst. With.; Auto. Pur.; Exch.- Tel.; Grp.-Acct.
VANG. INTERMED.-TERM MUNI BOND *(Vanguard Group)* The Vanguard Group/P.O. Box 2600 Valley Forge, PA 19482 800-523-7025/800-362-0530 (PA only)	Tax free income, primarily from high quality municipal bonds with an average maturity of 7-12 years.	1977	81	3000 Wire	50 Wire	Tel.;Wire; Ck. Writ.	*Dividends:* Auto.; M. *Other:* Syst. With.; Auto. Pur.; Exch.- Tel.; Grp.-Acct.
VANGUARD LONG-TERM MUNI BOND *(Vanguard Group)* The Vanguard Group/P.O. Box 2600 Valley Forge, PA 19482 800-523-7025/800-362-0530 (PA only)	Tax free income, primarily from high quality municipal bonds with an average maturity of more than 25 years.	1977	172	3000 Wire	50 Wire	Tel.; Wire; Ck. Writ.	*Dividends:* Auto.; M. *Other:* Syst. With.; Auto. Pur.; Exch.- Tel.; Grp.-Acct.
VANGUARD SHORT-TERM MUNI BOND *(Vanguard Group)* The Vanguard Group/P.O. Box 2600 Valley Forge, PA 19482 800-523-7025/800-362-0530 (PA only)	Tax free income, primarily from high quality municipal bonds with an average maturity of less than 1 year.	1977	253	3000 Wire	50 Wire	Tel.; Wire; Ck. Writ.	*Dividends:* Auto.; M. *Other:* Syst. With.; Auto. Pur.; Exch.- Tel.; Grp.-Acct.

173

INCOME FUNDS...
FOR HIGH CURRENT INCOME,
LONG TERM INVESTMENT

GENERALLY USED BY:

Investors seeking safety of principal with long term investment goals *and* high current income.

WHAT THEY BUY:

Corporate bonds or high dividend paying stocks.

HOW THEY DIFFER:

Bonds in the funds' portfolios may vary in quality and length of maturity; each fund takes varying degrees of risk in order to achieve its investment goals; some funds may specialize in or emphasize one type of fixed income investment such as all preferred stocks or U.S. Government obligations.

UNIQUE FEATURES:

High income sought by these funds lends itself particularly to systematic withdrawal plans if supplement to current income is needed; or this high level of income can be used to build the assets in the account more quickly through reinvestment of their dividends; some funds offer check writing redemptions.

Fund Name (Advisor) Address and Telephone Number	Investment Objective and Policy	Year First Offered	Assets Mil. 12/31/82	Purchase Requirements Initial	Purchase Requirements Subsq.	Redemption Procedures	Services
AMERICAN INVESTORS INCOME (*American Investors Corp.*) 88 Field Point Rd. P.O. Box 2500 Greenwich, CT 06836 800-243-5353/203-622-1600	High current income. Capital appreciation secondary. Diversified investments in generous yielding lower rated bonds and pfd. stocks.	1976	$ 14	$400 Tel. Wire	$20 Tel. Wire	Tel.; Written; Sig. Guar. over $5M.	*Dividends:* Auto.; Q. *Ret. Plans:* Keo, IRA, Corp. *Other:* Syst. With.; Auto. Pur.; Exch.-Tel.
BOSTON COMPANY GOVERNMENT INCOME FUND (*The Boston Co. Advisors, Inc.*) One Boston Place Boston, MA 02106 800-343-6324/617-956-9740	High current income, safety of principal and liquidity; invests exclusively in U.S. Government obligations, maturing in 5 years or less.	1979	4	1000	0	Writ. with Sig. Guar.	*Dividends:* Auto.; Q. *Ret. Plans:* Keo, IRA, Corp. *Other:* Syst. With.; Auto. Pur.
CALVERT FUND (*Calvert Asset Management Co., Inc.*) 1700 Pennsylvania Ave., NW Washington, D.C. 20006 800-368-2748/301-951-4820	2 portfolios: Equity seeks cap. apprec. Income portfolio maximizes long-term bonds and other income sec. of med. grade and higher quality.	1982	1	2000	250	Tel .; Wire; Ck. Writ.; Writ. with Sig. Guar.	*Dividends:* Auto.; Q. *Ret. Plans:* Keo, IRA, Corp. *Other:* Syst. With.; Grp. Acct., Auto. Pur. Exch.-Tel. or Writ.; E.F.T.
CAP. PRES. TREA. NOTE TRUST (*Benham Management Corp.*) 755 Page Mill Rd. Palo Alto, CA 94304 800-4-SAFETY/800-348-0002 (AK and HI only)	Safety: U.S. Treasury Notes, bills and repurchase agreements. Maturities between 13 months and 4 years.	1980	12	1000	100 Wire	Tel; Wire; Writ . with Sig. Guar.	*Dividends:* Auto.; Q.
CAPAMERICA, FUND, INC. (*Bull & Bear Mgmt. Corp.*) 11 Hanover Square New York, NY 10005 800-431-6060/800-942-6911 (NY only)	Invests in high quality common stks, convertible sec. and bonds for current income and long-term growth of capital and income.	1961	4	1000	25 Tel.	Written; Sig. Guar. over $1M	*Dividends:* Auto.; Q., 403(b) *Ret. Plans:* Keo., IRA, 403(b) *Other:* Exch.-Tel., Syst. With Auto. Pur.
ENERGY & UTILITY SHARES, INC. (*Stratton Management Co.*) Butler & Skippack, Box 550 Blue Bell, PA 19422 215-542-8025	Seeks high rate of return from energy and utility related equities; monthly income.	1971	8	1000	100	Writ. with Sig. Guar. over $500 or if certifs. issued.	*Dividends:* Auto., M. *Ret. Plans:* Keo., IRA, 403(b) *Other:* Syst. With.; Exch.-Tel.
FIDELITY CORPORATE BOND FUND (*Fidelity Group*) 82 Devonshire St. Boston, MA 02109 800-225-6190/617-523-1919	Income: At least 80% of assets in investment-grade (rated BBB or better) debt securities.	1977	161	2500	250	Tel.; Writ. with Sig. Guar.	*Dividends:* Auto.; M. *Ret. Plans:* Keo., IRA Corp., 403(b) *Other:* Syst. With.; Exch.-Tel.

Fund Name (Advisor) Address and Telephone Number	Investment Objective and Policy	Year First Offered	Assets Mil. 12/31/82	Purchase Requirements Initial	Purchase Requirements Subsq.	Redemption Procedures	Services
FIDELITY GOV. SECURITIES FUND LTD. (*Fidelity Group*) 82 Devonshire St. Boston, MA 02109 800-225-6190/617-523-1919	Income from obligations issued by U.S. Govt., its agencies, or instrumentalities; income is exempt from state and local income taxes in all states.	1979	89	1000	250	Tel.; Wire; Writ. with Sig. Guar.	*Dividends:* Auto.; M. *Ret. Plans:* Keo., IRA Corp., 403(b) *Other:* Syst. With.; Exch.-Tel.
FIDELITY HIGH INCOME (*Fidelity Group*) 82 Devonshire St. Boston, MA 02109 800-225-6190/617-523-1919	High current income diversified portfolio of high-yielding, fixed-income corporate securities.	1977	186	2500	250	Tel.; Writ. with Sig. Guar.	*Dividends:* Auto.; M. *Ret. Plans:* Keo., IRA, Corp. 403(b) *Other:* Syst. With.; Exch.-Tel.
FIDELITY QUALIFIED DIVIDEND FUND (*Fidelity Group*) 82 Devonshire St. Boston, MA 02109 800-225-6190/617-523-1919	High current income for corporations eligible to take the 85% dividends received exclusion.	1981	47	50,000	0	Tel.; Writ. with Sig. Guar.	*Dividends:* Auto.; credited daily, pd. M. *Other:* Exch.-Tel.; scaled mgmt. & ser. fee, fully tax-deduct.
FIDELITY THRIFT TRUST (*Fidelity Group*) 82 Devonshire St. Boston, MA 02109 800-225-6190/617-523-1919	Income: Corporate obligations (AA or better), Gov. securities, and money market instruments; maturity not to exceed ten years.	1975	$ 87	$1000	$ 250	Tel.; Writ. with Sig. Guar Ck. Writing	*Dividends:* Auto.; M. *Ret. Plans:* Keo., IRA, Corp. 403(b) *Other:* Syst. With.; Exch.-Tel.
FINANCIAL BOND SHARES (*Financial Programs, Inc.*) P.O. Box 2040 Denver, CO 80201 800-525-9831/303-779-1233	High level of current income through bonds and other debt securities. Potential capital appreciation is secondary.	1976	7	1000	100	Written	*Dividends:* Auto.; Q. *Ret. Plans:* Keo.; IRA, Corp. 403(b) *Other:* Auto. Pur.; Exch.-Tel.
FINANCIAL INDUSTRIAL INCOME (*Financial Programs, Inc.*) P.O. Box 2040 Denver, CO 80201 800-525-9831/303-779-1233	Current income with capital growth given additional consideration.	1960	192	500	25	Written	*Dividends:* Auto.; Q. *Ret. Plans:* Keo.; IRA, Corp. 403(b) *Other:* Auto. Pur.; Syst. With.; Exch.-Tel.
FOUNDERS INCOME FUND, INC. (*Founders Mutual Depositor Corp.*) 655 Broadway Denver, CO 80203 800-525-2440/303-595-3963	Income consistent with invest quality. Purchases divid. paying stocks and other income securities. Also writes covered call options.	1967	6	250 500 By Tel.	25 500 By Tel.	Writ. with Sig. Guar.	*Dividends:* Auto.:Q. *Ret. Plans:* Keo..IRA *Other:* Auto. Pur.; Syst. With.; Exch.-Tel.

Fund	Objective	Year	(Assets)	Min. Initial	Min. Subseq.	Redemption	Dividends / Plans
LEXINGTON GNMA INCOME FUND (Lexington Management Corp.) Box 1515, 580 Sylvan Ave. Englewood Cliffs, NJ 07632 800-526-4791/800-932-0838 (NJ only)	High current income, liquidity, safety. Invests in mortgage-backed "Ginnie Mae" certificates guar. by U.S. Govt.	1973	12	1000	50	Writ. Sig. Guar. over $5M	*Dividends:* Auto.; Q. *Ret. Plans:* Keo., IRA *Other:*-Syst. With.; Auto. Pur.; Exch.-Tel.
LIBERTY FUND, INC. (Neuberger & Berman Management Inc.) 342 Madison Ave. New York, NY 10172 212-850-8300	High level of current income, diversified portfolio of high yielding, lower rated fixed income securities.	1956	8	250; 500 By Tel.	25; 500 By Tel.	Writ. with Sig. Guar. Tel.	*Dividends:* Auto.; Q. *Ret. Plans:* Keo., Corp., IRA. *Other:* Syst. With.; Exch.-Tel.
MAIRS & POWER INCOME FUND (Mairs And Power, Inc.) W-2062 1st Nat'l Bank Bldg. St. Paul, MN 55101 612-222-8478	Income	1961	2	1000	50	Writ.; Sig. Guar.	*Dividends:* Auto.; Q. *Ret. Plans:* Keo., IRA
NEWTON INCOME FUND, INC. (Heritage Investment Advisors, Inc.) 733 N. Van Buren St. Milwaukee, WI 53202 414-347-1141/800-242-7229 (WI only)	Above-average current income consistent with preservation of capital.	1970	6	500	50	Tel.; Writ. with Sig. Guar.	*Dividends:* Auto.; Q. *Ret. Plans:* Keo., IRA, 403(b) *Other:* Syst. With.; Auto Pur.
NORTH STAR BOND FUND INC. (Investment Advisers Inc.) 1100 Dain Tower, Box 1160 Minneapolis, MN 55440 612-371-7780	Taxable income, corporate and government bonds.	1977	10	1000	100	Written	*Dividends:* Auto.; Q. *Ret. Plans:* Keo., IRA, Corp., 403(b) *Other:* Exch.-Writ.
T. ROWE PRICE NEW INCOME FUND (T. Rowe Price Associates, Inc.) 100 East Pratt St. Baltimore, MD 21202 800-638-5660/301-547-2308	High current income with reasonable stability through investment grade fixed income securities.	1973	611	1000 Wire	100 Tel.; Wire	Tel., Tlgm., Wire Ck. Writ.; Writ. with Sig. Guar. over $10M	*Dividends:* Auto.; M. *Ret. Plans:* Keo., IRA, Corp., 403(b), Municipal *Other:*-Syst. With.; Auto Pur. Grp.-Acct.; Exch.-Tel.
PRO INCOME FUND, INC. (PRO Services, Inc.) 1107 Bethlehem Pk. c/o PRO Services Flourtown, PA 19031 800-523-0864/215-836-1300	Income: Seeks the highest investment income available consistent with preservation of principal.	1974	24	300	0 Tel.	Tel.; Writ. with Sig. Guar.	*Dividends:* Auto.; Q. *Ret. Plans:* Keo., IRA, Corp. 403(b) *Other:* Syst. With.; Auto. Pur.; Exch.-Tel.
RETIRE. PLAN. FDS. AMER/BOND (Chicago Title & Trust Co.) 111 W. Washington Street Chicago, IL 60602 1-800-621-1110/312-630-2540	Growth in capital through appreciation and income investment in fixed income securities; available only to tax-qualified retirement plans.	1978	2	250	250	Written	*Dividends:* Auto.; Q. *Ret. Plans:* Keo., IRA Corp. 403(b) *Other:* Exch.-Tel.

177

Fund Name (Advisor) Address and Telephone Number	Investment Objective and Policy	Year First Offered	Assets Mil. 12/31/82	Purchase Requirements Initial	Purchase Requirements Subsq.	Redemption Procedures	Services
SAFECO INCOME FUND, INC. (*Safeco Asset Management Co.*) Safeco Plaza T15 NL Seattle, WA 98185 800-426-6730	**Seek high current income plus capital growth. Invests primarily in convertible and common securities of medium to large companies.**	1968	17	200	25	Writ. with Sig. Guar.	*Dividends:* Auto.; Q. *Ret. Plans:* Keo., IRA, Corp. *Other:* Syst. With.; Auto. Pur.; Exch.-Writ.
SAFECO SPECIAL BOND FUND, INC. (*Safeco Asset Management Co.*) Safeco Plaza T15 NL Seattle, WA 98185 800-426-6730	**High level of income consistent with preservation of capital. Invests in BBB or higher rated debt sec. with 10 yrs. or less to maturing.**	1969	2	200	25	Writ. with Sig. Guar.	*Dividends:* Auto.; Q. *Ret. Plans:* Keo., IRA, Corp. *Other:* Syst. With.; Auto. Pur.; Exch.-Writ.
SCUDDER INCOME FUND, INC. (*Scudder, Stevens & Clark, Inv. Counsel*) 175 Federal St. Boston, MA 02110 800-225-2470/617-482-3990	**Income: To provide income with due consideration to the prudent investment of the capital.**	1928	$ 91	$ 1000	$ 0 Tel. over 500	Tel.; Writ. with Sig. Guar.	*Dividends:* Auto.; Q. *Ret. Plans:* Keo., IRA, Corp., 403(b), 401(k) *Other:* Syst. With.; Exch.-Tel.
SCUDDER TARGET FUND (*Scudder, Stevens & Clark*) 175 Federal Street Boston, MA 02110 800-225-2471/617-482-3990	**Current income, capital preserv. and capital apprec. by investment in debt obligations maturing by a target year.**	1982	.1	1000	0	Tel.; Writ. with Sig. Guar.	*Dividends:* Auto., M. *Ret. Plans:* Keo., IRA, Corp., 403(b), 401(k) *Other:* Syst. With.; Exch.-Tel.
SOUTHWESTERN INVESTORS INCOME FUND, INC. (*Tenneco Asset Management Company*) 777 Walker, 2 Shell Plaza #2000 Houston, TX 77002 713-757-5675/713-757-5679	**Maximum current income without exposing capital to unnecessary risk through investments in fixed-income securities.**	1968	8	0	0	Writ. with no sign. guar. if shares are in unissued form.	*Dividends:* Auto.; S/A *Ret. Plans:* Keo., IRA, 403(b) *Other:* Syst. with.; Auto. Pur.; Exch.-Writ.; Var. Ann. (qual. plans only)
STEINROE BOND FUND, INC. (*Stein Roe & Farnham*) 150 S. Wacker Drive Chicago, IL 60606 800-621-0320/312-368-7826	**High current income. Invests primarily in marketable debt securities.**	1978	59	2500	100	Writ. with Sig. Guar.	*Dividends:* Auto.; Q. *Ret. Plans:* Keo., IRA, Corp. *Other:* Syst. With.; Grp.-Acct.; Exch. Writ.

178

Fund / Manager / Address	Objective	Year		Min.		Redemption	Dividends / Ret. Plans / Other
STRONG TOTAL RETURN FUND *(Strong/Corneliuson Cap. Mgmt. Inc.)* 815 E. Mason Street Milwaukee, WI 53202 414-765-0620	Highest total return consistent with capital preservation. Return generated by short term trading of fixed income and equity securities.	1982	4	250	200	Writ. with Sig. Guar.	*Dividends:* Auto.; Q. *Ret. Plans:* IRA, Keo., Corp., 403(b) *Other:* Syst. With.; Auto. Pur.
TWENTIETH CENTURY U.S. GOVERNMENTS *(Investors Research Corporation)* P.O. Box 200 Kansas City, MO 64141 816-531-5575	Seeks income by investing in securities of the U.S. Government and its agencies.	1982	.1	1000	100	Writ. with Sig. Guar.	*Dividends:* Auto.; A *Ret. Plans:* Keo., IRA, 403(b) *Other:* Syst. With.; Auto. Pur.; Exch.-Writ.
UNIFIED INCOME FUND, INC. *(Unified Management Corporation)* Guaranty Bldg., Indianapolis, IN 46204 317-634-3300/800-428-4492	Current income and capital appreciation. Invests without quality restrictions. May buy stock and write options.	1977	3	500	25	Tel.; Writ.	*Dividends:* Auto.; S/A. *Ret. Plans:* Keo., IRA, Corp. 403(b) *Other:* Syst. With.; Auto Pur.; Exch.-Tel.
USAA MUTUAL/INCOME *(USAA Investment Mgmt. Co.)* Box 33277 San Antonio, TX 78233 800-531-8181/800-292-8181 (TX only)	Maximum current income without undue risk to principal. Flexible, diversified portfolio, high yields relative to risk.	1974	27	1000	25	Tel.; Wire; Writ. with Sig. Guar.	*Dividends:* Auto.; Q. *Ret. Plans:* Keo., IRA, 403(b), Corp. *Other:* Syst. With.; Auto. Pur.; Exch.-Tel.
VALUE LINE BOND FUND, INC. *(Arnold Bernhard & Co., Inc.)* 711 Third Avenue New York, NY 10017 800-223-0818/800-522-5217 (NY only)	High current income and capital appreciation by investing in high and good grade bonds.	1981	62	1000	250	Writ. with Sig. Guar.	*Dividends:* Auto.; Q. *Ret. Plans:* Keo, IRA, 403(b) *Other:* Syst. with.; Exch.-Writ. or Tel.
VALUE LINE INCOME FUND, INC. *(Arnold Bernhard & Co., Inc.)* 711 Third Avenue New York, NY 10017 800-223-0818/800-522-5217 (NY only)	Current income but capital appreciation is an important, though secondary, objective.	1952	94	250	0	Writ. with Sig. Guar.	*Dividends:* Auto.; Q. *Ret. Plans:* Keo., IRA, 430(b) *Other:* Syst. With.; Exch.-Writ. or Tel.
VANGUARD GNMA PORTFOLIO *(Wellington Management Company)* The Vanguard Group/P.O. Box 2600 Valley Forge, PA 19482 800-523-7025/800-362-0530 (PA only)	Current income, primarily from mortgage-backed securities, whose timely payment of interest and principal is guaranteed by the U.S. Government.	1980	79	3000 Wire	50 Wire	Writ. with Sig. Guar.	*Dividends:* Auto.; M. *Ret. Plans:* Keo., IRA, Corp., 403(b) *Other:* Syst. With.; Auto. Pur.; Exch.-Tel. Grp.-Acct.
VANGUARD HIGH YIELD BOND *(Wellington Management Company)* The Vanguard Group/P.O. Box 2600 Valley Forge, PA 19482 800-523-7025/800-362-0530 (PA only)	Current income, primarily from high yielding medium and lower quality bonds.	1978	43	3000 Wire	50 Wire	Writ. with Sig. Guar.	*Dividends:* Auto.; M. *Ret. Plans:* Keo., IRA, Corp. 403(b) *Other:* Syst. With.; Auto. Pur.; Exch.-Tel. Grp-Acct.

Fund Name (Advisor) Address and Telephone Number	Investment Objective and Policy	Year First Offered	Assets Mil. 12/31/82	Purchase Requirements Initial	Purchase Requirements Subsq.	Redemption Procedures	Services
VANGUARD INVSTMNT. GRADE BOND *(Wellington Management Company)* The Vanguard Group/P.O. Box 2600 Valley Forge, PA 19482 800-523-7025/800-362-0530 (PA only)	High current income, primarily corporate bonds.	1973	62	3000 Wire	50 Wire	Writ. with Sig. Guar.	*Dividends:* Auto.; M. *Ret. Plans:* Keo., IRA, Corp., 403(b) *Other:* Syst. With.; Auto. Pur. Exch.-Tel.; Grp. Acct.
VANGUARD QUALIFIED DIV. I *(Wellington Management Company)* The Vanguard Group/P.O. Box 2600 Valley Forge, PA 19482 800-523-7025/800-362-0530 (PA only)	Maximize income (from all sources) which qualified for the 85% corporate dividend exclusion, by investing in common stocks.	1975	29	3000 Wire	50 Wire	Writ. with Sig. Guar.	*Dividends:* Auto.; Q. *Ret. Plans:* Keo., IRA, Corp., 403(b) *Other:* Syst. With.; Auto. Pur.; Exch.-Tel.; Grp.-Acct.
VANGUARD QUALIFIED DIV. II *(Wellington Management Company)* The Vanguard Group/P.O. Box 2600 Valley Forge, PA 19482 800-523-7025/800-362-0530 (PA only)	Maximize income (from all sources) which qualified for the 85% corporate dividend exclusion, by investing in preferred stocks.	1975	$ 45	$ 3000 Wire	$50 Wire	Writ. with Sig. Guar.	*Dividends:* Auto.; Q. *Ret. Plans:* Keo., IRA, Corp., 403(b) *Other:* Syst. With.; Auto. Pur.; Exch.-Tel.; Grp.-Acct.
VANGUARD SHORT TERM BOND *(Vanguard Group)* The Vanguard Group/P.O. Box 2600 Valley Forge, PA 19482 800-523-7025/800-362-0530 (PA only)	High current income through short-term fixed income investments.	1982	33	3000	50	Tel.; Wire.; Ck. Writ.	*Dividends:* Auto.; M. *Ret. Plans:* Keo., IRA, Corp. 403(b) *Other:* Syst. With.; Auto. Pur.; Exch. Tel.; Grp.-Acct.
WISCONSIN INCOME FUND, INC. *(Nicholas Company, Inc.)* 312 East Wisconsin Ave. Milwaukee, WI 53202 414-272-6133	High current income consistent with conservation of capital.	1929	13	500	50	Written; Sig. Guar. on Cert. only	*Dividends:* Auto.; Q. *Ret. Plans:* Keo., IRA *Other:* Syst. With.; Exch.-Writ.

BALANCED FUNDS...
FOR LONG TERM GROWTH OF CAPITAL AND INCOME THROUGH A BALANCED INVESTMENT OF STOCKS AND BONDS

GENERALLY USED BY:

Investors seeking long term commitments that provide growth and income.

WHAT THEY BUY:

A balance of fixed income investments (bonds or preferred stocks) and common stocks.

HOW THEY DIFFER:

Each fund has a different emphasis on generating income versus growth, and the degree of risk taken to achieve their stated goals.

UNIQUE FEATURES:

These funds provide a *complete* package of common stocks and bonds in one fund.

Fund Name (Advisor) Address and Telephone Number	Investment Objective and Policy	Year First Offered	Assets Mil. 12/31/82	Purchase Requirements		Redemption Procedures	Services
				Initial	Subsq.		
FIDELITY EQUITY-INCOME FUND *(Fidelity Group)* 82 Devonshire St. Boston, MA 02109 800-225-6190/617-523-1919	Growth and Income: at least 80% in income-producing equity securities with remainder generally in convertible securities.	1966	$356	$1000	$250	Writ. with Sig. Guar.	*Dividends:* Auto.; Q. *Ret. Plans:* Keo., IRA, Corp., 403(b) *Other:* Syst. With.; Auto. Pur.; Exch.-Tel.
FIDELITY PURITAN FUND *(Fidelity Group)* 82 Devonshire St. Boston, MA 02109 800-225-6190/617-523-1919	Growth and Income: primary emphasis on income growth from high yielding common stocks, convertibles and fixed-income securities.	1946	720	1000	250	Writ. with Sig. Guar.	*Dividends:* Auto.; Q. *Ret. Plans:* Keo., IRA, Corp., 403(b) *Other:* Syst. With.; Auto. Pur.; Exch.-Tel.
LOOMIS-SAYLES MUTUAL FUND *(Loomis, Sayles & Co.)* Box 449, Back Bay Annex Boston, MA 02117 617-267-6600	Reasonable long-term capital appreciation and current income return, without undue risk.	1929	87	250	50 Tel.	Writ.; Sig. Guar. Over $10M	*Dividends:* Auto.; Q. *Ret. Plans:* Keo., IRA *Other:*Syst. With.; Auto. Pur.
"NEW BEGINNING" INCOME FUND, INC. *(Sit Investment Associates, Inc.)* 1714 First Bank Place West Minneapolis, MN 55402 612-332-3223	Income, capital preserv. and growth. Variable ratios of stocks, convertibles, bonds; max. 80% equities, max. 50% (10 yr. mat. or less).	1982	1	10M	500 2M IRA shrhlds Bk wire or Writ.	Writ. with Sig. Guar.	*Dividends:* Auto.; Q. *Ret. Plans:* Keo, IRA
NORTH STAR STOCK FUND, INC. *(Investment Advisers, Inc.)* 1100 Dain Tower, Box 1160 Minneapolis, MN 55440 612-371-7780	Growth with a secondary emphasis on income. Common stocks.	1971	29	1000	100	Writ.	*Dividends:* Auto.; S/A *Ret. Plans:* Keo., IRA, Corp., 403(b) *Other:* Exch.-Writ.
THE ONE HUNDRED AND ONE FUND *(Berger Associates, Inc.)* 899 Logan St. Denver, CO 80203 303-837-1020	Managed investments in successful and highly profitable corporations, with emphasis upon higher current dividend return.	1966	1	250 Wire	50 Tel.; Wire	Writ. with Sig. Guar.	*Dividends:* Auto.; A. *Ret. Plans:* IRA, Keo. *Other:* Syst. With.; Exch.-Tel.
PINE STREET FUND INC. *(Wood, Struthers & Winthrop Mgmt.)* 140 Broadway New York, NY 10005 800-221-7780/212-902-4396	Income & growth. Emphasis on stocks but also use Gov't. agency and corporate bonds & money market instruments.	1949	43	500 Tel.	50 Tel.	Writ.; Sig. Guar. over $500	*Dividends:* Auto.; Q. *Ret. Plans:* Keo., IRA *Other:* Syst. With.

Fund	Objective	Year			Redemption	Dividends / Plans
SELECTED AMERICAN SHARES, INC. *(Burton J. Vincent, Chesley & Co.)* 105 W. Adams St. Chicago, IL 60603 1-800-621-7321/1-800-972-1092 (IL only)	Combination of growth of capital and income. Investment among common and preferred stocks, and bonds.	1933	77	1000	100	Writ. with Sig. Guar.	*Dividends:* Auto.; Q. *Ret. Plans:* Keo., IRA, Corp. *Other:* Syst. With.; Auto. Pur.; Exch.-Writ./Tel.
STEIN ROE & FARNHAM BAL. FUND *(Stein Roe & Farnham)* 150 S. Wacker Dr. Chicago, IL 60606 800-621-0320/312-368-7826	Maintain and increase capital while providing income. Diversified investments: bonds, preferred and common stocks.	1949	85	2500	100	Writ.; with Sig. Guar.	*Dividends:* Auto.; Q. *Ret. Plans:* Keo., IRA, Corp. *Other:* Exch.-Writ/Tel.; Syst. With.; Grp.-Acct.
STRONG INVESTMENT FUND *(Strong/Corneliuson Cap. Mgmt., Inc.)* 815 E. Mason St. Milwaukee, WI 53202 414-765-0620	Combination of capital growth and income. Max. 65% in equities; balance in fixed income securities. Investments limited to high quality corp.	1982	4	250	200	Writ. with Sig. Guar.	*Dividends:* Auto.; Q. *Ret. Plans:* IRA, Keo., Corp., 403(b) *Other:* Auto. Pur.; Syst. With.
UNIFIED MUTUAL SHARES, INC. *(Unified Management Corporation)* Guaranty Bldg. Indianapolis, IN 46204 800-428-4492/317-634-3300	Capital growth and current income. Flexible with emphasis on high quality stocks and convertibles; uses covered option writing.	1963	8	200	25	Tel.; Written	*Dividends:* Auto.; S/A *Ret. Plans:* Keo., IRA, 403(b), Corp. *Other:* Syst. With.; Auto. Pur.; Exch.-Tel.
VANGUARD/WELLESLEY INCOME FUND *(Wellington Management Company)* The Vanguard Group/P.O. Box 2600 Valley Forge, PA 19482 800-523-7025/800-362-0530 (PA only)	Seeks as much current income as is consistent with reasonable risk; 60-70% fixed income securities; balance in high yielding stocks.	1970	$ 94	$ 500 Wire	$ 50 Wire	Writ. with Sig. Guar.	*Dividends:* Auto.; Q. *Ret. Plans:* Keo., IRA, Corp., 403(b) *Other:* Syst. With.; Auto. Pur.; Exch.-Tel.; Grp.-Acct.
VANGUARD WELLINGTON FUND *(Wellington Management Company)* The Vanguard Group/P.O. Box 2600 Valley Forge, PA 19482 800-523-7025/800-362-0530 (PA only)	Conservation of principal; reasonable income; profits without undue risk. 60-70% in common stocks; balance in fixed-income securities.	1928	558	500 Wire	50 Wire	Writ. with Sig. Guar.	*Dividends:* Auto.; Q. *Ret. Plans:* Keo., IRA, Corp., 403(b) *Other:* Syst. With.; Auto. Pur.; Exch.-Tel.; Grp.-Acct.

GROWTH FUNDS...
FOR LONG TERM GROWTH OF CAPITAL AND-OR INCOME THROUGH COMMON STOCKS

GENERALLY USED BY:

Investors seeking to offset inflation through long term investments; often used to build assets for retirement, to cover college costs, or other potential needs.

WHAT THEY BUY:

Common stocks, or securities convertible into common stocks; some funds occasionally use bonds or other securities to meet growth or income objectives.

HOW THEY DIFFER:

Growth funds differ from each other in the investment policies and strategies they use in seeking the growth of your money.

UNIQUE FEATURES:

All types of investment plans are available through these funds. Most frequently used is the automatic reinvestment of dividends which helps the growth of your investment.

Fund Name (Advisor) Address and Telephone Number	Investment Objective and Policy	Year First Offered	Assets Mil. 12/31/82	Purchase Requirements Initial	Purchase Requirements Subsq.	Redemption Procedures	Services
ACORN FUND (*Harris Associates, Inc.*) 120 S. La Salle St. Chicago, IL 60603 312-621-0630	Capital growth — Seeks smaller growth companies with financial strength whose investment qualities have not been widely recognized.	1970	$ 132	$1000	$200 Tel.	Writ . with Sig. Guar.	*Dividends:* Auto.; S/A *Ret. Plans:* Keo., IRA *Other:* Auto. Pur.; Syst. With.
ADV FUND, INC. (*ADV Management Co., Inc.*) One New York Plaza New York, NY 10004 212-908-9582	To achieve a return consisting of capital appreciation and current income.	1967	21	250	50	Writ with Sig. Guar.	*Dividends:* Auto., Q *Ret. Plans:*Keo, IRA *Other:* Auto. Pur.; Syst. With.
AFUTURE FUND, INC. (*Carlisle-Asher Management Co.*) Legal Arts Bldg. Front & Lemon Sts. Media, PA 19063 800-523-7594/215-565-3131	Seeks growth of capital thru investments in superior earnings companies and the use of market timing techniques.	1968	33	500	30 Tel.	Tel. Writ.; Sig. Guar.	*Dividends:* Auto.; A. *Ret. Plans:* Keo, IRA *Other:* Syst. With.
AMERICAN EXPRESS GROWTH FUND (*The Boston Company Advisors Inc.*) One Boston Place Boston, MA 02106 617-956-9748	Seeks to achieve long-term growth of capital through investments primarily in common stocks.	1982	2	1000	100	Writ. with Sig. Guar. Tel.	*Dividends:* Q. *Ret. Plan:* IRA
AMERICAN INVESTORS FUND, INC. (*American Investors Corp.*) 88 Field Point Rd. P.O. Box 2500 Greenwich, CT 06836 800-243-5353/203-622-1600	Growth of investment capital. Emphasis on timing and selecting securities believed to have best potential for capital appreciation.	1958	131	400 Tel. Wire	20 Tel. Wire	Tel.; Written; Sig. Guar. over $5M	*Dividends: Auto.; A.* *Ret. Plans:* Keo., IRA, Corp. *Other:* Syst. With.; Auto. Pur.; Exch.-Tel.
ANALYTIC OPTIONED EQUITY FUND (*Analytic Investment Mgt.*) 2222 Martin St., Suite 230 Irvine, CA 92715 714-833-0294	Seeks greater total return with less risk by writing covered call options and cash secured puts on its div. high quality stock portfolio.	1978	29	25M No min. for IRA, Corp., Keo	1000	Tel.; Wire; Writ. with Sig. Guar.	*Dividends:* Auto.; Q. *Ret. Plans:* Keo., Corp., IRA. *Other:* Syst. With.
ARMSTRONG ASSOCIATES, INC. (*Portfolios Inc.*) 311 N. Market St. Dallas, TX 75202 214-744-5558	Capital growth by investing primarily in common stocks and securities convertible into common stock.	1968	10	500	50	Writ. with Sig. Guar.	*Dividends:* Auto.. A. *Ret. Plans:* Keo., IRA, Corp. *Other:* Syst. With.; Auto. Pur.

185

Fund Name (Advisor) Address and Telephone Number	Investment Objective and Policy	Year First Offered	Assets Mil. 12/31/82	Purchase Requirements Initial	Purchase Requirements Subsq.	Redemption Procedures	Services
BASIC GROWTH FUND, INC. (Basic Money Mgmt. Corp.) 505 Northern Blvd. Great Neck, NY 11021 516-466-9571	Growth of capital thru long-term investment.	1962	.1	100	25	Writ. with Sig. Guar.	Dividends: Auto.; A.
BEACON HILL MUTUAL FUND, INC. (Beacon Hill Management, Inc.) 75 Federal St. Boston, MA 02110 617-482-0795	Growth — specialize in quality growth stocks — flexible but generally investing in common stocks.	1964	2	0	0	Writ. with Sig. Guar.	Dividends: Auto.; A. Ret. Plans: Keo., IRA Other: Syst. With.
BOSTON CO. CAPITAL APPRECIATION (The Boston Company Advisors, Inc.) One Boston Place Boston, MA 02106 800-343-6324/617-956-9740	Long-term growth of capital with current income secondary. Invests primarily in common stock.	1947	213	1000	0	Writ. Sig. Guar. Tel. Exch.	Dividends: Auto.; Q. Ret. Plans: Keo., IRA, Corp. Other: Syst. With.; Auto. Pur. Cap. Gains. A
CAPITAL SHARES, INC. (Bull & Bear Mgmt. Group) 11 Hanover Square New York, NY 10005 800-431-6060/800-942-6911 (NY only)	Invests in emerging growth companies and special situations for long-term capital appreciation.	1959	$ 73	$ 1000	$ 25 Tel.	Written; Sig. Guar. over $1M	Dividends: Auto.; A. Ret. Plans: Keo, IRA, 403(b) Other: Exch.-Tel., Syst. With. Auto. Pur.
CHARTER FUND, INC. (Fund Management Company) 2100 Republic Bank Tower Dallas, TX 75201 214-742-6567	Capital appreciation by investing in common stocks.	1968	60	2000	25	Writ.	Dividends: Auto.; A Ret. Plans: Keo.; IRA 403(b) Other: Syst. With.;
DE VEGH MUTUAL FUND, INC. (Wood Struthers & Winthrop Mgt.) 140 Broadway New York, NY 10005 800-221-7780/212-902-4396	Long term capital appreciation.	1950	62	250	100	Writ. with Sig. Guar. over $500	Dividends: Auto.; S/A Ret. Plans: Keo., IRA Other: Syst. With.; Auto. Pur.
THE DIVIDEND/GROWTH FUND, INC. (AIM Management Co.) 11400 Rockville Pike, Suite 300 Rockville, MD 20852 301-770-1600	Primary income orientation with growth secondary. Emphasis on fundamentally sound stocks, income tax-sheltered.	1968	3	50	0	Writ. with Sig. Guar.	Dividends: Auto.; A. Ret. Plans: Keo., IRA Other: Syst. With.

186

Fund	Objective	Year	No.	Min. Initial	Min. Subseq.	Redemption	Features
THE DREXEL BURNHAM FUND *(Drexel Burnham Lambert Mgt. Corp.)* 60 Broad St. New York, NY 10004 212-483-1436	Capital appreciation mainly long term with income secondary emphasizing a flexible approach but generally common stocks.	1960	48	1000	250	Writ. with Sig. Guar.	*Dividends:* Auto.; Q. *Ret. Plans:* Keo., IRA *Other:* Syst. With.
ENERGY FUND INCORPORATED *(Neuberger & Berman Management)* 342 Madison Ave. New York, NY 10173 212-850-8300	Long-term capital appreciation; primarily investing in common stocks whose activities are related to the field of energy.	1955	316	100; 500 By Tel.	25; 500 By Tel.	Writ. with Sig. Guar.	*Dividends:* Auto.: A. *Ret. Plans:* Keo., IRA, Corp. *Other:* Syst. With.: Exch.-Tel.
FIDELITY ASSET INVEST. TRUST *(Fidelity Group)* 82 Devonshire St. Boston, MA 02109 800-225-6190/617-523-1919	Growth: specializes in securities whose market value is less than their book value.	1978	48	1000	250	Writ. with Sig. Guar.	*Dividends:* Auto.; A. *Ret. Plans:* Keo., IRA, Corp.; 403(b) *Other:* Syst. With.; Auto. Pur.; Exch.-Tel.
FIDELITY CONTRAFUND INC. *(Fidelity Group)* 82 Devonshire St. Boston, MA 02109 800-225-6190/617-523-1919	Growth from contrarian strategy: seeks solid investment values among stocks currently out of favor with other investors.	1967	73	1000	250	Writ. with Sig. Guar.	*Dividends:* Auto.: A. *Ret. Plans:* Keo., IRA, Corp. 403(b) *Other:* Syst. With.: Auto. Pur.; Exch.-Tel.
FIDELITY FUND *(Fidelity Group)* 82 Devonshire St. Boston, MA 02109 800-225-6190/617-523-1919	Growth with Income: Invests primarily in dividend-paying common stocks and convertible securities of well-known companies.	1930	588	1000	250	Writ. with Sig. Guar.	*Dividends:* Auto.; Q. *Ret. Plans:* Keo., IRA, Corp. 403(b) *Other:* Syst. With.; Auto. Pur.; Exch.-Tel.
FIDELITY MERCURY FUND *(Fidelity Group)* 82 Devonshire St. Boston, MA 02109 800-225-6190/617-523-1919	Growth: Agressive. Stocks and securities of above-average growth characteristics.	1983	.1	1000	250	EFT, Tel.; Writ. with Sig. Guar. Wire	*Dividends:* Auto.: A *Ret. Plans:* Keo, IRA, 403(b) *Other:* Syst. With.: Auto. Pur.; Exch.-Tel.
FIDELITY TREND FUND *(Fidelity Group)* 82 Devonshire St. Boston, MA 02109 800-225-6190/617-523-1919	Growth: Seeks long-term growth by considering market, industry and company trends.	1958	554	1000	250	Writ. with Sig. Guar.	*Dividends:* Auto.: A. *Ret. Plans:* Keo., IRA, Corp. 403(b) *Other:* Syst. With.; Auto. Pur.; Exch.-Tel.
FINANCIAL DYNAMICS FUND *(Financial Programs, Inc.)* P.O. Box 2040 Denver, CO 80201 800-525-9831/303-779-1233	For the aggressive investor seeking capital growth through speculative investment policies.	1967	70	500	25	Written	*Dividends:* Auto.; A. *Ret. Plans:* Keo., IRA, Corp. 403(b) *Other:* Auto. Pur.; Exch.-Tel.

Fund Name (Advisor) Address and Telephone Number	Investment Objective and Policy	Year First Offered	Assets Mil. 12/31/82	Purchase Requirements Initial	Purchase Requirements Subsq.	Redemption Procedures	Services
FINANCIAL INDUSTRIAL FUND, INC. *(Financial Programs, Inc.)* P.O. Box 2040 Denver, CO 80201 800-525-9831/303-779-1233	Long-term capital growth, with income.	1935	344	1000	100	Written	*Dividends:* Auto.; Q *Ret. Plans:* Keo. IRA, Corp. 403(b) *Other:* Syst. with; Auto. Pur.; Exch.-Tel.
FINOMIC INVESTMENT FUND *(Investment Advisors Inc.)* 1100 Louisiana, 4550 First Intl. Plz. Houston, TX 77002 713-659-2611	Capital appreciation. Primarily in common stocks of small to medium size companies generally located in the Sunbelt.	1972	5	750	50	Writ. with Sig. Guar.	*Dividends:* Auto.; A. *Ret. Plans:* Keo., IRA, Corp. *Other:* Syst. With.; Auto. Pur.
FIRST MUTUAL FUND, INC. *(Trainer Wortham & Co., Inc.)* 50 South Main St. Providence, RI 02903 401-521-4342	Growth with income secondary; investments made in companies with growth characteristics and some attention given to market timing.	1959	$ 2	$200	$ 100 Tel.	Writ. with Sig. Guar.	*Dividends:* Auto.; S/A
FLEX-FUND *(R. Meeder & Assoc., Inc.)* 3366 Riverside Drive Columbus, OH 43221 614-457-8100	Long-term capital growth thru invest. in common stocks. Also bonds or money market instru. for defensive purposes.	1982	16	5000	500	Writ. & Tel.	*Dividends:* Auto.; A. *Ret. Plans:* Keo. IRA *Other:* Syst. With.; Sub-Acctg.
THE 44 WALL STREET FUND, INC. *(Forty Four Mgt.)* 150 Broadway New York, NY 10038 800-221-7836/212-267-2820	Long-term cap. apprec. — using limited no. of common stock companies with above aver. potential and which are fundamentally attractive.	1969	201	25,000	100 Tel.	Tel.; Writ. with Sig. Guar.	*Dividends:* Auto.; A. *Ret. Plans:* Keo.; IRA.; 403(b) (exist. share-owners only) *Other:* Syst. With.; Auto. Pur.; Exch.-Tel.
FOUNDERS GROWTH FUND, INC. *(Founders Mutual Depositor Corp.)* 655 Broadway Denver, CO 80203 800-525-2440/303-595-3863	Capital appreciation with income secondary. Purchases common stocks or convertible securities of established companies.	1967	39	250; 500 By Tel.	25; 500 By Tel.	Writ. with Sig. Guar.	*Dividends:* Auto.; A. *Ret. Plans:* Keo.; IRA *Other:* Auto. Pur.; Syst. With.; Exch.-Tel.
FOUNDERS SPECIAL FUND, INC. *(Founders Mutual Depositor Corp.)* 655 Broadway Denver, CO 80203 800-525-2440/303-595-3863	Max. cap. apprec. through common stocks of companies relatively small in terms of assets and earnings. Also may leverage investments.	1969	1	250; 500 By Tel.	25; 500 By Tel.	Writ. with Sig. Guar.	*Dividends:* Auto.; A. *Ret. Plans:* Keo.; IRA *Other:* Auto. Pur.; Syst. With.; Exch.-Tel.

Fund	Objective	Year	No.	Min. Initial	Min. Subseq.	Redemption	Dividends / Ret. Plans / Other
GAMING SPORTS & GROWTH FUND (*Valley Forge Management Corp.*) 1375 Anthony Wayne Drive Wayne, PA 19087 215-688-6839	Capital appreciation through investment in gaming and/or sports oriented companies.	1978	1	500	100	Writ. with Sig. Guar.	*Dividends:* Auto.; A. *Other:* Auto. Pur.
GATEWAY OPTION INCOME FUND (*Gateway Investment Advisers, Inc.*) 1120 Carew Tower Cincinnati, OH 45202 513-621-7774	Earns a high current return with less risk by writing covered call options. Income qualifies for 85% corporate dividend exclusion.	1977	21	500	100	Writ. with Sig. Guar.	*Dividends:* Auto.; Q. *Ret. Plans:* Keo., IRA *Other:* Syst. With.
G. T. PACIFIC FUND, INC. (*G. T. Capital Management, Inc.*) 601 Montgomery St., Suite 1400 San Francisco, CA 94111 415-392-6181	Long-term growth through investment in diversified portfolio of Far Eastern Securities.	1977	14	500	100	Tel.; Writ. with Sig. Guar.	*Dividends:* Auto.: A. *Ret. Plans:* IRA *Other:* Auto. Pur.; Syst. With.
GENERAL SECURITIES, INC. (*Craig-Hallum, Inc.*) 133 South Seventh St. Minneapolis, MN 55402 612-332-1212	Capital appreciation and security of principal — Flexible to use stocks and sometimes fixed income securities — also covered options.	1951	13	100	10 Tel.	Writ. with Sig. Guar.	*Dividends:* Auto.; Q. *Ret. Plans:* Keo., IRA, 403(b) *Other:* Syst. With.; Auto. Pur.
GOLCONDA INVESTORS LTD. (*Bull and Bear Group*) 11 Hanover Square New York, NY 10005 800-431-6060/800-942-6911 (NY only)	Specialized; invests in gold bullion and internationally diversified portfolio of gold mining shares.	1974	23	1000	25 Tel.	Written; Sig. Guar. over $1M	*Dividends:* Auto.; S/A. *Ret. Plans:* Keo., IRA, 403(b) *Other:* Exch.-Tel. Syst. With.; Auto. Pur.
GOOD AND BAD TIMES FUND (*Growth Research and Management*) Box 29467 San Antonio, TX 78229 800-531-5777/512-696-1234	Preservation of capital and capital appreciation. Current income secondary. Invests in low debt, financially sound, successfully managed companies.	1981	5	500	50	Tel.; Writ.; Sig. Guar. Over $5M	*Dividends:* Auto.; S/A *Ret. Plans:* Keo., IRA, 403(b) *Other:* Syst. With.; Auto. Pur.; Exch.-Tel.
GROWTH INDUSTRY SHARES (*William Blair & Company*) 135 S. LaSalle St. Chicago, IL 60603 312-346-4830	Appreciation of capital and growth of income through growth companies; diversification among different size companies.	1946	54	200	25	Writ; Sig. Guar. over $5M	*Dividends:* Auto.; Q. *Ret. Plans:* Keo., IRA *Other:* Auto. Pur.; Syst. With.
GUARDIAN MUTUAL FUND, INC. (*Neuberger & Berman Management*) 342 Madison Ave. New York, NY 10173 212-850-8300	Capital appreciation with income secondary; common stocks of seasoned companies, flexibility to shift to fixed income securities.	1950	229	200; 500 By Tel.	50; 500 By Tel.	Writ. with Sig. Guar.	*Dividends:* Auto.; Q. *Ret. Plans:* Keo., IRA, Corp. *Other:* Syst. With.; Exch.-Tel.

Fund Name (Advisor) Address and Telephone Number	Investment Objective and Policy	Year First Offered	Assets Mil. 12/31/82	Purchase Requirements Initial	Purchase Requirements Subsq.	Redemption Procedures	Services
HARTWELL GROWTH FUND, INC. (Hartwell Management Co., Inc.) 50 Rockefeller Plaza New York, NY 10020 212-247-8740	Capital appreciation. Invests primarily in intermediate size growth companies.	1965	10	300	50	Writ. with Sig. Guar.	Dividends: Auto.; A. Ret. Plans: IRA Other: Syst. With.; Auto. Pur.
HARTWELL LEVERAGE FUND, INC. (Hartwell Management Co., Inc.) 50 Rockefeller Plaza New York, NY 10020 212-247-8740	Capital appreciation. Flexible policy emphasizing appreciation potential.	1968	36	5000	50	Writ. with Sig. Guar.	Dividends: Auto.; A. Ret. Plans: IRA Other: Auto. Pur.
IVY FUND, INC. (Grantham et. al.., & Furman et. al.) 40 Industrial Pk. Rd. Hingham, MA 02043 617-749-1416	Growth. The fund seeks to achieve long-term growth of capital primarily through investment in equity securities.	1961	$77	$500	$100	Writ. with Sig. Guar.	Dividends: Auto.; A. Ret. Plans: Keo., IRA Other: Syst. With.
JANUS FUND, INC. (Janus Management Corp.) 789 Sherman St. Denver, CO 80203 800-525-3713/303-837-1774	Growth of capital. Takes positions in a limited number of securities.	1970	102	1000	100	Writ. with Sig. Guar.	Dividends: Auto.; A. Ret. Plans: Keo., IRA Other: Exch.-Tel.; Syst. With.; Auto. Pur.
LEHMAN CAPITAL FUND (Lehman Management Co., Inc.) 55 Water St. New York, NY 10041 212-558-2031	Capital appreciation; essentially common stocks with above average market appreciation potential.	1976	63	2500	1000	Writ. Sig. Guar.	Dividends: Auto.; A. Ret. Plans: Keo. IRA Other: Exch.-Tel. or Writ.
LEXINGTON GOLDFUND, INC. (Lexington Management Corp.) P.O. Box 1515, 580 Sylvan Ave. Englewood Cliffs, NJ 07632 800-526-4791/800-932-0838 (NJ only)	Capital appreciation, income secondary. Invests exclusively in gold bullion and gold mining stocks.	1979	4	1000	50	Writ.; Sig. Guar. over $5M	Dividends: Auto.; S/A Ret. Plans: Keo., IRA Other: Syst. With.; Auto. Pur.; Exch.-Mail
LEXINGTON GROWTH FUND, INC. (Lexington Mgmt. Corp.) Box 1515, 580 Sylvan Ave. Englewood Cliffs, NJ 07632 800-526-4791/800-932-0838 (NJ only)	Capital appreciation; invests in common stocks believed to be undervalued and offering better than average growth possibilities.	1969	28	1000	50	Writ.; Sig. Guar. over $5M	Dividends: Auto.; A. Ret. Plans: Keo., IRA Other: Syst. With.; Auto. Pur.; Exch.-Tel.

Fund	Objective	Year	No.	Min. Init.	Min. Add.	Redemption	Distributions / Plans
LEXINGTON RESEARCH FUND, INC. *(Lexington Mgmt. Corp.)* Box 1515, 580 Sylvan Ave. Englewood Cliffs, NJ 07632 800-526-4791/800-932-0838 (NJ only)	Long-term capital appreciation; invests in common stocks of large, ably managed, well-financed companies.	1939	93	1000	50	Writ.; Sig. Guar. over $5M	*Dividends:* Auto.; Q. *Ret. Plans:* Keo., IRA *Other:* Syst. With.; Auto. Pur.; Exch.-Tel.
LINDNER FUND, INC. *(Lindner Management Corp.)* 200 South Bemiston St. Louis, MO 63105 314-727-5305	Growth. Seeks optimum combination of low price-earnings ratio and growth.	1973	160	2000	100 Tel.	Tel. Written;	*Dividends:* Auto.; A. *Ret. Plans:* IRA *Other:* Syst. With.
MAIRS & POWER GROWTH FUND *(Mairs and Power, Inc.)* W-2062 1st Nat'l Bank Bldg. St. Paul, MN 55101 612-222-8478	Growth.	1958	17	1000	50	Writ. Sig. Guar.	*Dividend:* Auto.; S/A *Ret. Plans:* Keo., IRA
MANHATTAN FUND, INC. *(Neuberger & Berman Management)* 342 Madison Ave. New York, NY 10173 212-850-8300	Capital appreciation.	1966	66	250; 500 By Tel.	25; 500 By Tel.	Writ. with Sig. Guar.	*Dividends:* Auto.; A. *Ret. Plans:* Keo., Corp., IRA *Other:* Syst. With.; Exch.-Tel.
MEDICAL TECHNOLOGY FUND, INC. *(PRO Services, Inc.)* 1107 Bethlehem Pk., c/o PRO Services Flourtown, PA 19031 800-523-0864/215-836-1300	Growth through companies engaged in products or services related to technology for medicine or health care.	1979	34	1000	0 Tel.	Tel. Writ. with Sig. Guar.	*Dividends:* Auto.; A. *Ret. Plans:* Keo., IRA, Corp., 403(b) *Other:* Syst. With.; Auto. Pur.; Exch.-Tel.
MUTUAL QUALIFIED INCOME FUND *(Heine Securities Corp.)* 26 Broadway New York, NY 10004 212-908-4048	Income and capital apprec., either short or long term.	1980	29	1000	0 Tel.	Writ.; Sig. Guar.	*Dividends:* Auto.; S/A *Ret. Plans:* Keo., IRA
MUTUAL SHARES CORP. *(Heine Securities Corp.)* 26 Broadway New York, NY 10004 212-908-4048	Long term capital appreciation. Income secondary. Invest in common, preferred & debt securities at prices less than intrinsic value.	1949	154	1000	0 Tel.	Writ. with Sig. Guar.	*Dividends:* Auto.; S/A *Ret. Plans:* Keo., IRA *Other:* Syst. With.
NAT'L AVIATION & TECH. CORP. *(American Fund Advisors, Inc.)* 50 Broad St. New York, NY 10004 212-482-8100	Capital growth. Invests in aviation related companies and companies which use technology extensively in product development or operations.	1928	95	500	0 Tel.; Wire Over $500	Writ. with Sig. Guar.	*Dividends:* Auto.; S/A *Ret. Plans:* Keo., IRA, Corp. *Other:* Syst., With.; Exch.-Tel.

Fund Name (Advisor) Address and Telephone Number	Investment Objective and Policy	Year First Offered	Assets Mil. 12/31/82	Purchase Requirements Initial	Purchase Requirements Subsq.	Redemption Procedures	Services
NEUWIRTH FUND, INC. (Wood, Struthers & Winthrop Mgt.) 140 Broadway New York, NY 10005 800-221-7780/212-902-4396	Capital growth. Common stock of established companies with growth characteristics; also emerging growth companies.	1966	20	500	50	Writ. with Sig. Guar. over $500	Dividends: Auto.; A. Ret. Plans: Keo., IRA Other: Syst. With.
"NEW BEGINNING" GROWTH FUND, INC. (Sit Investment Associates, Inc.) 1714 First Bank Place West Minneapolis, MN 55402 612-332-3223	Long-term capital growth. Emphasis on small, emerging-growth and larger special situation equity investments.	1982	2	10M	500 2M IRA shrhlds Bk wire or Writ.	Writ. with Sig. Guar.	Dividends: Auto.; A. Ret. Plans: Keo., IRA
NEWTON GROWTH FUND, INC. (Heritage Investment Advisors, Inc.) 733 N. Van Buren St. Milwaukee, WI 53202 414-347-1141/800-242-7229 (WI only)	Long-term growth of capital, current income of lesser importance.	1960	$ 21	$ 500	$ 50	Tel.; Writ. with. Sig. Guar.	Dividends: Auto.; A. Ret. Plans: Keo., IRA, 403(b) Other: Syst. With.; Auto. Pur.
NICHOLAS FUND, INC. (Nicholas Company, Inc.) 312 East Wisconsin Ave. Milwaukee, WI 53202 414-272-6133	Growth. Concentrates in common stocks of small and medium size companies.	1969	98	500	100	Writ.; Sig. Guar. certificates only	Dividends: Auto.; A. Ret. Plans: Keo., IRA Other: Exch.-Tel.
NORTH STAR REGIONAL FUND (Investment Advisers, Inc.) 1100 Dain Tower, Box 1160 Minneapolis, MN 55440 612-371-7780	Growth; common stocks primarily from seven state upper midwest region.	1980	30	2500	100	Writ.	Dividends: Auto.; S/A Ret. Plans: Keo., IRA, Corp., 403(b) Other: Exch.-Writ.
NOVA FUND, INC. (Granaham-Everitt Investments, Inc.) 303 Wyman Street Waltham, MA 02152 617-890-4415	Long term growth.	1980	22	2000	0	Writ., Sig. Guar.	Dividends: Auto.; A. Ret. Plans: IRA Other: Auto. Pur.
THE ONE HUNDRED FUND, INC. (Berger Associates, Inc.) 899 Logan St. Denver, CO 80203 303-837-1020	Managed investments in successful and highly profitable corporations, with emphasis upon retained earnings.	1966	11	250 Wire.	50 Tel., Wire	Writ. with Sig. Guar.	Dividends: Auto.; A. Ret. Plans: Keo., IRA Other: Syst. With.; Exch.-Tel.

192

Fund	Objective	Year		Min. Initial	Min. Subsequent	Redemption	Dividends / Ret. Plans / Other
ONE WILLIAM STREET FUND (*Lehman Management Co., Inc.*) 55 Water St. New York, NY 10041 212-558-2020	Long-term growth of capital; income secondary, through common stock investment.	1958	332	500	50	Writ. Sig. Guar. over $5M	*Dividends:* Auto.; Q. *Ret. Plans:* Keo., IRA *Other:* Syst. With.; Auto. Pur.; Exch. Tel. or Writ.
THE PARTNERS FUND, INC. (*Neuberger & Berman Management*) 342 Madison Ave. New York, NY 10173 212-850-8300	Capital growth. Emphasis on common stocks with a portion of assets in stocks selected for short-term gain potential.	1968	110	250; 500 By Tel.	0; 500 By Tel.	Writ. with Sig. Guar.	*Dividends:* Auto.; A *Ret. Plans:* Keo., IRA, Corp. *Other:* Syst. With.; Exch.-Tel.
PENN SQUARE MUTUAL FUND (*Penn Square Mgmt. Corp.*) Berkshire Towers, Box 1419 Reading, PA 19603 800-523-8440/215-376-6771	Long-term capital growth. Investments principally in common stocks of larger companies considered undervalued on a fundamental basis.	1958	155	250	0	Writ.	*Dividends :* Auto.; Q. *Ret. Plans:* Keo., IRA, Corp., 403(b) *Other:* Syst. With.
PENNSYLVANIA MUTUAL FUND, INC. (*Quest Advisory Corp.*) 1414 Ave. of Americas New York, NY 10019 800-221-4268/212-355-7311	Capital appreciation. Invests in common stocks with special emphasis on securities of medium-sized companies purchased on value basis.	1962	48	1000	50; 500 Tel.	Writ. with Sig. Guar.	*Dividends:* Auto.; A. *Ret. Plans:* Keo., IRA, 403(b) *Other:* Syst. With.; Auto. Pur.
PLITREND FUND, INC. (*Tenneco Asset Management Company*) 777 Walker, 2 Shell Plza., #2000 Houston, TX 77002 713-757-5675/713-757-5679	Long-term capital appreciation through investments in the common stock of companies (including less well known companies).	1952	60	0	0	Writ. with no Sig. Guar. if shares are in unissued form.	*Dividends:* Auto.; S/A *Ret. Plans:* Keo., IRA, 403(b) *Other:* Syst. With.; Auto. Pur.; Exch.-Writ.; Var. Ann. (qual. plans only)
T. ROWE PRICE GROWTH STOCK (*T. Rowe Price Associates, Inc.*) 100 East Pratt St. Baltimore, MD 21202 800-638-5660/301-547-2308	Long-term capital appreciation and increased future income through investment in well-established growth companies.	1950	1008	500 Wire	50 Tel.; Wire	Writ. with Sig. Guar. over $10M	*Dividends:* Auto.; A. *Ret. Plans:* Keo., IRA, Corp., 403(b). Municipal *Other:* Syst. With.; Auto. Pur.; Grp.-Acct.; Exch.-Tel.
T. ROWE PRICE GROWTH & INCOME FUND (*T. Rowe Price Associates, Inc.*) 100 East Pratt St. Baltimore, MD 21202 800-638-5660/301-547-2308	Long-term cap. growth, reasonable current div. level, and growth of future income thru invest. in income-producing common stocks.	1982	1942	1000 Wire	100 Tel.; Wire	Tel.; Wire, Tlgm.; Writ. with Sig. Guar. over $10M	*Dividends:* Auto.; Q. *Ret. Plans:* Keo., IRA, Corp.; 403(b); Municipal *Other:* Syst. With.; Auto. Pur.; Exch.-Tel.; Grp.-Acct.
T. ROWE PRICE INTERNAT'L FUND (*T. Rowe Price Associates, Inc.*) 100 East Pratt St. Baltimore, MD 21202 800-638-5660/301-547-2308	Total return from long-term growth of capital and income through investment in foreign securities.	1980	101	5000 Wire	1000 Tel.; Wire	Writ.; Sig. Guar. over $10M	*Dividends:* Auto.; A. *Ret. Plans:* Keo., IRA, Corp., 403(b). Municipal *Other:* Exch.-Tel.; Telgm.; Grp. Acct.

Fund Name (Advisor) Address and Telephone Number	Investment Objective and Policy	Year First Offered	Assets Mil. 12/31/82	Purchase Requirements Initial	Purchase Requirements Subsq.	Redemption Procedures	Services
T. ROWE PRICE NEW ERA FUND *(T. Rowe Price Associates, Inc.)* 100 East Pratt St. Baltimore, MD 21202 800-638-5660/301-547-2308	Long-term capital appreciation through investment primarily in companies that own or develop natural resources.	1969	412	1000 Wire	100 Tel.; Wire	Writ. with Sig. Guar. over $10M	*Dividends:* Auto.; A. *Ret. Plans:* Keo., IRA, Corp., 403(b), Municipal *Other:* Syst. With.; Auto. Pur.; Grp.-Acct.; Exch.-Tel.
T. ROWE PRICE NEW HORIZONS FUND *(T. Rowe Price Associates, Inc.)* 100 East Pratt St. Baltimore, MD 21202 800-638-5660/301-547-2308	Long-term capital appreciation through investment in newer, smaller companies with potential to become major growth companies.	1960	1199	1000 Wire	100 Tel.; Wire	Writ. with Sig. Guar. over $10M	*Dividends:* Auto.; A. *Ret. Plans:* Keo., IRA, Corp., 403(b), Municipal *Other:* Syst. With.; Auto. Pur.; Grp.-Acct.; Exch.-Tel.
PRO FUND, INC. *(PRO Services, Inc.)* 1107 Bethlehem Pike Flourtown, PA 19031 800-523-0864/215-836-1300	Growth. Invests primarily in common stocks believed by management to have potential for capital appreciation.	1967	$ 40	$ 300	$ 0 Tel.	Tel.; Writ. with. Sig. Guar.	*Dividends:* Auto.; Q. *Ret. Plans:* Keo., IRA, Corp., 403(b) *Other:* Syst. With.; Auto. Pur.; Exch.-Tel.
THE RAINBOW FUND, INC. *(Robert Furman)* 60 Broad St. New York, NY 10004 212-558-1585	Growth of capital. A non-diversified fund primarily investing in common stocks, and leveraging investments through option strategies.	1967	1	600	50	Writ. with Sig. Guar.	*Dividends:* Auto.; A. *Ret. Plans:* Keo., IRA *Other:* Syst. With.
RETIRE. PLAN OF AMER/EQUIT. *(Chicago Title & Trust Co.)* 111 W. Washington Street Chicago, IL 60602 1-800-621-1110/312-630-2540	Growth in capital through appreciation and reinvestment of income in common stocks; available only to tax-sheltered retirement plans.	1978	2	250	250	Writ.	*Dividends:* Auto.; Q. *Ret. Plans:* Keo., IRA Corp., 403(b) *Other:* Exch.-Tel.
SAFECO EQUITY FUND, INC. *(Safeco Asset Management Co.)* Safeco Plaza T15 NL Seattle, WA 98185 800-426-6730	Growth & income; Invests in well known companies providing above average yields and growth prospects.	1932	30	200	25	Writ. with Sig. Guar.	*Dividends:* Auto.; Q. *Ret. Plans:* Keo., IRA, Corp. *Other:* Syst. With.; Auto. Pur.; Exch.-Writ.
SAFECO GROWTH FUND, INC. *(Safeco Asset Management Co.)* Safeco Plaza T15 NL Seattle, WA 98185 800-426-6730	Invests in medium to small companies having good growth prospects for coming 3 to 5 yrs.	1967	48	200	25	Writ. with Sig. Guar.	*Dividends:* Auto.; S/A *Ret. Plans:* Keo., IRA, Corp. *Other:* Syst. With.; Auto. Pur.; Exch.-Writ.

194

Fund	Objective	Founded	No.	Min.	Subseq.	Redemption	Services
SCUDDER CAPITAL GROWTH FUND *(Scudder, Stevens & Clark)* 175 Federal St. Boston, MA 02110 800-225-2470/617-482-3990	Growth. Emphasizes common stocks of above-average risk.	1957	171	1000	0 Tel. over $500	Tel.; Writ. with Sig. Guar.	*Dividends:* Auto.; A. *Ret. Plans:* Keo., IRA, 403(b), Corp., 401(k) *Other:* Syst. With.; Auto. Pur.; Exch.-Tel.
SCUDDER COMMON STOCK FUND *(Scudder, Stevens & Clark)* 175 Federal St. Boston, MA 02110 800-225-2470/617-482-3990	Growth. Common stocks, readily marketable securities of leading companies.	1929	188	1000	0 Tel. over $500	Tel.; Writ. with Sig. Guar.	*Dividends:* Auto.; S/A *Ret. Plans:* Keo., IRA, 403(b), Corp., 401(k) *Other:* Syst. With.; Auto. Pur.; Exch.-Tel.
SCUDDER DEVELOPMENT FUND *(Scudder, Stevens & Clark)* 175 Federal St. Boston, MA 02110 800-225-2470/617-482-3990	Growth. Consists primarily of marketable equity securities of small or little known companies.	1971	168	1000	0 Tel. over $500	Writ. with Sig. Guar.	*Dividends:* Auto.; A. *Ret. Plans:* Keo., IRA, 403(b), Corp., 401(k) *Other:* Exch.-Tel.
SCUDDER INTERNATIONAL FUND *(Scudder, Stevens & Clark)* 175 Federal St. Boston, MA 02110 800-225-2470/617-482-3990	Growth. Specializes in common stocks of non-U.S. companies and economies.	1954	79	1000	0 Tel. over $500	Tel.; Writ with Sig. Guar.	*Dividends:* Auto.; A. *Ret. Plans:* Keo., IRA, 403(b), Corp., 401(k) *Other:* Syst. With.; Exch.-Tel.
SELECTED SPECIAL SHARES, INC. *(Burton J. Vincent, Chesley & Co.)* 105 W. Adams St. Chicago, IL 60603 1-800-621-7321/1-800-972-1092 (IL only)	Capital growth. Investing in securities which afford maximum opportunity for appreciation.	1968	31	1000	100	Writ. with Sig. Guar.	*Dividends:* Auto.; A. *Ret. Plans:* Keo., IRA, Corp. *Other:* Syst. With.; Auto. Pur.; Exch.-Writ. and Tel.
SHERMAN, DEAN FUND *(Sherman, Dean Mgmt. & Res.)* 120 Broadway New York, NY 10271 212-577-3850	The primary objective of the fund is capital appreciation. Income is of secondary importance.	1968	5	1000	100	Writ. with Sig. Guar.	*Dividends:* Auto.; A. *Ret. Plans:* Keo., IRA
STEINROE & FARN. CAP. OPPOR. *(Stein Roe & Farnham)* 150 S. Wacker Dr. Chicago, IL 60606 800-621-0320/312-368-7826	Long-term capital appreciation. Invests in common stocks of both seasoned and smaller companies.	1963	199	2500	100	Writ. with Sig. Guar.	*Dividends:* Auto.; A. *Ret. Plans:* Keo., IRA, Corp. *Other:* Syst. With.; Grp.-Acct.; Exch. Writ.-Tel.
STEINROE SPECIAL FUND, INC. *(Stein Roe & Farnham)* 150 S. Wacker Dr. Chicago, IL 60606 800-621-0320/312-368-7826	Max. cap. apprec.; invests in companies expected to benefit from special factors or trends or having unusual capital apprec. potential.	1968	78	2500	100	Writ. with Sig. Guar.	*Dividends:* Auto.; A. *Ret. Plans:* Keo., IRA, Corp. *Other:* Syst. With.; Grp.-Acct.; Exch.-Writ./Tel.

Fund Name (Advisor) Address and Telephone Number	Investment Objective and Policy	Year First Offered	Assets Mil. 12/31/82	Purchase Requirements Initial	Purchase Requirements Subsq.	Redemption Procedures	Services
STEINROE & FARNHAM STOCK (*Stein Roe & Farnham*) 150 S. Wacker Dr. Chicago, IL 60606 800-621-0320/312-368-7826	Long-term capital appreciation. Invests substantially all assets in common stocks and other equity-type securities.	1958	235	2500	100	Writ. with Sig. Guar.	*Dividends:* Auto.; Q. *Ret. Plans:* Keo., IRA, Corp. *Other:* Syst. With.; Grp.-Acct.; Exch. Writ./Tel.
STEINROE UNIVERSE FUND, INC. (*Stein Roe & Farnham*) 150 S. Wacker Dr. Chicago, IL 60606 800-621-0320/312-368-7826	Capital appreciation through investing in an unusually broad spectrum of common stocks utilizing a computerized selection process.	1980	193	5000	100	Writ. with Sig. Guar.	*Dividends:* Auto.; A. *Ret. Plans:* Keo., IRA, Corp. *Other:* Grp.-Acct. Exch.-Writ.
STRATTON GROWTH FUND (*Stratton Management Co.*) Butler & Skippack Box 550 Blue Bell, PA 19422 215-542-8025	Growth-primary; income-secondary. Value-oriented high yield, low P/E common stocks.	1972	$ 9	$ 1000	$ 100 Tel.	Writ. with Sig. Guar. over $500	*Dividends:* Auto.; A. *Ret. Plans:* Keo. IRA, 403(b) *Other:* Syst. With.; Exch.-Tel.
TUDOR FUND (*Tudor Management Co., Inc.*) One New York Plaza New York, NY 10004 212-908-9582	Capital appreciation. Write covered call options.	1969	38	250	50	Writ. with Sig. Guar.	*Dividends:* Auto.; A. *Ret. Plans:* Keo. IRA *Other:* Syst. With.
TWENTIETH CENTURY GROWTH (*Investors Research Corporation*) P.O. Box 200 Kansas City, MO 64141 816-531-5575	Capital growth. Common stocks believed to have above-average appreciation potential.	1958	439	0	0	Writ. with Sig. Guar.	*Dividends:* Auto.; A. *Ret. Plans:* Keo., IRA, 403(b) *Other:* Syst. With.; Auto. Pur.; Exch.-Writ.
TWENTIETH CENTURY SELECT (*Investors Research Corporation*) P.O. Box 200 Kansas City, MO 64141 816-531-5575	Satisfactory rate of return through dividend paying common stocks selected for appreciation potential.	1958	130	0	0	Writ. with Sig. Guar.	*Dividends:* Auto.; A. *Ret. Plans:* Keo., IRA, 403(b) *Other:* Syst. With.; Auto. Pur.; Exch.-Writ.
TWENTIETH CENTURY ULTRA (*Investors Research Corporation*) P.O. Box 200 Kansas City, MO 64141 816-531-5575	Capital growth. Common stocks believed to have above average appreciation potential.	1981	113	0	0	Writ. with Sig. Guar.	*Dividends:* Auto.; A. *Ret. Plans:* Keo., IRA, 403(b) *Other:* Syst. With.; Auto. Pur.; Exch.-Writ.

Fund	Objective	Year	No.	Min.		Redemption	Dividends / Plans
UNIFIED ACCUMULATION FUND (*Unified Management Corporation*) Guaranty Bldg. Indianapolis, IN 46204 317-634-3300/800-428-4492	Tax shel. capital appreciation. Flexible invest. in high-yield stocks, corp. and gov. bonds. Income and capital gains accumulate tax-free.	1978	3	1000	25	Tel.; Writ.	*Dividends:* Accum. Tax-Free *Ret. Plans:* Keo., IRA, Corp. 403(b) *Other:* Syst. With.; Auto. Pur.; Exch.-Tel.
UNIFIED GROWTH FUND, INC. (*Unified Management Corporation*) Guaranty Bldg. Indianapolis, IN 46204 317-634-3300/800-428-4492	Capital appreciation. Medium to smaller companies with above-average growth in sales and earnings. Attention to timing.	1970	5	200	25	Tel.; Writ.	*Dividends:* Auto.: A. *Ret. Plans:* Keo., IRA, 403(b), Corp. *Other:* Syst. With.; Auto. Pur.; Exch.-Tel.
UNITED SERVICES GOLD SHARES, INC. (*Growth Research and Management, Inc.*) Box 29467 San Antonio, TX 78229 800-531-5777/512-696-1234	Growth, Income. Specializes in gold shares and other precious metals. securities.	1970	198	500	50	Tel.; Writ.; Sig. Guar. over $5M	*Dividends:* Auto.: S/A *Ret. Plans:* Keo., IRA, 403(b) *Other:* Syst. With.; Auto. Pur.; Exch.-Tel.
USAA MUTUAL/GROWTH (*USAA Investment Mgmt. Co.*) P.O. Box 33277 San Antonio, TX 78233 800-531-8181/800-292-8181 (TX only)	Long-term growth of capital, income secondary; diversified and flexible — can take a defensive position.	1971	75	1000	25	Tel.; Wire; Writ. with Sig. Guar.	*Dividends:* Auto.: A. *Ret. Plans:* Keo., IRA, 403(b) *Other:* Syst. With.; Auto. Pur.; Exch.-Tel.
USAA MUTUAL/SUNBELT ERA (*USAA Investment Mgmt. Co.*) P.O. Box 33277 San Antonio, TX 78233 800-531-8181/800-292-8181 (TX only)	Capital appreciation; invests in common stocks of emerging companies located in Sunbelt regions of U.S. which have high potential for future growth.	1981	16	1000	25	Tel.; Wire; Writ. with Sig. Guar.	*Dividends:* Auto.: A. *Ret. Plans:* Keo., IRA, 403(b) *Other:* Syst. With.; Auto. Pur.; Exch.-Tel.
VALLEY FORGE FUND, INC (*Valley Forge Management Corp.*) P.O. Box 262 Valley Forge, PA 19481 215-688-6839	Capital appreciation through market timing. Will move into c.d.'s and/or debt securities to defend capital.	1971	2	300	100 Tel.	Tel.; Wire; Writ. with Sig. Guar.	*Dividends:* Auto.: A. *Ret. Plans:* IRA, Keo *Other:* Auto. Pur.
VALUE LINE FUND, INC. (*Arnold Bernhard & Co., Inc.*) 711 Third Avenue New York, NY 10017 800-223-0818/800-522-5217 (NY only)	Long-term growth of capital is primary objective. Current income is a secondary objective.	1949	109	250	0	Writ. with Sig. Guar.	*Dividends:* Auto.: Q. *Ret. Plans:* Keo., IRA, 403(b) *Other:* Syst. With.; Exch.-Writ. or Tel.
VALUE LINE LEVERAGED GROWTH (*Arnold Bernhard & Co., Inc.*) 711 Third Avenue New York, NY 10017 800-223-0818/800-522-5217 (NY only)	Fund's sole objective is capital growth by investing in stocks ranked #1 and #2 by The Value Line Investment Survey.	1972	115	250	0	Writ. with Sig. Guar.	*Dividends:* Auto.: A. *Ret. Plans:* Keo., IRA, 403(b) *Other:* Syst. With.; Exch.-Writ. or Tel.

Fund Name (Advisor) Address and Telephone Number	Investment Objective and Policy	Year First Offered	Assets Mil. 12/31/82	Purchase Requirements Initial	Subsq.	Redemption Procedures	Services
VALUE LINE SPECIAL SITUATIONS FD. *(Arnold Bernhard & Co., Inc.)* 711 Third Avenue New York, NY 10017 800-223-0818/800-522-5217 (NY only)	The *sole* investment objective is long term growth of capital through investing in what are considered to be special situations.	1956	200	250	0	Writ. with Sig. Guar.	*Dividends:* Auto.; A. *Ret. Plans:* Keo., IRA., 403(b) *Other:* Syst. With.; Exch.-Writ. or Tel.
VANGUARD EXPLORER FUND *(Wellington Management Company)* The Vanguard Group/P.O. Box 2600 Valley Forge, PA 19482 800-523-7025/800-362-0530 (PA only)	Long term capital growth by investing in small, unseasoned or embryonic companies.	1967	96	3000 Wire	100 Wire	Writ. with Sig. Guar.	*Dividends:* Auto.; A. *Ret. Plans:* Keo., IRA Corp., 403(b) *Other:* Syst. With.; Auto. Pur.; Exch.-Writ.; Grp.-Acct.
VANGUARD/INVEST FUND *(Wellington Management Company & Schroder Capital Management)* The Vanguard Group/P.O. Box 2600 Valley Forge, PA 19482 800-523-7025/800-362-0530 (PA only)	Seeks long-term cap. growth by investing in U.S. and foreign common stocks for appreciation.	1961	149	500 Wire	50 Wire	Writ. with Sig. Guar.	*Dividends:* Auto.; A. *Ret. Plans:* Keo., IRA, Corp., 403(b) *Other:* Syst. With.; Auto. Pur.; Exch.-Tel.; Grp.-Acct.
VANGUARD/W.L. MORGAN GROWTH *(Wellington Management Company)* The Vanguard Group/P.O. Box 2600 Valley Forge, PA 19482 800-523-7025/800-362-0530 (PA only)	Seeks long-term growth of capital, by investing in companies believed to have above-average growth potential.	1968	289	500 Wire	50 Wire	Writ. with Sig. Guar.	*Dividends:* Auto.; A. *Ret. Plans:* Keo., IRA Corp., 403(b) *Other:* Syst. With.; Auto. Pur.; Exch.-Tel.; Grp.-Acct.
VANGUARD/TR. COMMINGLED EQUITY *(Batterymarch Financial Management)* The Vanguard Group/P.O. Box 2600 Valley Forge, PA 19482 800-523-7025/800-362-0530 (PA only)	Seeks max. long-term total return through equities of undervalued securities. Disciplined portfolio construction, comput, modeling.	1980	191	25M Wire	1M Wire	Writ. with Sig. Guar.	*Dividends:* Auto.; Q. *Ret. Plans:* Keo., IRA Corp., 403(b) *Other:* Syst. With.; Exch.-Tel.; Grp.-Acct.
VANGUARD/WINDSOR FUND *(Wellington Management Company)* The Vanguard Group/P.O. Box 2600 Valley Forge, PA 19482 800-523-7025/800-362-0530 (PA only)	Long-term growth of capital and income, by investing in companies with favorable prospects but currently undervalued in the market.	1958	1175	500 Wire	50 Wire	Writ. with Sig. Guar.	*Dividends:* Auto.; S/A *Ret. Plans:* Keo., IRA Corp., 403(b) *Other:* Syst. With.; Auto. Pur.; Exch.-Tel.; Grp.-Acct.
VARIABLE STOCK FUND, INC. *(Monarch Investment Mgmt. Corp.)* 1250 State St. Springfield, MA 01133 413-785-5811	Capital appreciation with income secondary using primarily common stocks; to complement ownership of fixed obligations.	1957	6	50	25	Writ. with Sig. Guar.	*Dividends:* Auto.; A. *Ret. Plans:* Keo., IRA, Corp. *Other:* Auto. Pur.

RETIREMENT PLANNING WITH
NO-LOAD MUTUAL FUNDS

No-Load Mutual Funds are ideal investments for tax-sheltering your income now and for watching your retirement reservoir swell—tax-free—until you draw from it.

Individual Retirement Accounts (IRAs)

Everyone who works is now eligible for an Individual Retirement Account (IRA). There are three basic kinds of IRA plans:

1. You can set up an IRA for yourself and shelter up to $2,000 per year or 100% of your income, whichever is less. (Remember that although the maximum deduction is $2,000, you can invest less if you choose. Many no-load funds require only $250 or less to open an IRA account.)

2. You can set up a "spousal" IRA (which is really two separate accounts) and shelter up to an additional $250 per year, for a total deduction of $2,250, if your spouse is not a wage earner.

3. If both you and your spouse are wage earners, you can shelter up to $2,000 in separate accounts each year, for a total deduction on your joint return of $4,000.

Withdrawals from an IRA may begin at any time, but if you remove money before age 59½, you'll pay a 10% penalty. You *must,* however, start withdrawals no later than age 70½.

In addition to an IRA, you may also be eligible for one of the other retirement plans listed in this section. If you are, you can participate in that plan and still put away the full amount into your IRA.

Simplified Employee Pension (SEP)

A Simplified Employee Pension (SEP) is an IRA plan to which both an employee and employer may contribute. Under a SEP, the employee can take a deduction for contributions to the account made by the employer to the extent of $15,000 or 15% of the employee's compensation, whichever is less. In addition, the employee may deduct contributions to the SEP up to the lesser of $2,000 or 100% of compensation.

Generally, a SEP must include all employees who have reached age 25 and worked for the employer at least three of the past five years.

Self Employed Retirement Plans (Keogh Plans)

Keogh plans permit qualified self-employed individuals and their employees to annually invest up to $15,000 or 15% of their income, whichever is less, in a tax-sheltered retirement plan. If you are a business owner, doctor, lawyer, or free-lancer, for example, you may qualify for a Keogh. If you are employed by a firm but earn other income through consultant's or director's fees, that income may also qualify for a Keogh plan.

403(b)

This plan is only for employees of certain not-for-profit organizations, such as hospitals, churches, schools, and charitable foundations. Those eligible may defer taxes on part of their income—often as much as 20% or more, depending on certain conditions of employment. A 403(b) can be set up only through your employer with your authorization.

Municipal Deferred Compensation Plans (State and Local Government Workers)

After a local or state government has passed the necessary legislation, its employees are eligible to participate in a Defer-

200

red Compensation Plan to which they may contribute up to 25% of their salary, with a maximum of 17,500 per year. In addition to being excellent for retirement savings, these plans may be suitable for use before then, because money can be withdrawn from the plan without penalty whenever an employee leaves the job. So people who plan to start a business or raise a family, for example, may also benefit from a Deferred Compensation Plan.

Employees within 3 years of retirement, who did not fulfill the amount they were eligible to defer in past years, may defer larger amounts to make up the difference. In no case, though, can the deferral be more than $15,000 per year. The maximum deferral for employees who have both a Deferred Compensation Plan and a 403(b) is reduced by the amount contributed to the 403(b). Contributions to an IRA or Keogh Plan, however, do not affect a Deferred Compensation Plan.

401(k)

A 401(k) plan is available to employees of all types of businesses, and must be set up through your employer—it cannot be done individually.

Your company's 401(k) plan can be either a "cash election" profit-sharing or stock bonus plan, or a salary reduction plan such as a thrift plan. No federal income tax is paid on amounts that employees elect (by salary reduction agreement or otherwise) to contribute to the plan. In addition, all contributions to the 401(k) plan accumulate tax-free until withdrawal. In addition the 401(k) has other important advantages.

Be sure to get full explanations from your tax consultant and from the fund you've chosen before you invest in any of the retirement plans described here.

NO-LOAD SERVICES

No-load mutual funds offer you many advantages and convenient shareholder services not available through other types of investments. The following summary of services and advantages applies to most no-load funds. Please check the individual listings to see the particular services offered by each fund.

•**Diversification.** The fund reduces your risk by investing in many different securities. This degree of diversification is often difficult for individuals to achieve on their own.

•**Professional Management.** Your money is managed by professionals who work on a full-time basis to help achieve your investment objectives.

•**Convenience.** You own only one security (shares in the fund itself) rather than several and still enjoy the many services offered by no-load mutual funds.

•**No Sales Charge.** 100% of your money goes to work immediately for you.

•**Privacy.** You deal directly with the no-load mutual fund of your choice. You do not have to go through bank trust departments, securities salesmen or other middlemen. In other words, your investments are strictly your own business.

•**Knowing Where You Stand.** No-load mutual funds provide regular reports to you. Your share value is generally available by telephone every business day, and in many cases, is printed in *The Wall Street Journal* and the business sections of many daily newspapers.

•**Liquidity.** On every business day you can redeem your no-load mutual fund shares at their current net asset value.

•**Variety.** This Directory shows the wide variety of no-load mutual funds available to you—serving virtually every investment objective.

•**Investing Services.** You can open your account by mail, telephone or bank wire depending upon the fund involved. And frequently, you can add to your investment in the same manner or by pre-authorized payroll deduction of pre-authorized drafts against your checking account.

•**Exchange Services.** Many no-load mutual funds will allow you to exchange your shares from one fund within the fund group to another as your investment objectives change or as you change your viewpoint of current market conditions.

•**Dividend Option Services.** You may receive your dividends in cash or have them reinvested in additional fund shares, so you can enjoy the benefits of automatic compounding.

•**Withdrawal Services.** You may redeem your shares by letter, telephone, bank wire or check depending upon the fund involved. You may also choose a "Systematic Withdrawal Plan," so you can withdraw money on a regular monthly basis enabling you to supplement your current income.

•**Retirement Plan Services.** You can use shares of many no-load mutual funds to fund both individual and corporate tax-sheltered retirement plans. Many funds have established and maintain IRS-approved, tax-sheltered retirement plans at very low cost or you may use your own plan.

•**Personal Services.** The funds provide all record-keeping, dividend and interest collection and safekeeping of securities, so that you no longer have to bother with these tasks. Moreover, fund personnel are always available by telephone to answer any questions you may have about your account.

The following are some recent innovations of no-load mutual funds, being offered by an increasing number of funds:

•**ATMs.** Automatic Transaction Machines, allowing you to perform transactions 24 hours a day, 7 days a week, at locations convenient to you.

•**Home Computer Access.** You can buy and redeem shares,

check account balances, and examine the fund's portfolio using your home computer.

•**Walk-In Branches.** Conveniently located offices, with long hours, where you can perform transactions of all types, face-to-face with your fund's service representatives.

•**Sweep Accounts.** A relationship between your no-load mutual fund and your bank account in which money exceeding the minimum requirement for your bank account is automatically swept into your money market fund. You're able to take advantage of both accounts, and all the work is done for you.

•**Asset Management Accounts.** All your financial service needs can be taken care of in one account: from discount brokerage service and credit card account, to unlimited check writing and automatic bill paying.

•**Automatic Direct Deposit.** At your request, you can arrange for deposit of certain checks, such as a monthly social security check, directly into your no-load mutual fund account. Your money goes to work for you immediately, and you no longer need worry about depositing a check.

GLOSSARY OF MUTUAL FUND TERMS

Adviser: The organization which is employed by a mutual fund to give professional advice on its investments and management of its assets.

Aggressive Growth Fund: A mutual fund which seeks maximum capital appreciation through the use of investment techniques involving greater than ordinary risk, such as borrowing money in order to provide leverage, short selling, hedging, options and warrants.

Automatic Reinvestment: The option available to mutual fund shareholders whereby fund income dividends and capital gains distributions are automatically put back into the fund to buy new shares and thereby build up holdings; has the effect of compounding.

Balanced Fund: A mutual fund which has an investment policy of "balancing" its portfolio, generally by including bonds, preferred stocks and common stocks.

Bond Fund: A mutual fund whose portfolio consists primarily of bonds. The emphasis of such funds is normally on income rather than growth.

Capital Gains Distributions: Payments to mutual fund shareholders of gains realized on the sale of the fund's portfolio securities. These amounts usually are paid once a year.

Capital Growth: An increase in market value of a mutual fund's securities which is reflected in the net asset value of fund shares. This is a specific long-term objective of many mutual funds.

Common Stock Fund: A mutual fund whose portfolio consists primarily of common stocks. The emphasis of such funds is usually on growth.

Conversion Privilege: See Exchange Privilege.

Custodian: The organization (usually a bank) which holds in custody and safekeeping the securities and other assets of a mutual fund.

Deferred Compensation Plan: A tax-sheltered investment plan to which employees of state and local governments can defer up to 25% of their salary, with a maximum contribution of $7,500 per year.

Diversification: The mutual fund policy of spreading its investments among a number of different securities to reduce the risks inherent in investing.

Dollar-Cost Averaging: Investing equal amounts of money at regular intervals regardless of whether the stock market is moving upward or downward. This reduces average share costs to the investor who acquires more shares in periods of lower securities prices and fewer shares in periods of high prices.

Exchange Privilege: Enables a mutual fund shareholder to transfer his investment from one fund to another within the same fund group if his needs or objectives change, generally with a small transaction charge.

Growth Fund: A mutual fund whose primary investment objective is long-term growth of capital. It invests principally in common stocks with growth potential.

Growth-and-Income Fund: A mutual fund whose aim is to provide for a degree of both income and long-term growth.

Income Dividends: Payments to mutual fund shareholders of dividends, interest and short-term capital gains earned on the fund's portfolio securites after deduction of operating expenses.

Income Fund: A mutual fund whose primary investment objective is current income rather than growth of capital. It usually invests in stocks and bonds that normally pay higher dividends and interest.

Index Fund: A mutual fund whose investment objective is to match the composite investment performance of a large group of publicly-traded common stocks, generally those represented by the Standard & Poor's 500 Composite Stock Price Index.

Individual Retirement Account: A Retirement program for all employed individuals regardless of coverage under employer or government retirement plans. An individual may contribute and deduct from his or her income tax an amount up to the lesser of 100 percent of compensation or $2,000. An individual retirement account may be funded with mutual fund shares.

Investment Adviser: See Adviser.

Investment Company: A corporation, trust or partnership in which investors pool their money to obtain professional management and diversification of their investments. Mutual funds are the most popular type of investment company. Also see Mutual Fund.

Investment Objective: The goal—e.g., long-term capital growth, current income, etc.—which an investor or a mutual fund pursues.

Koegh Plan: A retirement program for self-employed individuals and their employees based on tax-savings provisions. A Keogh plan may be funded with mutual fund shares. (Also known as H.R. 10 Plans.)

Liquid Asset Fund: See Money Market Fund.

Management Fee: The amount paid by a mutual fund to the investment adviser for its services. The annual average fee industrywide varies between one-half of one percent to one percent of the fund's assets.

Money Market Fund: Also called a liquid asset or cash fund, it is a mutual fund whose primary objective is to make higher interest securities available to the average investor who wants immediate income and high investment safety. This is accomplished through the purchase of high-yield money market instruments such as U.S. government securities, bank certificates of deposit and commercial paper.

Municipal Bond Fund: A mutual fund which invests in a broad range of tax-exempt bonds issued by states, cities and other local governments. The interest obtained from these bonds is passed through to shareowners free of federal tax. The fund's objective is current tax-free income.

Mutual Fund: An open-end investment company that ordinarily stands ready to buy back (redeem) its shares at their current net asset value; the value of the shares depends on the market value of the fund's portfolio securities at the time. Also, most mutual funds continuously offer new shares to investors. Also see Investment Company.

Net Asset Value Per Share: The market worth of a mutual fund's total assets—securities, cash and any accrued earnings —after deduction of liabilities, divided by the number of shares outstanding.

No-Load Fund: A mutual fund selling its shares at net asset value without the addition of sales charges.

Option Income Fund: The investment objective of these funds is to seek a high current return by investing primarily in dividend-paying common stocks on which call options are traded on national securities exchanges. Current return generally consists of dividends, premiums from expired call options, net short-term gains from sales of portfolio securities or exercises of options or otherwise, and any profits from closing purchase transactions.

Payroll Deduction Plan: An arrangement whereby an employee may accumulate shares in a mutual fund by authorizing his employer to deduct and transfer to the fund a specified amount from his salary at stated times.

Prospectus: The official booklet which describes the mutual fund and offers its shares for sale. It contains information as required by the Securities and Exchange Commission on such subjects as the fund's investment objectives and policies, services, investment restrictions, officers and directors, how shares can be bought and redeemed, its charges and its financial statements.

Qualified Retirement Plan: A private retirement plan that meets the rules and regulations of the Internal Revenue Service. Contributions to a qualified retirement plan are in almost all cases tax-deductible and earnings on such contributions are always tax sheltered until withdrawal.

Redemption Price: The price at which a mutual fund's shares are redeemed (bought back) by the fund. The redemption price usually means the current net asset value per share.

Reinvestment Privilege: A service provided by most mutual funds for the automatic reinvestment of a shareholder's income dividends and capital gains distributions in additional shares.

Rollover IRA: A special tax shelter for lump-sum payments from qualified retirement plans. This payment can be rolled-over into an IRA without being immediately taxed, if done within 60 days of payment. The $2,000 annual IRA maximum does not apply to Rollover accounts.

Section 401(k) Plan: A tax-deferred retirement plan available to employees of all types of businesses. A company's 401(k) plan can be either a "cash election"; profit sharing or stock bonus plan, or a salary reduction plan. A 401(k) carries many advantages for both employer and employee that other retirement plans do not.

Section 403(b) Plan: Section 403(b) of the Internal Revenue Code permits employees of certain charitable organizations and public school systems to establish tax-sheltered retirement programs which may be funded with mutual fund shares.

Short-Term Municipal Bond Fund: These funds invest in municipal bonds with maturities not exceeding two years. They are also known as Tax-Exempt Money Market Funds.

Simplified Employee Pension: A program in which employers who have not established a qualified retirement plan may contribute up to $15,000 or 15% of compensation, whichever is less, to individual retirement accounts of their employees.

Specialty Fund: A mutual fund specializing in the securities of certain industries, special types of securities or in regional investments.

Spousal IRA: An IRA to which you can shelter up to an additional $250 per year, for a total deduction of $2,250, if your spouse is not a wage earner.

Transfer Agent: The organization which is employed by a mutual fund to prepare and maintain records relating to the accounts for its shareholders.

Unissued Shares: A modern share-recording system which eliminates the need for mutual fund share certificates but gives the fund shareowner a record of his holdings.

Withdrawal Plans: Many mutual funds offer withdrawal programs whereby shareholders receive payments from their investments at regular intervals. These payments typcially are drawn from the fund's dividends and capital gains distributions, if any, and from principal, to the extent necessary.

Voluntary Plan: A flexible accumulation plan in which there is no definite time period or total amount to be invested.

CHAPTER EIGHT

REAL ESTATE INVESTING

Primed for a new boom like the metals, real estate tends to move with, and often in front of, a rapid spiral in inflation. It has been traditionally the best hedge against high inflation.

Real estate investing has created more millionaires and multi-millionaires in America, than any other investment vehicle. That's the good news! The bad news is that in a period of disinflation (recession), real estate's upward mobility often comes to a screeching halt. The last one in (the buyer) prior to the market taking a downturn, or moving sideways for prolonged periods of time, can get hurt.

If you believe the American economy is headed for monetary stabilization and a very modest, controlled rate of inflation as was the case during the "Eisenhower years" of the 1950's, don't expect real estate to be the "go-go" investment that it was during most of the 1970's. If you honestly believe inflation will be held to a minimum, your only smart real estate holdings would be your own home and, perhaps, those one-in-a-thousand type exceptional buys that almost guarantee an investor a nice return.

If, on the other hand, you expect inflation to really heat up by the mid to late 1980's, as many leading financial advisors do, you can greatly profit from many select real estate opportunities.

The author feels that double-digit inflation will again be a reality, unless both military spending and welfare-state spending are curtailed. It's hard to have both guns and butter, and it's impossible to finance socialistic welfare and "entitlement" programs without inflating the nation's money supply.

211

In addition to believing that inflation, but not necessary run-away inflation, will return by 1986 or sooner, real estate investing today has another big factor in its favor.

By 1986 it is widely estimated that there will be nearly a two-million unit housing shortage in the U.S.A. This will obviously help create wealth for people owning good rental properties that are unburdened by rent control laws or unbearable negative cash-flow positions. There is no incentive for an investor to operate where rent control laws are in effect. Also, too high a negative on your property (the "negative" being the amount you have to add to the rents collected to make your mortgage payment) can turn what may appear to be a good buy into a cash-gobbling monster.

CHOOSING RENTAL PROPERTIES

In rental income property you can choose from a variety of buildings such as:

    Luxury apartment buildings
    Luxury condos
    Middle-class apartments
    Middle-class condos
    Inner-city housing
    Single family housing

Although there is an unmistakable trend pointing developers and investors in the direction of expensive, luxury condominiums and apartments, Hidden-Profit wealth-seekers should never overlook the huge potential profits in older, middle-class buildings.

Further, it is much easier to swing a small cash or NO CASH down arrangement for an older building. Inner-city buildings also are often available on excellent terms and at good prices, but you must proceed with caution. Be on guard against buying in a decaying neighborhood. All neighborhoods in cities across the United States are in transition. They are going in one direction or another. They are:

(A) Going up in value (renovation) or

(B) Going down in value (the process of decay)

While it is possible to spot a Hidden-Profit property in a decaying neighborhood - spruce things up a little and then bail out with a nice profit before the neighborhood really goes to the dogs - this kind of buy-in/sell-out-quick investing is more than a little risky. And, if you play with matches on a regular basis, eventually you'll burn your fingers! Invest smart! Put your time, talent, and money into neighborhoods that are showing signs of improvement. It's smarter, safer and generally more profitable.

Single-family houses are also a proven source of rental profits, both new and old houses. They deserve as much consideration as older buildings and usually can be picked up for much less. Maintenance costs are lower, tenant problems are held to a minimum and taxes, utilities and other considerations are usually quite favorable.

The major potential disadvantage is that with a single-family dwelling, if you're not fully rented, you're fully vacant.

HOW TO ACCUMULATE SINGLE-FAMILY UNITS

•Look for resales or repossessions in newspaper real estate advertising. Pay particular attention to new ads (be an early bird and watch for new listings) that advertise "for sale by owner" resales.

•Check out the cash needed—some of the sellers will accept small cash down payments.

•Try to find FHA and bank resales and repossessions—many have no legal fees—or old low-interest, assumable mortgages.

Once you locate one or more such houses, inspect them. Look for major defects, such as:

- Leaky roof
- Cracked foundations
- Flooded basements
- Broken beams
- Defective heating system
- Heating/air-conditioning problems

Don't worry about minor defects—you can get your tenants to:
- Paint the inside or outside of the house
- Fix minor leaks
- Trim the grass, hedges, etc.

Now here's a valuable tip you can keep in mind whenever you are working out a deal for a no-down payment house:

Buy the materials and supplies (lumber, paint, etc.) for your tenants and they'll do most of the minor repairs the house needs while helping paying off the house for you and giving you a profit in the form of income and tax savings!

For best results, *always* have an attorney on hand when you take over *any* real estate. In some repossessions the attorney may be furnished you free of charge by the:
- Bank
- Mortgage firm
- Government agency
- Seller

If you're short of cash and have to pay the attorney (which you *won't* have to do often), get the attorney to agree to allow you to pay him out of the rent you receive. This will delay your payment and save you from having to put up any cash. Also, *always* shop around for a competent attorney in real estate/taxation who charges reasonable rates.

Yes, you *can* make attractive profits from single-family houses. Just be sure to:
- Take over with little or *no* cash down
- Aim for *volume* income

•Get your tenants to do much of the work on the house
•Have an attorney at your side when contracts are prepared

YOU CAN BUILD A FORTUNE IN
MULTIPLE DWELLINGS

A *multiple dwelling* is any building having two, or more, families. Two-family units are also called duplexes; three-family, triplexes, etc. But when real estate people talk about multiple-family buildings they're usually talking about 20-, 30-, 50-, or even 300-unit buildings.

Let me—for a moment—show you the arithmetic of multiple units. Suppose that you have 1,000 rental units in 20 buildings. (This is easy because all you need is 20 buildings each having 50 apartments. This gives you a total of [20 buildings] x [50 apartments] = 1,000 apartments.)

Now if the *average* rent per apartment is $300 a month (which is *low* rent today), your monthly gross income will be ($300 per apartment) (1,000 apartments) = $300,000. In a year you'll take in ($300,000 per month x 12 months) = $3,600,000. And, friend, it's easy to take over buildings having 1,000, or more apartments—if you're willing to work hard at your real estate business! (One real estate wealth-builder I know of has 2,500 such apartments!)

The real beauty of the multiple-family building can be summed up for you thus:
•You can start with little or NO cash down
•Competition is modest, most folks buy single family dwellings only
•Pressures are few if you "hand pick" your renters
•Cash flow is substantial
•You have big tax advantages
•Inflation improves your investment and income
•You don't have to work 8-hour days

215

•You have an unlimited world for expansion—if you want to take on a large number of buildings, the first one is always the biggest obstacle
•You make money—big money—while having lots of time for other activities.

GETTING STARTED FROM SCRATCH

Cold hard cash is still important in building a fortune today. The dollar is greatly devalued, but is still in big demand. Many Hidden-Profit wealth-builders believe they are doomed to failure before they really start because of a lack of start-up cash. Let me tell you the truth - and please, let it sink in. Having lots of cash money is an enviable position to be in. However, great ideas, energy, desire and lots of "git and grit" are more important than start-up capital! The man (or woman) with bright ideas and determination is unstoppable.

My friend, Vince Bartolone, recently went from zero to one million dollar wealth in less than three years. Vince rose from the bottom of the heap to the top of the hill. With only a grade school education and only marginal reading and writing ability, Vince was forced to accept work as a fruit picker in his native Michigan.

Vince Bartolone really started from scratch. Some would even say "from poverty." He lacked almost every discernment, he even lacked indoor plumbing! Devoid of rich relatives, lacking educational skills, without important contacts, he was a most unlikely success candidate. However, there is one vital tool he clung to: Desire! He never gave up his desire for success or his faith in himself. Vince is living proof how potent desire and faith mixed with imagination and action can be. Today Vince Bartolone is one of America's leading financial consultants in the field of real estate, wealth-building, and personal motivation. His books, tapes, and seminars are in constant demand from coast to coast.

His popular book, "Your Million Dollar Success Blueprint" and "How To Be a Millionaire" Manual and cassette tape course are a fantastic tribute to what a man or woman can accomplish once the person uses "mind power" and "will power" in the pursuit of wealth goals. Vince went from zero to one million dollars in less than three years—and so can you.

"Your Million Dollar Success Blueprint" by Vince Bartolone is available for $9.95. Order from: Profit Ideas, 8361 Vickers, Suite 304, San Diego, CA 92111. Profit ideas will also send information on the "How to be a Millionaire" manuals and tapes.

He is a real-life, living testimonial to the power of positive thinking and positive action! Like Vince is so fond of saying, "This is your lucky day; opportunity confronts you now." This is the truth. Now, what will you do about it?

You can get good, solid, profitable rental multiple-dwelling buildings in large cities anywhere if you look for properties which are:
•In changing neighborhoods
•Abandoned by owners
•Being "carried" by the city or state
•Being "carried" by banks
•In foreclosure!

You can get a number of good buildings from such sources just by making a phone call or a short visit. Once you take over the building, with *no* cash down, you are on your way to your first million dollars in real estate.

"But why will they let me take over a good building with no cash down?" you ask. "Good question," I reply.

Learn this fact of real estate life here and now.

No bank, mortgage lender, city or state, wants to be in the business of operating a building if their major purpose in life is something else—as it usually is. A fantastic deal to you may be a burden off their backs.

So when a bank, mortgage lender, city, or state is forced to "take-over" a building because the owner can't pay for it, the first step the organization takes is to look for someone to take the building off their hands. That someone could be *you!*

To make a fortune in real estate starting from scratch, take these tried and proven steps:

1. Locate one or more suitable buildings by using your local large-city newspaper, or some of the smaller weekly papers in your area.

2. Inspect the building

3. Offer to take over the building if it appears to be sound and rentable

4. Once you have possession of the building take steps to find any additional tenants needed

5. Collect a suitable rent security—one to three months' rent from each tenant if the former owners had no rent security

6. Take over the rent security from the present tenant in the building if the security is held by the seller

7. Arrange for all future rents to be paid to you by mail

8. Have any needed repairs made to the building

9. Scout around for the next building and repeat the winning process.

COLLECT CASH FROM THIN AIR

Frank Eller had a common problem—no cash. He tried all sorts of lenders but his poor credit history prevented him from getting the loan he needed. Reading his local large-city newspaper, he saw several ads for no-cash down buildings. Since one of the buildings was in his neighborhood, Frank de-

218

cided to check it out. To his amazement this sturdy, if old, building:
•Was 100% rented
•Contained 100 apartments
•Had $45,000 in rent security on deposit
•Was available for *no cash*
•Could be had by just signing a few papers
•Did *not* require a credit check

After checking out the building, Frank went home almost reeling with joy. Here was a gold-mine of cash (the rent security account would put $45,000 into *his* bank in his security-account name—more money than he ever had in his life before). Yet he felt full of fear. questions ran through his mind:
•What if something went wrong with the building?
•Suppose all the tenants moved out?
•Would the taxes go up?
•Could the tenants stop paying rent?

1. With 100 apartments at an average rental of $300 per month, the monthly income would be $30,000, the annual income $360,000.

2. The $45,000 rent security could—in some states—be used as a compensating balance for a loan of five times that amount, or $225,000, provided Frank paid his tenants interest on their rent security (a legal requirement in some states). And—if he was lucky—Frank might be able to borrow as much as ten times $45,000 from a "hungry" bank!

3. He could get a $360,000-per-year income and $45,000 cash without a credit investigation.

The cold, hard facts about multiple-unit rental property are:

1. Every building has something "wrong" with it. But in older buildings the "wrongness" was usually corrected long ago. So really very, very little can go wrong with such a build-

ing, unless it is "ancient" and in a state of decay!

2. Few buildings are ever vacated 100% by their tenants if the buildings are well kept, warmly heated, and repaired when necessary. It is usually easy to maintain the 80% occupancy which is needed to break even (that is, pay all expenses in such a building).

3. Real estate taxes almost always go up. To take care of this, you just put a clause in each lease, allowing you to raise rents when the taxes go up a certain amount. This is another good reason why you should not invest in fixed "rent control" areas.

USE OPM TO TAKE OVER PROPERTY

You may not like the kinds of buildings you can get on zero cash. Or there may not be any such buildings available in your area. So, if you still want to go into rental property, you'll have to put up some cash to take over one or more buildings. And if you don't have this cash you'll have to use OPM—Other People's Money.

In rental real estate OPM can take several forms, such as:

1. A purchase-money (PM) mortgage
2. A personal loan for the down payment
3. A business loan for the down payment
4. Mortgaging out with 100%, or better, financing—also called a windfall.

Let's take a look at each form of OPM to see how you can use it to build your real estate empire.

GET THE SELLER TO HELP YOU BUY

Many sellers of real estate are anxious to sell their property. Why? For hundreds of reasons, including:

•They don't know how to handle their tenants.
•They think real estate holdings "hold them down."
•They want to move.
•They want to cash out and invest elsewhere.

RENOVATION - HOW TO INCREASE THE VALUE OF A HIDDEN PROFIT PROPERTY (HPP)

The secret to success in buying and selling used housing is renovation at as reasonable a price as possible.

You should know the difference between a "run-down" appearance (often offering the investor the opportunity to buy substantially below current market value) and a structurally unsound property. One needs only cosmetic changes to make it look great, the other may be beyond cost effective repair.

If the property only needs some cleaning, fixing, and painting, you may have a great HPP and the opportunity to make a substantial profit.

There are three good reasons why a property should be renovated:

Good appearance of property is important for three vital reasons:

1. Value is increased for resale
2. Renters are easier to attract
3. Loan value is substantially increased.

Here are the basics of making a property look good again:

Do away with immediate eyesores! Haul away the trash!

Mow the lawn and plant new grass seed if called for. A beautiful green lawn surrounding any property is a tremendous asset.

Clean all units and make repairs as needed.

Apply a new coat of paint wherever it is needed.

Drapes, windowshades, carpets and other "dressings," even if purchased used or at discount houses, can greatly improve the overall look.

Improvements do cost some money and often a fair amount of labor is required. However, if you search for bargains and do some or all of the work yourself, expenses can be held to a required minimum. Never underestimate the value of "cosmetic changes."

Early in 1981, Ted Larsen of San Diego bought a rundown-looking, 4-unit apartment complex near downtown San Diego. Rents were low, but the previous owner still had trouble keeping the rundown building full of tenants. Ted had a plan that proved to be very profitable. He bought the building at $130,000 (substantially below market value) and with only $13,000 as a down payment. By doing most of the work himself, he was able to completely renovate, including fresh paint inside and out, for another $4,500. Since this building was located in a "C" (commercial) zone, Ted knew he had a true Hidden Profit Wealth-Builder on his hands. By switching his building from a low-rent residential to high-rent commercial building, Ted was able to stock his four units with an accountant, an attorney, an artist and an ad agency. Where once residential rents were in the $175 to $225 range, Ted now gets three times that much ($600 to $750 each) from his new commercial clients. A sparkling example of the money-making power of combining improvements and renovating to a Hidden Profit property and then switching it over to its highest potential.

PAINT IT RIGHT

A new coat of paint adds far more value than its cost to the inside or outside of any property. Light colors are best, highlighted by darker colors for the trim. Avoid both dark colors for the general theme or "unusual" combinations of colors. Remember: Personal preferences aside, use color combinations acceptable to the masses. Light colors have a warm, bright, comfortable feeling appreciated by most people.

LIGHT UP

On most properties, improved lighting is a must! Look for sales on lighting fixtures and bulbs. You will always impress potential new tenants by placing a large pair of fixtures at the doorstep.

STRUCTURAL RENOVATIONS

The cracked slab (foundation) is something to be wary of. Many lenders, including V.A. and F.H.A., refuse to lend on properties with a cracked slab. Worse yet, it's often hard to get a fair price for such a property when you wish to sell.

If you notice a crack on the outside wall of the stucco, it's time to play Sherlock Holmes and check the foundation for cracks, especially if the property is on expansive soil (a soil test on any property is always recommended).

New stucco on an older home or building can be a camouflage. To check for cracked slab floors when carpeting is layed throughout, use "upholstery pins." These pins, 1/16" in diameter and 4" long, can be stuck into the carpet in any area that appears to be uneven. Probing with the pin should locate any possible problem.

BATHROOM FIXTURES

Most people, especially the ladies, are turned off by old-fashioned, out-dated bathroom fixtures. Check the salvage yards of any big city and you will be amazed at the great bargains available. A complete pullman is often available for less than $50, a shower door for $25, etc. Salvage yards can allow you to buy excellent bathroom fixtures, also lighting and other renovation items at 10¢ on the dollar! Worth checking out!

OTHER IMPROVEMENTS

•Mirrors are an excellent way to make rooms look twice their actual size.

•Paneling a wall can often be a major "cosmetic" improvement.

•Garage additions. Today more Americans own more cars than ever. It is not unusual for a family of four to own two automobiles plus a camper. Enlarging the size of the garage can add value to any property and often be the single most important factor to swing a sale.

•Adding a patio is another excellent way to command a much higher price. It is not uncommon to get back four or five times the cost of putting in a patio at the time of resale.

•Swimming pools. Contrary to popular belief, adding a swimming pool to a property will seldom result in obtaining more money at the time of resale. At best, you can expect to recoup your cost, and at the worst, you may turn off several potential buyers (senior citizens, families with very young children, etc. who do not want a pool). The only exception in which a pool adds value to a property seems to be a multiple-unit complex (8 or more units), in which case a pool is usually desirable.

A GOOD "HANDYMAN" IS GOOD TO HAVE

Professional union labor commands top pay. A 1983 national government statistic puts the average hourly wage of skilled laborers (a composite of electricians, plumbers, masonry workers, carpenters, etc.) at $24 per hour. That can be too costly for a beginning wealth-builder. The solution: Find a competent handyman to assist you in your renovating projects.

Look in your local newspaper's "Situations Wanted" classified section. Moonlighting labor often advertises there. Then too, you can place a "help wanted" ad. A good handyman is not always real easy to find, but if you persist, you'll locate a good one, and a good handyman will be a tremendous asset. For starters, most handymen, even the top producers, usually charge only about one-half the going rate for the service involved.

People are greatly influenced by outward appearances. Fortunately, often just a little time and a little money can turn a "rundown property" into a brilliant diamond. Plants, a green lawn, soap, water, wallpaper, paneling, paint, etc. can add value far beyond their actual cost. Dirt and neglect can actually be the number one alert signal that a Hidden Profit Wealth-Builder has been found. Clean it up and renovate it with loving care and the profits you reap can be spectacular!

MULTIPLE-UNIT INVESTING

Although real estate offers investments in many areas, the primary action will most likely be in multi-unit investing. A large housing shortage gives the real estate speculator (remember: no matter how good the deal looks, there still is - and always will be - a degree of risk involved) a good chance to make money.

There are four things an investor needs to know about any investment opportunity:

1. What are the main risks?

2. What will be the return on investment (ROR)?

3. What are the leverage factors?

4. is this investment expected to stay in front of future anticipated inflation?

MORE APARTMENTS NEEDED

Providing housing is a very basic service. It ranks next to food as the major consideration of every human's life. Real estate investing in general, and apartment investing in particular, has a long and impressive, safe, sound, and overall profitable track record for creating wealth.

Certain areas of the nation, particularly the "sun belt" states of the West and Southwest, are undergoing major increases in population. California cities such as San Diego, San Jose, and Sacramento, are booming, as is Phoenix and Tucson, Arizona, Las Vegas and Reno, Nevada, and several cities in Texas and New Mexico.

THE LEVERAGE FACTOR

In real estate there is a big advantage which may be gained in the use of borrowed money. It also is called leverage. Banks and savings and loan associations make use of this principle when they loan the money in your savings account to someone else at a higher rate of interest. The differential between these two interest rates represents the leverage factor or the gross profit. Apartments on the present market, in some locations, can be bought for from 15 percent to 20 percent down. The balance of the purchase price is in the form of a loan extended by a lending institution, the former owner, or by the assumption of loans used in previous financing. The leverage factor is possible and present to the extent of these loans. It is a powerful force if properly used, and the opportunities it presents should not be overlooked.

Leverage, of course, is also present with many other types of investments, but usually with different effects. The leverage factor is working when we buy stock on margin, or when we buy a commodities contract, or when we buy real estate on option, but generally these investments are of a highly volatile type and your entire investment can be wiped out as easily as it can make a profit for you. This is not true of apartments.

THE HEDGE AGAINST INFLATION

Any investment that does not offer a "hedge" against inflation is of dubious value. Since we all are losing purchasing power due to inflation, it is wise to put your money in inflation-proof investments. Apartment investing has a great record as a leading hedge against inflation. An apartment investment has a built-in advantage in that rent increases almost always outpace the regular inflation rate - one of the few investments inflation does not adversely effect.

TAX SHELTERS

Depreciation of apartment buildings offers the real estate investor a great tax shelter. A good accountant with a real estate background can point out the tax advantages of every potential apartment investment and should be consulted prior to purchase. As we go to press with this Guide, new liberalized real estate tax laws have been introduced by the Reagan administration.

The most prominent and beneficial benefit for real estate entrepreneurs is the depreciable life on all real property. The reduction to 15-year depreciation has been very advantageous to the investor. Consult a competent real estate accountant

227

and/or attorney for advice on all tax laws in effect at the time you plan to purchase. Tax laws change frequently.

KNOW THY VALUE

Knowing the present and future value of any building is the key to success in apartment real estate. Perhaps the best method to determine value is to evaluate the three essential elements:

1. the land
2. the building
3. the improvements (standard extras)

The standard extras are those things which are normally, but not necessarily, furnished by the apartment owner. These include stove, refrigerator, curtain rods and fixtures, curtains and drapes, capeting, etc. Such things as water heaters, furnaces, air conditioning units, kitchen cabinets and sinks are considered part of the building itself. So with this to start with we are ready to set up a standard against which we can measure any apartment building. The exact standard we use is not the important thing. The important thing is that we use the standard consistently. If we were going to measure length, for example, we could pick any arbitrary length for our standard and it would serve our purpose as long as we did not deviate from that standard. So it makes no difference that two appraisers of income property may not use the same standards in all details. The important thing is that each appraiser uses his own standard, whatever it may be, in every case. He then has a comparable against which he can measure every apartment building, and he has something to work with when he needs to compare one building against another.

IMPORTANT LOCATION INFORMATION

Your preliminary analysis of any possible apartment complex can usually be conducted by phone with the seller or his broker. Once we have our prelminiary data from the broker or the owner, we can make a decision based on the early data of whether to gather more information or drop out of the particular deal.

If we decide to gather more information on the property, the next major consideration ought to be location.

The first thing that should concern us is the immediate neighborhood in which the building is located. The obtainable rent for any apartment in a modest or poor neighborhood will not rent for much more than others that are near it. Tenants like to live in nice neighborhoods. They will pay $400 a month to live in a nice building in a choice neighborhood, but they will not pay $400 to live in the slums no matter how nice the apartment might be.

Professional real estate appraisers tell us that any neighborhood passes through three distinct periods: a period of growth (integration), followed by a static period (equilibrium), followed by a period of decline or decay (disintegration). Neighborhood has an important influence on apartment value and it must not be overlooked.

Class I
Neighborhood

Integration—The integration period is a period of growth and development. The buildings are new, rents are prime; the tenants rank high on the economic scale. The expense ratio is low.

Class II
Neighborhood

Equilibrium—A neighborhood in equilibrium has passed the peak of its development. It has begun to feel the pinch of competition from new developments. The expense ratio is increasing.

Class III Neighborhood	Disintegration—A disintegrating neighborhood is one in which decline and decay have definitely set in. Tenants are at the lowest end of the economic scale. Rents are low. The expense ratio is high.

Once we have decided the type of neighborhood in which our building is located we should consider whether it conforms to that neighborhood and give it a plus or minus rating for any nonconformity. A new building in a declining neighborhood does not conform. Its newness is a plus factor. Similarly, an older building which just happens to be in the path of a new development does not conform. Its age would be a minus factor. The value of any building will always be affected to some degree by the type, value and age of the buildings which surround it.

If you are as familiar with your city as you should be before you attempt to buy an apartment building, the address alone should tip you off about the neighborhood it is located in. Never, but never, underestimate the importance of neighborhood. Location is vital in real estate investing.

NEIGHBORHOOD AND EXPENSE RATIO

In general, in considering a Class I building, we are being realistic if we estimate that the expenses of operation will range from 35 percent to 45 percent of the effective gross income. For a Class II building this will range from 46 percent to 56 percent, and for a Class III building from 57 percent to 67 percent. Since net income is the only real test of value, it is easy to see why we must be careful in estimating value from a

230

gross income figure alone.

Some apartment buyers use a formula based upon their belief that annual gross income should be at least 15 percent of total value. If we can assume a 35 percent expense ratio it is a good figure to use. To find the value then (comparative value, not market value), of the building using gross income, our formula would be as follows:

$$\frac{\text{Annual Gross Income}}{15}$$

If the gross income from the building was $30,000, our estimated value would be as follows:

$$\frac{\$30,000}{15} \times 100 = \$200,000$$

or to simplify the formula—

$$\frac{\$30,000}{.15} = \$200,000$$

However, the 15 percent figure would be valid only for a building with an expense ratio which did not exceed 35 percent. For a building in a Class II neighborhood, with an expected expense ratio of 50 percent, you would need to use .20 as a denominator in the formula, and for a Class III building, with an expected 67 percent expense ratio, 30 would be a more realistic figure to use. With this as a guide we can now compare the estimated values of three properties having the same gross income but which are located in different neighborhoods.

231

	Ratio			Expense
Class I				
Neighborhood	35%	$\dfrac{\$30,000}{.15}$	=	$200,000
Class II				
Neighborhood	50%	$\dfrac{\$30,000}{.20}$	=	$150,000
Class III				
Neighborhood	67%	$\dfrac{\$30,000}{.30}$	=	$100,000

The wide difference in the relative value of these three apartment buildings in different areas is due to many factors. Tenants in a Class III neighborhood are generally at the lower end of the economic scale, and it is one of the business facts of life that they have less respect for the property of other people. Also, the buildings are older, as is the neighborhood itself, and repair and maintenance costs are rising rapidly. Water heaters, heating and cooling plants, plumbing and roofs are some of the things likely to give trouble, and of course, the number of years that the property will produce income has been greatly reduced.

We have conveniently divided neighborhoods into three classifications, but it is intended only as a guide. There are always factors other than neighborhood, and there will be shadings between the various classifications, but if we can rate our building as to its probable expense ration (35 percent to 67 percent) we will have gone a long way toward determining its probable value as compared with other buildings. Nearly always the owner will furnish figures which he designates as expenses of operation but they are seldom reliable figures to use and it is imperative that we have some method of checking the figures he has given us.

MANY METHODS FOR DETERMINING VALUE

There are many methods for determining value widely used by real estate people and apartment buyers. some use an annual gross income multiplier, such as 6.6. Others us a monthly gross income multiplier of 80, but if these methods are compared with the method explained earlier in this chapter you will find that they yield approximately the same results.

Original illustration $\dfrac{\$30,000}{.15}$ = $200,000
(35% exp. ratio)

Using annual gross $30,000   x   6.6   = $198,000
multiplier

Using monthly gross $\dfrac{\$30,000}{12}$ x   80   = $200,000
multiplier

These are the more commonly used methods, but they are not the only ones. I know of one real estate firm that uses a very elaborate table which supposedly takes into consideration such factors as the number of units, the rent scale and whether they are furnished or unfurnished. Banks and savings and loan associations sometimes use a system based upon per unit rent scale alone, though usually there is some assumption as to the minimum number of units, the expense ratio, vacancy factor, etc. In each case the attempt is to make something simple out of a problem which is really not simple at all, as we shall see in later chapters.

233

New tax law coming from the Reagan administration is greatly benefitting real estate entrepreneurs. Be certain to obtain advice from a real estate attorney or accountant prior to investment time.

My feeling is that a better tax break is the positive action being given to offset the planned negative impact of allowing financial institutions to refuse to accept assumable loans. While we salute favorable new tax rulings, we think everyone concerned with real estate (and that's most Americans!) should strongly oppose giving up assumable loan rights. Assumable loans are very vital to the real estate industry. Eliminating assumable loans will be as harmful to the entire industry as "rent control" is to apartment owners.

USING OPTION-TO-PURCHASE TACTIC FOR APARTMENT INVESTING

The investor with very little or no money to invest in apartments or other real estate has a powerful tool in the option approach. The use of an option is not the only way for such a person to reach for profits, but it is a highly recommended approach. A key factor is that you can gain control of an apartment complex for a limited period of time with very little money committed and with no obligations or further liability if the option is not exercised.

There are several possible reasons for wanting to gain control. You may wish to gain control to allow needed time to structure the overall project and to line up the financing. Without having control of the property, you might find, after a considerable amount of work, that it was sold to another just before you arranged the necessary financing to purchase it.

Another important reason for using the option aproach is to allow you to make a more thorough investigation. For example, the seller may have incorrectly stated that his property can be rezoned easily, say, to allow the construction of additional apartment units on the same site and that there is no filled ground on the property. Whether he has deliberately or innocently misrepresented, it is important you, as an investor, find it out before completing the purchase. You might be able to recoup your money and the money you persuaded others to invest after closing a deal, but lawsuits are expensive and non-productive. An entrepreneur must maintain his reputation for ferreting out profitable deals. He must keep his attention on productive efforts only. Your time, money and reputation are all important; avoid non-productive encounters.

You should, of course, consider all possible uses of available real estate. Always consider the highest and best use of a property and analyze it with respect to profits for yourself. In many cases, you will need time to determine that there is a market for your planned use of the property. An option, tying up the property for a specified time period, will give you time to evaluate it thoroughly. And, of course, an option ensures that the property will be available to you if it stands up under your investigation. The risk you take is that the amount you pay for the option may be forfeited if you decide not to exercise it and not to consummate the purchase. In most cases, the money paid for the option is non-refundable.

HOW TO USE OPTIONS

Options-to-purchase real property are usually short term agreements between a potential buyer and a seller and always must be regulated by a specific time interval. The option should specify the total purchase price, the terms of payment and all other buying/selling consideration. It also must specify the amount of money (consideration) paid for the option itself. If no consideration is mentioned, the option is not valid. Any consideration, even only one dollar, can make the option valid. Also, the option must mention if the consideration paid is to apply toward the total purchase price if the option is exercised. If the option is not exercised within the time period given, the consideration becomes the rightful property of the party that granted the option, and that party is free to offer for sale or sell to anyone.

Following is the general format used in drawing up an option-to-purchase:

OPTION TO PURCHASE A PROPERTY

AGREEMENT made this _____ **day of** _____,
19____, between ____*(name)*____, ____*(address)*____,
hereinafter described as Seller and ____*(name)*____,
____*(address)*____, hereinafter described as Buyer.

WITNESSETH,

1) that for and in consideration of the sum of one dollar ($1.00) in hand paid and other valuable considerations, the receipt and sufficiency of which are hereby acknowledged by Seller, Seller offers and agrees to sell and convey to Buyer, and hereby grants to Buyer the exclusive and irrevocable option, right and privilege of purchasing, under the conditions hereinafter provided, the following land with the buildings and improvements there on, located in the _____*(city)*_____ of _____ County, State of _____, described as:
_____*(legal description)*_____
for the sum of _____ dollars ($_____); the amount being in addition to the one dollar ($1.00) above mentioned.

2) Notice of election to purchase hereunder shall be given by Buyer in writing by delivering said written notice in person or by registered mail to Seller on or before ____(time)____, _____, 19_____.

The key points to be covered in an option agreement were discussed previously in this part. Knowing when to use the option approach is also important. Fundamentally, an option should be used in those instances when you need additional time and when you wish to ensure that the property is yours if you choose to purchase it within the specified time limit. There should be many times when the option approach can be used to increase your profits in real estate.

One entrepreneur might use an option to gain time to secure advantageous financing with high leverage for himself, perhaps by forming a syndicate. Another may wish to carry out a more thorough investigation and analysis. You may have heard rumors of possible confiscation of the property by government for a school, highway right-of-way, or other use. If you plan to put the property to its highest and best use, you may need to check zoning, the possibility of a change in zoning, and other government regulations. The option approach gives time, if needed, to double check the market's future for your intended investment.

SEVEN KEYS TO SUCCESSFUL APARTMENT BUILDING INVESTING—USING OPTIONS

1. The best bets in apartment investments are those which are being mismanaged in one way or another. For instance, a manager may have failed to increase rents (and hence, return on investment) at a rate at least equaling inflation rates. Another may have allowed some "junking" by tenants, e.g., automobiles being repaired in exposed parking areas or junk

furniture on exposed balconies. The number of ways of mis-management is large. Fortune builders look for such apart-ments, buy them, correct management's mistakes, and make big profits.

2. Leverage is the insider's key to building a fortune in apartment investing. Using leverage enables you to make profits with other people's money. It allows you to multiply the return on investment on your own money.

3. An ambitious entrepreneur will even leverage apartment financing to infinity—to the point where he has no money of his own invested.

4. The key to faster and more satisfactory progress to wealth through apartment investing is to select only those in-vestments and modes of financing which meet your own goals and desires.

5. Compared with other types of real estate investments, apartment buildings are comparatively easier to finance and to get high leverage from. More money is available from a larger number of sources for financing apartment buildings.

6. An option to purchase an apartment building allows op-timization of an investment on the "upside." It provides time to consider all possible ways to structure the project and time to optimize the details of financing for your own benefit.

7. An option-to-purchase allows protection on the "down-side." It provides for time to evaluate the neighborhood's fu-ture, the rent being charged, and to find any other present or future negative factors which would adversely affect your in-vestment.

REMEMBER THESE POINTS

•The option approach allows you to gain temporary control of property; use it to your advantage.
•Use time gained to check market factors of optioned proper-ty.

•Always consider the possibility of obtaining an option if it is needed for any reason.

•An option allows time to structure a project.

•Option time can be used to ensure that desired financing is available.

•Option time can be used to check zoning and other government regulations.

•An option itself is a salable item.

•Increase your leverage in a project by using an option.

•Option approach can keep your position more flexible until it is exercised.

•Have an attorney, one with real estate experience, prepare the option document to assure compliance with law and yield non-ambiguous agreements.

•Laws vary from state to state and laws change with time.

•You, as an entrepreneur, must make the business decisions; you live with the consequences.

•Marginal areas tend to turn into blighted areas.

•Carefully evaluate the future quality of an area; avoid creeping blight.

NOTE: Much of the information in this chapter on real estate was taken from the Profit Ideas Book, ''Real Estate Wealth-building Opportunities'' by Russ Von Hoelscher (© 1984 by Profit Ideas).

CHAPTER NINE

HARD ASSETS

It's a very good idea to put something besides paper into your investment portfolio. Gold, silver, diamonds, precious and semi-precious stones, collectible coins, and similar tangible items are called hard assets. In times of high inflation, hard assets or "hard money" can offer real protection against the onslaught of cheap paper money.

GOLD

Gold should be considered as a store, not as a medium for speculation. This does not mean there isn't a time to buy and a time to sell, there definitely is! I am saying that gold is not an ideal commodity for constant buy-sell, in-and-out spot plays. Gold is symbolic with wealth but it actually is more than that. It is a means to represent and preserve wealth that has already been obtained.

The world is on a gold standard. It has been on the gold standard. As long as human beings populate this planet, it will probably always be on a gold standard, Sometimes governments attempt to abandon this standard. You no doubt have read about and noticed the rise and fall of many governments world wide. At the same time, people from all lands adhere to the gold standard. The citizens of the world recognize gold's intrinsic value.

Governments are unable to enforce monetary edicts in the world market place. They usually cannot even make their own people blindly follow their dictates.

In 1933, the depression was showing signs of loosening its grip on the United States, and the economy was ready to make a sharp rebound. Unfortunately, this was the time President Roosevelt decided to make yet another drastic economical move...the dollar was to be devalued. Throughout the Great Depression of 1929-1933, the gold backing of the dollar was 20 percent. Next Roosevelt would sharply devaluate the dollar by raising the price of gold.

The government guaranteed that the price of gold would remain at $35 per ounce. From 1933 to 1949 gold flowed into the American Treasury from all parts of the world. During this period $35 per ounce was considered high and other nation's were eager to trade their gold for our devalued dollars.

After 1949, the price was considered too low and a reverse trend took place. Our Treasury sold far more gold than it bought. Foreign nations now wanted our gold and not our dollars. Uncle Sam continued to send gold to anyone who wanted it (except U.S. citizens) at the $35 per ounce rate.

From 1934 to 1950 there was no logical reason to use gold as a hedge against inflation. The American dollar was very strong. From 1950 till this present day, the opposite is fact. This seems only natural to hard money advocates. They are fond of stating: **"Sooner or later gold, and only gold, is the standard!"**

Since 1975, it has been legal for Americans to own gold. Tens of thousands, including government officials and the most wealthy, always maintained gold positions. Since 1975 just plain "folks" are allowed to own gold and countless numbers of them are doing just that.

During the 1970's a growing flock of hard money advocates led by Harry Browne, Jim Dines, Howard Ruff, Douglas Casey, and others used their books and/or newsletters to preach the hard money doctrine. The Results - more public awareness concerning gold and other hard assets.

The double-digit inflation synonymous with the President Jimmy Carter white house years (1976-1980) sent most hard assets soaring! Inflation greatly reduces "paper money" (savings, currency, notes, etc.) and increases the value of tangible assets - land with or without improvements, metals, coins, diamonds, and gems. Even everyday commodities such as food, clothing, shoes, toothpaste, and toilet paper rapidly gain in value as the dollar is devaluated.

I believe prudent investors should acquaint themselves with the works of Ruff, Browne, Casey, and other responsible crisis investing types. On the other hand, I repudiate any advice that would have you heading for the hills, armed to the teeth, and ready to do battle with anyone who might come near your water, food, gold, or guns.

A wise person wants to be informed of all possibilities and positions, while maintaining a rational outlook. This great country of ours has survived a horrible economic depression before, not to mention two World Wars and a million and one other difficulties. It remains intact, and we can believe it will remain intact for a long time to come. God willing. Nevertheless, gold and other hard assets make a great hedge in the war against inflation.

I expect gold to be a solid investment for the 80's. It has a proven track record of many centuries and the political, social, and economic condition of the 1980's will keep it strong. We expect gold to continue to rise, with occasional corrections. $1,000 per ounce or even much higher, would not surprise me. Before 1990 rolls around, gold could easily be at $1,800 per ounce or higher.

IS GOLD FOR YOU?

Soon after gold reached its historic high-level mark at the beginning of 1980, its market value fell by $300 an ounce. As this is being written (fall 1983), gold has begun to rebound and is currently near $450 per ounce. While some prognosticators are predicting a steady upswing in gold prices, we take a somewhat different view. We believe gold will continue to move upward, but with several "corrections" enroute. Obviously, if the Fed is able to strengthen the U.S. dollar substantially, gold will climb modestly. If the dollar continues to lose purchasing power and national and/or world events become bleak, gold will rise sharply. Gold is both an anti-inflation and "crisis" metal.

Gold deserves your full investment consideration; however, realize that it is of a highly speculative nature, and be ready to experience rapid rises and declines in value. Over the long pull, I'm bullish on gold, just as I am on the entire American economy. Your strategy for investing in gold should not depend on the imminent collapse of society as we know it, God forbid, but rather on the overall value of gold and the high interest in it from people all over the globe.

GOLD COINS

There are two basic types of gold coins: (1) bullion coins; (2) collector's coins.

Bullion coins are valuable for their gold content. These coins are traded by investors through recognized dealers and are often issued by nations of the world as legal tender.

Bullion coins are the simplest method for gold investors to buy the precious yellow stuff. The most popular gold bullion coin today is the South African Krugerrand, a gold coin whose gold bullion content is one troy ounce. Since this coin is exactly one troy ounce of gold, and because it is readily available throughout the world, it has become the favorite of gold investors everywhere.

Before you can possibly make an intelligent buy in gold

coins, you have to know the current price of gold. in this country, that usually means the current price on the London market, though there are also gold markets in Paris, New York, Zurich, and other places. Most reputable coin dealers will post the current price in their shops, which is one reason why it pays to buy only from a major, widely recognized trader. Once you know what gold is selling for at the moment, you know the worth of the gold in the coin. But besides the price of the gold, there is a dealer's premium to be paid on each coin you buy. Quite simply, this is how coin dealers make their money. The price for which they buy coins is always slightly lower than the price for which they sell. Furthermore, the premium may differ from customer to customer and from moment to moment. If you buy several coins a day, a dealer who knows you will probably give you a discount because of the volume of business you generate. Or the size of the premium may be determined by what's happening to the gold market. If the dealer thinks the price of your coins is going down, he stands to take a loss, and may charge you more of a selling fee. If the market is bullish, the dealer's premium may be a bit less.

What all this means is that if you buy a Krugerrand for say $600, your actual price to the dealer will be about $620. But if you want to sell the same coin back to the same dealer the next day, and the price of gold is still $600 an ounce, you won't be able to get $620 from the dealer. The price at which the dealer will be willing to buy back your Krugerrand will be somewhat between $590 and $595. Obviously, what you want to do is hang onto your coin until the price of gold has risen at least enough to cover the premium differential and make you some profit. How long this will be is anyone's guess, but the decision to invest in gold coins (or any gold) implies that you must think the long-run direction of the gold market is up.

RECOMMENDED COINS

As mentioned previously, the Krugerrands are the most popular bullion coins; they comprise the largest market. The coin was first struck in South Africa in 1967. Since 1969, it has been widely circulated throughout the world. Since it is exactly one troy ounce, the price of each one of the coins and the daily gold market price are very close. This makes it quite simple for speculators to add to or subtract from the value of their holdings. The Krugerrand now accounts for nearly 70% of the sales in bullion coins, worldwide.

In addition to the South African Krugerrand, the following coins are of proven merit:

•*The Austrian Crown:* Along with the Hungarian Crown, ranks a distant second to the Krugerrand in worldwide popularity. It is the 100 Corona coin that commands most of the market, though Austria and Hungary make gold coins of other denominations. These coins contain .9802 ounces of fine gold, making them slightly less valuable as bullion than Krugerrands. Unlike the Krugerrand, however, the Austrian/ Hungarian coins are not legal tender. They are copies of coins issued by the Austro/Hungarian Empire, which hasn't even existed as a nation since the end of the First World War.

100 Coronas are made by both Austria, at the official government mint in Vienna, and by Hungary, at the mint in Budapest. They are usually thought of as the same coin and traded at the same price. Like the Krugerrand, the Austro/Hungarian coin has a relatively low dealer premium, usually in the range of 3%-4%. Currently, the coronas account for about nine percent of the international market.

Austrian ducats, coins with about a quarter of the gold content of the crowns, claim a much smaller share of the market. None of the Austro/Hungarian coins are exchangeable directly for goods, since they aren't legal tender of any existing nation.

•*The Mexican Peso:* The most popular of the gold coins issued by Mexico is the 50-peso coin, which contains 1.2057 ounces of fine gold. Mexico also makes a 20-peso gold piece which contains about .48 ounces of gold. Currently, the 50-peso piece accounts for about 7% of the trade in bullion coins. Because it is a large coin, it is always more expensive than the other popular issues. There is usually a dealer premium on the 50-peso coin ranging up to 15%. The first 50-peso gold coins were issued in 1921 to commemorate Mexico's 100th anniversary. Because of this, the coin has been known ever since as the "centenario." The centenario is the most popular coin with South American gold-hoarders, and it is traded daily in Europe. All centenarios are dated 1974, the year the government began re-issuing the coin as a restrike, or copy of the original issue.

•*The British Sovereign:* This coin, containing .2354 ounces of fine gold has been minted continuously in England since 1817.

•*The Canadian Maple Leaf:* This coin has become popular since it was introduced to the international markets. It is fast becoming the top competitor to the powerful Krugerrand. The Maple Leaf, like the Krugerrand, contains one ounce of fine gold. Also, it is legal tender and not a restrike.

Potential political instability in southern Africa may be a major factor in the Maple Leaf's rising popularity with gold traders. Although quite new, it is very much in demand. If South Africa ever falls, the fate of the Krugerrand will be uncertain. For the sake of the Free World, we would not like to see that brave nation go down.

COLLECTOR'S COINS

Many hard money advocates like gold bullion coinage far above collector's coins. Nevertheless, a market in collector's coins continues to flourish. Those who fancy coins with rarity value and fine gold value have made the U.S. Double Eagle, also called the Liberty Head, their choice investment. Originally this coin was a $20 gold piece. Now (fall 1983), it is worth close to $1,000 depending on its date and condition.

In 1907, the coin was re-designed by the sculptor Augustis Saint-Gaudens, after which it became known as the St. Gaudens gold piece. On one side, the Double Eagle bears the American Eagle, and on the other the whole figure of Miss Liberty. The Liberty Head has not been struck since 1907 and the St. Gaudens has not been struck since 1932, when the U.S. forbade its citizens to hold gold. Both coins are close in size to today's bullion coins, containing slightly less than an ounce of fine gold. The premium on a Double Eagle today may be as much as 40 percent, while the premium on a bullion coin is almost never more than 15 percent. The rarity value makes the Double Eagle a good investment, even with the additional premium.

The Double Eagle has been hoarded in Europe for years, and it has been counterfeited by many underworld types, particularly in Lebanon and in Italy. For this reason, you should be especially careful to buy this coin from a large, well-known dealer.

OTHER U.S. GOLD PIECES

Several other official government gold coins were issued before 1932, including the Quarter Eagle, the half Eagle, and the Eagle, worth $2.50, $5.00, and $10.00, respectively at the time of issue. Once the possession of gold was forbidden to

U.S. citizens, these became collector's items, and when the price of gold was allowed to rise with market demand, they became increasingly valuable for bullion content. Now that U.S. citizens may hold gold in all forms, all of these coins are being sought for rarity and for fine gold value.

In a representative market sampling in the summer of 1983, these approximate prices were being paid for U.S. gold coins:

$ 1 gold piece........................$ 300.00
$ 2.50 gold piece....................$ 325.00
$ 4 gold piece.......................$14,000.00
$ 5 gold piece.......................$ 275.00
$10 gold piece.......................$ 500.00
$20 gold piece.......................$ 1,000.00
$50 gold piece.......................$ 6,500.00

The above prices are subject to rapid change, consult a reputable dealer.

The appearance of an individual coin is imporant in determining what price it will bring, so if you are in possession of any rare gold coins, here are the various grades the dealers use to determine the condition of coins:

PE: meaning plate finish. This is the best grade, also known casually as mint condition. It should look as though it had never left the mint or been handled at all, and it must have been struck from new dies in perfect condition themselves.

UNC: uncirculated.

BU: bright, uncirculated.

AU: almost uncirculated, showing barely detectable signs of wear.

EF: extremely fine; just one grade below AU, with bright clean looks, but clear signs of handling.

VF: very fine, but showing either some flaw or signs of circulation.

F: fine. Though all these grades seem to be terms of approval, fine-grade is actually the lowest acceptable grade for collectors, except in the case of very rare coins. Most experienced collectors will gladly pay more for the higher grades, knowing that these may upgrade the whole collection if and when they decide to sell.

GOLD BULLION

Purchasing gold bars (bullion) has become very popular with many Americans during the past few years of high inflation. Wars and rumors of wars have been a big factor that made gold bars popular with Europeans and Asians. It is the gold bullion trade (dominated by large investors), that pushes gold prices up or down on the world market.

GOLD STOCK

When gold stock investing is mentioned, many people think about the many South African mines that offer common stock. However, I think of a well-managed mutual fund that gives the investor a better opportunity to make money. Gold stocks usually follow the trend set by the bullion itself.

This gives the investor a chance to see the direction gold prices are moving toward. More often than not, the shares outperform the bullion. They also may pay a nice dividend, and when you buy a mutual fund you are also buying expert management who endeavors to know all they can about the companies.

Another way to invest in gold stocks is to "crap shoot" with Canadian and American gold mine corporations. These *OTC* shares are often traded on penny stock exchanges in Salt Lake City, Denver, and Spokane. Risk is extremely high, but so are the rewards. A 50-cent stock that soars to $50 is a long-shot player's dream come true. You've been forewarned. Don't invest any money unless you can afford to lose it all (very possible).

The smart money is spread around with shares in several small gold and/or silver mines. If you own stock in ten companies and one hits pay dirt big, you might make money even if the other nine close the shafts and walk away.

GOLD COMMODITY FUTURES

I seriously doubt if this is for you unless you're a risk-loving gambler. It is my belief that for every person who trades gold commodity futures successfully, there are fifty others who lose their shirts in this volatile market. Not even worth considering for anyone except the most speculative-seeking investor.

SILVER

When gold makes a bold move, silver usually follows, sometimes even outperforming its big brother in the precious metals family. I am very high on silver as an investment. I expect it to again reach, or surpass, its 1980 high of $50 per ounce before the 1980's become history. And $100 an ounce is not an impossibility during the next five or six years.

Silver soared 800 percent in value during a twelve-month period (1979-1980). Many hard money people are extremely high on this metal, and it appears to be primed for steady, if not spectacular increases in value. Silver's spectacular 800 percent run-up was greatly fueled by massive hoarding and a super-rich family's attempt to control the market.

The Hunt family of Dallas, Texas (the heirs of H.L. Hunt, the Texas oil billionaire) has been hoarding silver and speculating on silver futures for years. Early in 1980, trading in silver futures was temporarily suspended because the Hunt people held more futures contracts than there was silver to back them with. When you realize that both the Chicago Board of Trade and the New York Commodity Exchange each keep well over 50 million ounces of silver on hand to meet contracts, you know the Hunt family held contracts on vast amounts of silver. That is, until March 28, 1980, when the Hunt family failed to meet a hundred million dollars of margin calls from Bache and other brokerage firms. Finding themselves in a very awkward and precarious position, the brokerage firms began selling off the Hunt holdings. Quickly, the price of silver fell from a high of $50.00 per ounce to $10.00 per ounce. Thousands of small investors were left to cry in their beer and lick their wounds while "Bunky" Hunt and family were left to plan their next big financial coup.

In spite of the big drop in silver prices, both the short and long range outlook for silver looks promising.

Compared to gold, many investors think silver has been undervalued. Traditionally, the rise of silver prices has not been tandem with activity in the gold markets, but rather with other commodities such as feed, soybeans, and grain. Additionally, there is great industrial demand for silver. Silver is the best known conductor of electricity. Also silver is used in photography, photocopying, and throughout the electronics field.

Like gold, silver was kept at an artificially low price by Uncle Sam. By selling silver at a rock bottom rate.$1.293 per troy ounce—the Treasury hoped to keep folks from hoarding silver coins. Again, the government guessed wrong and three years after taking all silver out of the nation's coins, the government announced that it would henceforth sell silver at the market price. The price of silver did not immediately shoot through the roof, in part because the government did continue to sell, though at a higher price. By 1970, however, the government had stopped selling silver altogether, and the market, no longer under the influence of massive dumping, began its steady rise.

Today, several factors influence the continued rise in silver's worth. For one thing, no massive new surface mines are being discovered: there probably will never be another Comstock Lode. For another thing, industrial need, based on sophisticated uses in photography and electronics is really just getting underway. And the market in silver is less influenced by hysteria than the gold market is. Almost nobody is hoarding silver with the expectation that any currency will ever be based on it again. Finally, as long as inflation continues—and there are few signs that it will do anything else—silver will continue to be an effective hedge and small investors will continue to keep the price up.

As with investments in gold, there are basically three ways to put your money in silver: bullion, coins, and futures. (If the Hunts have left you any futures to buy, that is.) Because of price (silver is still much cheaper than platinum or gold) and availability, the silver market is easier for the small investor to enter than the market for any other precious metal.

Just remember, like the gold market, the silver market is subject to sudden dramatic swings. If you don't watch what you're doing all the time, watch prices, watch your own holdings, and *think*, you could be caught on a downturn. Our recommendation is to buy and hold for the long pull which looks like the true *silvery lining*.

SILVER BULLION

The spot or cash market for silver bullion is the standard by which all silver prices are determined. The price is posted every day, depending on demand. If you pay cash and accept delivery of silver bullion, you get plain, unminted bars, stamped with the weight and grade. Common sizes of silver bars are 10 (troy) ounces, 100 ounces, and 1,000 ounces. A 1,000-ounce bar weighs about 70 pounds, not easy to lift, but not too hard to manage for home storage. You can, of course, actually keep your silver bars at home, or you can rent space in a warehouse that specializes in the storage of precious metals, or you can rent a bank vault. Or you can purchase the silver from a dealer—often on a substantial margin—and store the silver with him. In that case, your silver is "unallocated," which is to say the dealer is obligated to give you your silver on demand, but not to give you any particular bar. If you buy on margin, of course, you must pay the remaining percentage of your account to take delivery on the bullion.

As with anything of intrinsic value, we think it's nice to have around our own house, providing that a safe place is made ready and not too many folks know we have the precious stuff.

254

SILVER FUTURES

Silver futures, like any futures of any commodity, are contracts to buy silver in the future. Buying silver contracts is a bullish move in which you are betting that the actual price of silver (at a future date) will be greater than today's price for silver futures. On the futures market, you are not required to put up the full purchase price of the silver at delivery, but only some percentage, as in a margin account.

If the futures market appears simple, it is really quite complex in practice and requires constant evaluation. Some speculators have several contracts for several future dates and manipulate their profit margins by matching off contracts for "near dates," while buying more "distant dates" contracts.

In a bull market, the more distant the prospective delivery date, the cheaper the contract.

SILVER COINS

There is a proper principle of economics known as "Gresham's Law" that states: *"Good money always forces bad money out of circulation."* That sums up what happened in the United States in the mid 1960's.

In 1966, the government began flooding the U.S. coin market with copper-clad coins with no silver content. Almost overnight most of the $500 million of pre-1965 coins with a 90% silver content fled the marketplace and ended up in home safes, old cookie jars, and bank safe deposit boxes throughout the nation.

In 1965, President Johnson signed the Coinage Act, which not only replaced silver coinage with a copper-nickel clad coin, but gave the Secretary of the Treasury power to forbid the melting down of silver coins.

With the introduction of the copper-nickel coins, the coin shortage was over. Silver coins gradually disappeared from circulation, snapped up either by private individuals or by the Treasury. These days, the 90% silver coins bring anywhere from 10 to 25 times their face value, depending on the spot price of silver.

The other category of silver coins is that of the numismatically valuable. As in the gold coin market, these are coins that have not only silver bullion content but also rarity value. Those coins whose price is closely related to their silver content are known as "common date" coins. The others are "collector's" coins. People who have collector's coins don't have to worry much about the rise and fall of the price of silver. Their coins will continue to gradually increase in value, if they are in good condition, regardless of fluctuations in the price of silver. Silver has been used as currency ever since coining began. Along with gold, silver is a synonym for money in many languages. These days, not many nations make silver coins, though Canada recently struck silver coins in connection with its hosting of the Olympic Games, and Mexico, which produces more silver than any other country, occasionally coins 100-peso pieces of silver. But there are still millions of silver coins from all ages and all nations. Some are legal tender in the countries of origin, but they seldom show up in circulation and are immediately snatched into hiding when they do. Most of the silver coins that haven't been melted down or sold are probably being hoarded against a day of need.

To date, no national government has issued a silver bullion coin comparable to the Maple Leaf or the Krugerrand. The Franklin Mint, the world's largest private mint, has for several years issued silver medals for memorabilia, but with the surge in silver prices, these medals and commemorative ingots have taken on new value among investors. A medal that originally cost only $10 may today be trading at a coin dealer for as much as twice that value. And its value as bullion may be even greater than that. All the Franklin Mint medals are .925 fine, which means that for every thousand parts in the medal, 925 are pure silver. Silver bars are normally .999 silver, but the Franklin Mint medals are sufficiently fine to make them a good storehouse of silver bullion value. Over fifty different silver medallions and ingots have been issued by Franklin over the years, and they vary considerably in weight and bullion content. Use good judgment and consult a reputable coin dealer before buying. A medal must be weighed and assayed before its true worth is known.

HOW TO BUY

When you decide to buy silver coins, you start by hunting for a real professional outfit with whom to do business.

The best place to buy bags of coins is from the largest and most respectable dealer you can find. Bag coins are a very low mark-up, high turnover business. Small dealers just can't compete with volume operators.

Bag prices, like the price of silver, change daily—often significantly. Unless a dealer is constantly buying and selling, he can't make money trading with only a minimum inventory. Small dealers merely place your order through a volume dealer and add a commission—and you don't need to pay more commission!

In order to locate dealers, refer to the yellow pages of your telephone book. Call up several of the apparently larger dealers. Ask questions. Make contacts. Get information.

You can also locate bag coin dealers by their advertisements in certain trade papers and newspapers. At any coin shop you can pick up a copy of *Coin World*, the trade paper of coin collectors. Many bag coin dealers advertise there as well as in *The Wall Street Journal, Barrons,* and the financial pages of metropolitan newspapers.

YOU BE THE DEALER

Want to buy your silver coins at the very best prices? Then *you* become the dealer!

Start buying directly from individuals who have small amounts to sell. In order to do this, just let it be known that you will buy any amount of silver coins. Pay 20% below market. And keep buying here and there until you get a bag—about 55 lbs., the standard trading unit—or as much silver as you desire.

Buying from individuals can be a rewarding way of investing a little money at a time in silver. You'll be surprised how many people have junk silver in small amounts that they don't know how to sell. And once you're known as always having cash, the word will get around. Of course, to make this plan work you really will need plenty of cash on hand. Once the word gets out that you have ready money to offer for silver coins, C.O.D., a steady stream of silver coin sellers will be seeking you out.

GOLD AND SILVER JEWELRY

Gold and silver jewelry, though dazzlingly beautiful, is not purely ornamental. The same is true of diamonds. Jewelry, perhaps because of its beauty, is the most imaginatively appealing form of wealth. Nomadic people, kings and queens on the run from a revolution, refugees of all kinds have always saved their jewelry if they saved nothing else, sewing it into the hems of garments before desperate flights across borders or into the trackless desert. Jewelry is a way of having and displaying wealth when times are good—after all you can wear it and use it instead of leaving it in a vault where its only function is to make its owner anxious. And when times are bad, jewelry is tangible and portable, perhaps the easiest form of great wealth to transport and keep hidden.

Liquidation of gold and silver coins has historically been easier than to sell the family jewels, but there are many instances of fantastic fortunes stored and transported as jewelry.

JEWELRY AS AN INVESTMENT

As already mentioned, the primary disadvantage of jewelry as an investment is its lack of instant (as is the case with coins) liquidity. Jewels are always sold for more than the market value of the materials, and the extra price reflects the value of design, conception, and the work itself. Just how much the work of an artist or an artisan is really worth is very hard for even an expert to judge. When you buy jewelry, you always run the risk of paying too much for the artistic value of the piece, and of not being able to recoup your investment should you be in a hurry to sell.

Buying jewelry is rather like buying paintings as an investment. It can be a very good idea, if you know what you are doing. Not only do you have your wealth safely invested in a commodity that is little affected by inflation, but you have something lovely to look at and enjoy until such time as you need the cash again. But aesthetic judgment is largely a matter of taste, and the successful investor in art must be able to delineate not only his or her own preferences, but also the probable tastes of the buying public in the future. You may buy a gold necklace that you believe to your dying day is the

259

most beautiful piece you have ever seen. But if nobody else thinks so, you won't be able to find a market. If this turns out to be the case, you may take a loss on your investment, though if the absolute market value of the materials has gone up enough, you may be able to do well in spite of the lack of artistic market.

Unless you consider yourself an expert on jewelry and taste, or unless you're rich enough, as Nelson Rockefeller was, so that your taste *creates* the market, do not invest in jewelry without expert advice. If the price of a piece is substantial, you should have it appraised by an independent expert, not connected with the dealer from whom you buy, before you put out any money at all. And, as in all investment transactions, buy only from the most reputable and well-known sellers. You may be offered a "sweet deal" on jewelry by some fly-by-night seller, but there is simply too much risk in the investment in the first place to further jeopardize your money by dealing with an unknown merchant. The individual investor should be cautioned over and over to put only as much money in gold or precious jewelry as he or she can afford to lose without changing his life style. You won't enjoy your gold investment piece if every time you look at it you wonder what you'll eat next year if the market goes down.

The additional caveat with gold jewelry is to buy at wholesale. If you have no source for wholesale jewelry, your investment is worth 50% less as soon as you buy it. That is, a piece that you buy today for $500 probably wholesales for around $250. Therefore, to resell it you would receive no more than $250, and possibly even less, since the resale market is often a "buyer's market" that favors the dealer.

SMART BUYING AND SELLING TIPS

There are some common sense rules to help you buy and you should:

• *Always check three dealers for the best price when you decide to buy.*
• *Only buy from dealers who buy back and who will quote you a buy-back price as readily as a selling price.*
• *Buy for cash. Don't get involved in buying on credit.*
• *Take delivery of your coins. Don't let someone else hold them for you. If the dealer goes broke—and several have— you'll have a hard time getting your coins delivered.*
• *Don't speculate. There are many ways of speculating on the New York Commodity Exchange in silver coins with only 10% cash down. There are also various leveraged plans run by dealers. This is high-risk speculation. Again, you're an investor, not a speculator, if you believe in the long range attractiveness of silver.*
• *Don't buy art. You want silver—not art. So don't get talked into buying one-ounce bars of silver honoring Mother's day, Father's day, or any other day. These bars sell for about three times the value of world spot silver—not a wise investment.*

DIAMONDS

Are "diamonds really forever?" Are they a sound investment? The answer must be both a "yes" and a "no."

The beauty and durability of diamonds has always fascinated human beings. People cherish their diamonds as much or more than any other possession. Diamonds are symbolic with wealth, high fashion, and other highly desired status symbols. However, during the past few decades the beauty of diamonds has taken a back seat, as they were viewed more in terms of their investment potential. Europeans and third-world businessmen started this trend and recently, Americans have jumped on the bandwagon, often without sufficient information or expertise to make sound buy/sell decisions.

Since investment-grade diamonds still offer substantial long-range potential, in spite of sharp (and to some devastating) market corrections during the early 1980's, you should learn more about this fascinating area of investing.

THE DIAMOND MONOPOLY

At least 85 percent of the world's diamonds are controlled by a powerful company simply known as the Central Selling Organization (CSO), or "the syndicate." The CSO is the marketing arm of the DeBeers Mining Company. Almost everyone, in almost every nation, eventually does business with this huge monopolistic cartel.

The reason for the perpetuation of the CSO's diamond monopoly is simple: the CSO gets diamond mine owners a better price for their gems than they could get if they sold their own output. If the CSO didn't, the syndicate would break apart.

This is how the CSO works. Ten times a year the CSO holds a "sight" or sale in a closely guarded office in London. At that time, the CSO sells enough diamonds to maintain a stable world diamond market—usually about five million carats annually.

Invited to the sale are an exclusive group of some 300 of the world's most prestigious diamond dealers. The CSO offers each dealer an assortment of rough or uncut stones at a stated price. Haggling is almost nonexistent. The dealer merely accepts or rejects the offer. Few offerings are ever rejected, however. Those who do so risk not being invited back.

Obviously, the CSO sales are ideal for the producers. But surprisingly, the diamond industry seems to welcome the monopolistic practices of the CSO, too. Instead of considering the CSO as some type of economic tyrant, the CSO is more often described as a benevolent dictator who maintains the integrity of the diamond and the industry in an often chaotic world.

In effect, the CSO has provided over forty years of stable or increasing diamond prices. The entire industry—cutters, dealers, and retailers—has benefited from this situation. Even the ultimate consumer holds his or her diamond in higher esteem because of the diamond's ever-increasing value.

Besides their upward price stability, diamonds, unlike silver and gold, can be conveniently carried in your pocket or purse or placed out of sight in a small safe hiding place.

DIAMOND DEMAND

With the CSO in total control of the world's diamond supply, demand is effectively regulated.

Diamonds have traditionally been in demand as jewelry; now they have become additionally desirable as a hedge against uncertainty. People in South Africa, Israel, and various Arab nations have recently bought huge quantities of investment-quality stones.

Diamonds have a monopoly-controlled supply and they are in great demand. For this reason, they deserve consideration as another dynamic 1980's investment.

PRICING

People love diamonds, but diamonds, like people, are not all alike. The truth is so much variation in color, cut, and clarity that a one-carat gem—a stone weighing one-fifth of a gram—can be graded anywhere from imperfect to flawless. Yet all grades are considered diamonds.

So, always remember: The price of a diamond is not determined by size alone. Overall quality decides value. Thus the price of a one-carat diamond can vary from a few hundred dollars to $25,000 at wholesale.

Since demand for different grades of diamonds varies, the price of all diamond grades has not climbed at the same rate during recent years. Generally, scarcer, higher quality stones, known as investment grades, have significantly outperformed the more plentiful poorer quality gems. But all diamond grade-pricing starts with the price of rough stones.

INVESTMENT-QUALITY DIAMONDS

Although the price increases for raw, uncut stones sold by the CSO have been substantial, it is the price increases made by investment-quality diamonds that are truly impressive. These increases, and anticipated continued gains, have led to speculation (as well as to investment) in quality gems. But these gains are hard to pin down.

A major problem is grading. Even a slight variation in grade can cause a considerable change in the price of a diamond. And there are over 100 possible combinations of color and clarity grades, without even considering the size of the stone or its cut. Consequently, there is little consistent price information for any specific grade of diamond—except for raw, uncut stones.

Besides, there is no central market for cut and polished diamonds from which to gather price information. Characteristically, rough stones bought from DeBeers are sold to cutters, who usually resell their cut and polished stones through fourteen worldwide informal diamond exchanges. The exchanges sell to wholesalers, who resell to retail jewelry manufacturers, who, in turn, supply jewelry stores.

The exchanges, however, are not formally structured institutions like the major stock exchanges. Rather, they more represent exlusive clubs who treasure their privacy as much as the precious stones they trade.

You can discover all sorts of figures purporting to show the price appreciation of cut, polished diamonds during recent years. Among the quotes will be slight differences. This is the nature of the industry. It is quite impossible to be exact with diamond prices and quotes, due to the many grades of the stone. This is at least partially because there is no standard diamond—only innumerable grades.

Not surprisingly, it is beyond the scope of this book to analyze price activity for different grades of diamonds—even if it was possible to do so. Moreover, you don't need this information for your basic investment program. The overall diamond price trends for raw diamonds and the impressive climb in the price of investment-quality stones should be enough to convince you of the one essential fact: Diamonds can be a very profitable investment—if they are bought and sold right!

BUYING DIAMONDS

For your basic investment program, you might consider owning a one carat or larger investment-quality diamond. This type of gem has had spectacular price growth in the past. And the supply-demand fundamentals for diamonds plus persistent, worldwide inflation indicate continued above average gains.

Be warned, however. The return that a diamond investment yields has not gone unnoticed. In their continuing search for ways to protect their wealth in an era of inflation, investors have been giving diamonds more and more attention. The action of the CSO in raising prices 40% in March, 1978, only confirms this increased activity.

For the first time in forty years, demand for diamonds is a stronger force in the marketplace than supply. The CSO can no longer control diamond prices by increasing the supply of stones in the world market. Many diamond merchants feel that the CSO simply doesn't have enough stones to be able to do so. Thus the benevolent dictator of the diamond market, the CSO, can no longer guarantee a stable diamond market.

I saw a problem developing. As inflation heated up, there would be short-term speculative excesses in diamonds. For thirty-five years diamonds had appreciated 15 percent or more yearly, but as the 1980's dawned, major correction was imminent.

GRADING STANDARDS

The four basic characteristics that determine the quality of a diamond are:

1. Carat
2. Color
3. Clarity
4. Cut

The "four C's" form the foundation for all diamond grading. The Gemological Institute of America (GIA), a non-profit gemological laboratory with offices in Los Angeles and New York, is highly respected by diamond traders and merchants. In recent years their grading has become the standard of the diamond world.

CARAT

A carat is the unit used to measure the weight of a diamond. It converts to about one-fifth of a metric system gram. But diamond weight is always given by the carat or in "points," which are equal to one hundredth of a carat. Example: 125 points = 1¼ carat!

There is another important size factor to consider when buying an investment-quality diamond: As size increases, there are disproportionally fewer stones. This means that there are more than twice as many one-carat diamonds as two-carat stones. Thus a two-carat diamond doesn't sell for the same price per carat as a one-carat stone. To illustrate, a one-carat flawless diamond sold for a medium price of $16,400 in 1977. A two-carat diamond traded for $56,280, or $28,140 per carat (both prices at wholesale). Note: During 1981-1982 diamonds went down substantially. Depreciation cut the value of some stones in half. Some smaller or poorly cut stones lost up to 200 percent of their value. This was the diamond industry.

And, as diamond size increases further, the price per carat continues to escalate. For example, the 107 carat, flawless, "Louis Cartier" diamond is insured for $5 million. That's roughly $45,000 a carat!

The diamond speculator should also never be misled by very small diamonds of a few points each mounted together in a cluster in a ring that add up to a total of "One Full Carat." Those tiny stones have only marginal value. Putting a group of them together does not add up to the high value of one fine stone. For example: A high quality ten-point stone may sell for $80 at wholesale. Thus, ten such stones (one carat in weight) might cost about $800. This is significantly below the $20,000 plus price of a one-carat flawless diamond. The true speculation value is in one carat or larger investment-grade diamonds, not in stones of less than 100 points (one carat).

CUT

There are five basic shapes of finished diamonds: round, oval, square, pear, and marquise. If you are buying a diamond as a "love gift," personal preference would, of course, determine the shape to buy. And rightfully so.

For investment purposes, however, you want the diamond shape that is most popular. And that's the round stone traditionally mounted in engagement rings. Not only is this shape in great demand, but it is less susceptible to change in value due to changes in fashions.

Regardless of the shape, relative brilliance is the result of cutting. A 100% cut means the diamond has all the brilliance possible for the basic shape. Anything less than a 100% cutting is known as cutting error and detracts from the potential brilliance of the stone, as well as from its ultimate value.

COLOR

Color is the ultimate factor in determining the quality of a diamond. An investment-quality diamond must be colorless or very near colorless. Stones of inferior quality have various amounts of yellow in them. The more yellow in the diamond, the poorer the quality and value. You may also have heard jewelers describe certain diamonds as "blue white diamonds." This is nothing but "sales talk," as there are no "blue white" diamonds.

To objectively define color in an ordinary diamond, a scale from D to A is used, as shown in the table below. This scale represents graduations of color from colorless to light yellow.

But fancy stones are not included in this scale. They are a special situation.

COLOR GRADING STANDARDS FOR DIAMONDS

Grade	Description
DEF	Colorless
GHIF	Near Colorless
KLM	Faint Yellow
NOPQR	Light Yellow
STUVWXYZ	Yellow
"Fancy stone"	Any Color

"Fancy stones" are unusual diamonds that must be evaluated individually. In this group would be diamonds with a pink, peach, green, or even a blue haze. Obviously, these color variations make them difficult to grade, appraise, and market. Avoid them. To color grade a diamond, a gemologist uses sample stones that represent each color grade. Then, with the naked eye, the gemologist compares the diamond to the samples. Obviously, there is the possibility of an error in human judgment and of "fudging" when a difference of one or two grades can significantly affect price.

In order to eliminate human factors, a scientific instrument such as the Diamond Photometer can be used to determine color grade. With this tool, grading is precise. You should accept nothing less than precise grading when you buy a stone.

Color grades for investment-quality diamonds are grades D through H. Any lesser grade may be personally desirable, but it's not investment quality. So, if possible, stick with color grades D through H.

CLARITY

Clarity is the degree to which a diamond is free of internal or external marks (technically known as inclusions) when light is passed through the stone. The fewer the imperfections, the rarer and more precious the stone. The United States Federal Trade Commission (FTC) has ruled that no diamond can be sold as flawless if any spot, blemish, or other type of imperfection is apparent under a ten-power magnifying glass (also called a "loop"). But standards for a lesser quality or clarity are not determined by the FTC. GIA standards are most readily accepted for grades below flawless.

Grades VS2 or higher are accepted as investment-quality diamonds. The prudent diamond investor will only purchase these grades.

CLARITY GRADING STANDARDS FOR DIAMONDS

Grade	Description
Flawless	Perfect stone. No imperfections.
VVS1	Very Very Slight Inclusion
VVS2	Slightly lower grade than VVS1
VS1	Very Slight Inclusion
VS2	Slightly lower grade of VS1
S1	Slight Inclusion
S12	Slightly lower grade of S1
I1,2,3	Grades of imperfect stones

HOW TO GET A DIAMOND GRADED

Even when you know exactly what you want *(a one-carat or larger round diamond with a D-H color grade, flawless to VS1-2 clarity, and a 58-facet, 100% cut)*, you may not be able to tell if you're getting it!

The best and recommended way to get a 100% accurate grading of your diamond is to request the GIA grade your stone (the cost is nominal) and issue an official Gemological Institute of America certification. There are two GIA labs in the U.S. that will certify diamonds of a carat or more. Smaller stones will not be accepted. Call or write either GIA lab for instructions on submitting gems:

11940 San Vincente Blvd., Los Angeles, CA 90049

580 Fifth Avenue, New York, NY 10046

Just keep in mind that the GIA certificate doesn't tell how much a diamond is worth. They do not appraise stones. All they do (and how important it is!) is grade a diamond accurately.

BROKERS

There are diamond brokers...and then there are *diamond brokers!* With increased interest in diamonds in the late 1970's and early 1980's, some marginal operators began entering this field. While most diamond brokers are honest and trustworthy, a few are not. Here are some tips that will help you select a reputable broker:

•*Reputable brokers talk and use GIA grading standards.* Get out of the office quickly of any "dealer" who uses terms like "high quality" or "fine quality." There is no substitute for GIA grading.

•*Ask about buy-back prices.* Any reputable broker will resell a diamond with a GIA certification. The difference between the brokers bid (buying price from you) and ask (sale price) should be 15%-20%, depending on sales commission and other transaction costs. But don't expect instant action. Most

271

brokers require an average of four weeks to make a sale. Be wary of anybody who guarantees you a profit when you buy a diamond. Nobody can do this.

•*Check financial responsibility.* Diamond brokers need an impeccable reputation for integrity and money. Request Dun & Bradstreet ratings and bank references to check for capitalization and number of years in the business. Seek established firms. Forget newcomers.

•*Expect to hold diamonds at least two years* in order for the stone to appreciate enough to cover sale costs and earn you a profit.

•*Buy only diamonds with GIA certification.* Again, accept nothing else. And be willing to pay the GIA to get it.

•*Check with as many brokers as you can before you buy an investment-quality diamond.* Always, of course, describe the diamond you seek with precise GIA grading standards. And, if you can, cross-check quotes with typical *Jeweler's Circular Keystone* diamond survey prices.

Although I'm basically bullish on diamonds as a sound investment, it is only fair that a few of the leading disadvantages of owning diamonds be pointed out.

DISADVANTAGES OF OWNING DIAMONDS

1. There is no central diamond exchange for trading diamonds to other speculators.

2. You must sell to a diamond merchant and must rely on his judgment and honesty in appraising the diamond. This is true whether you are buying or selling diamonds.

3. When you buy, you buy at retail price, and when you sell, you sell at wholesale price to the diamond merchant. Thus a very high price appreciation is necessary before you

272

can profit.

4. There is no objective measurement of a diamond's value. Five jewelers will give you five different estimates of value. Even if values given are reasonably close, almost always the appraisals will differ somewhat.

5. Since DeBeers is located in South Africa and much diamond production takes place there, the South African political situation could, in the future, change the diamond's value and price stability.

6. The recent "market crash" was devastating. It also proved even DeBeers could not halt a very sharp correction.

Another diamond-related problem is the recent boom in man-made diamonds. In 1969, a good-looking "counterfeit diamond" called Yttrium Aluminum Garnet (YAG) was introduced. By 1980 YAG's were selling briskly worldwide. A one carat YAG will cost around $50 as opposed to several thousands of dollars for a real diamond.

In spite of various investment problems, we are bullish on diamonds as an investment over the long pull. However, this is no arena for the wide-eyed plunger. Here knowledge and careful dealing is absolutely essential.

Diamonds can be a sparkling investment for some. A degree of stability has occurred in 1983 and prices are heading back up. Nevertheless, don't invest before you spend a lot of effort investigating. And, above all, this is not the best investment for the unsophisticated.

THE ADEN SISTERS GOLD REPORT

During the past seven years, one of the most successful research efforts on gold and gold-related investments has been conducted in Costa Rica in total secrecy by two unusual and

273

highly talented sisters, Mary Aden-Harter and Pamela Aden-Ayales. Under private sponsorship, working with a dedicated research staff, they have completed over 20,000 hours of computer-assisted research that has resulted in 60 in-depth studies on gold, silver, major currencies, world stock markets, currencies, interest rates and economic cycles.

Among the most startling results of their diligent research is the following report, a calculated prediction that the price of gold will soar during 1985-1986. Can you imagine gold at close to $5,000 an ounce by 1986? The Aden sisters can, and they back up their prediction with the following data.

While we do not give the following special report our "100% stamp of approval," we do present it here as unique investing information from a highly respected source, worthy of your consideration.

THE ECONOMIC CYCLE:
DEBT, INFLATION AND INTEREST RATES

Inflation is not caused by big business, labor unions, oil companies or farmers; these groups are only reacting to it. Inflation cannot be stopped by price controls or regulations. Ever-increasing government debt is the cause of worsening inflation and will not be stopped until government stops printing new money to finance larger deficits. In the meantime, slowdowns are only temporary; the long-term trend is up.

If the government were a corporation it would have gone bankrupt and closed its doors years ago. Neither an individual, corporation or a government can continue operating in the red without eventually paying the consequences. Currently, those consequences are inflation and all of its ugly repercussions. The problem is not only domestic; it affects the rest of the world. Debt and its side effects are the major problems

274

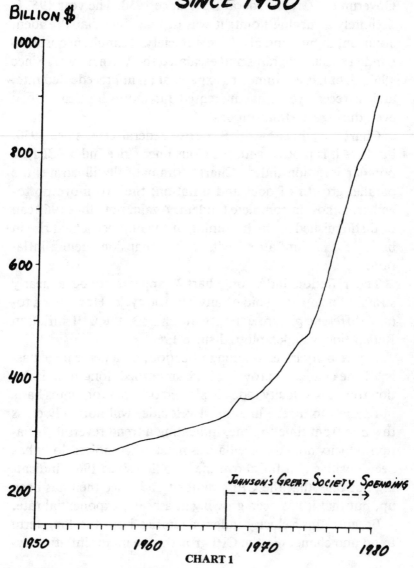

U.S. GOVERNMENT
GROSS FEDERAL DEBT
SINCE 1950

BILLION $

CHART 1

being faced by the present administration.

Government debt in the United States has been increasing for years. However, it was not until about 1967 that debt began increasing in earnest, as seen on chart 1, the United States Government Gross Federal Debt since 1950. The year 1967 is definitely a turning point; it was at that time that President Johnson, in building his "Great Society," simultaneously expanded social programs and escalated the Vietnam war. Since 1967, debt has continued to expand at an unprecedented rate, and in recent years has increased far more drastically than even during the Johnson era.

Chart 2 again shows U.S. Gross Federal Debt since 1950, but here it is plotted with the Consumer Price Index (CPI), a popular inflation index. Chart 2 dramatically illustrates the parallel growth of debt and inflation; the two move up together, almost in complete tandem. Again, note that 1967 can be distinguished as the beginning of the unprecedented rise in both debt *and* inflation, with debt expansion fueling inflation.

The inflation index on chart 2 appears to be a nearly straight line up and void of any specific cycle. However, a totally different picture emerges on chart 3, the CPI Inflation Rate Velocity Index plotted since 1967.

The velocity index is a magnification, on a percentage basis, of the change in growth of the smoothed, long-term inflation trend. A velocity index is plotted on a plus or minus basis in relation to a zero line; most velocities will normally cross this line from time to time, indicating a trend reversal. Inflation velocity does not oscillate as most other indices do; it has been positive and far above the zero line since 1967, indicating not only that the CPI's major trend since then has been up, but that it has been growing at a nearly exponential rate.

Because this velocity index magnifies both the long-term trend and changes in the CPI growth, the major inflation cy-

GROSS FEDERAL DEBT VS. CONSUMER PRICES

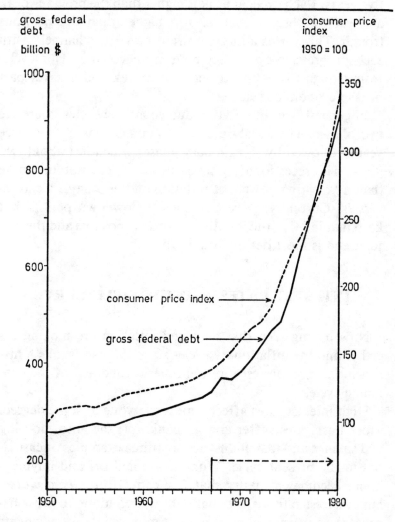

CHART 2

277

cle is seen. Most apparent is that there has been a consistent pattern of peaks and troughs since 1967. This is not random; a movement from peak to peak occurs approximately every five years. Each cyclical peak is higher than the previous peak and each cyclical trough is also higher than the previous trough. This forms a large, upward-moving "channel" with each progressive cycle becoming more volatile. This cycle, from trough to peak to trough, illustrates, and is a key part of, the economic cycle.

In general, within inflation and economic cycles, there are two phases. The inflation expansion phases last about three years, followed by recessionary phases which last about two years. The recessionary phases, however, are nothing more than a "slowing down" of inflation and not major trend reversals. Currently, we are in such a slowdown period, but keep in mind that the inflation velocity is positive and the major trend is most definitely still up.

INTEREST RATES AND THE YIELD CURVE

Now having seen that debt and inflation are moving together and the inflationary cycles since 1967, let's take a historical look at interest rates, another component of the economic cycle.

High interest rates affect almost everyone to some degree. More businesses suffer and go bankrupt; the auto, housing and savings and loan industries are prime examples of casualties in the present cycle. Workers are laid off and buying a home becomes a luxury that few can afford. Even worse, high interest rates assure that debt will continue to grow because the government must pay out more in interest payments for the money it is borrowing; interest payments on the debt are currently the third largest expense of the federal govern-

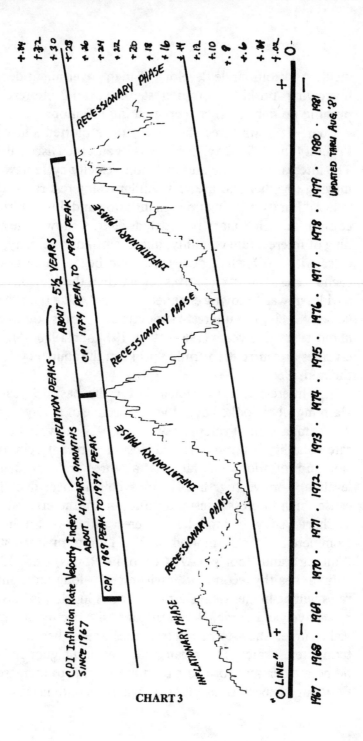

CPI Inflation Rate Velocity Index SINCE 1967

INFLATION PEAKS

ABOUT 4 YEARS 9 MONTHS — CPI 1969 PEAK TO 1974 PEAK

ABOUT 5½ YEARS — CPI 1974 PEAK TO 1980 PEAK

RECESSIONARY PHASE

INFLATIONARY PHASE

RECESSIONARY PHASE

INFLATIONARY PHASE

RECESSIONARY PHASE

INFLATIONARY PHASE

"O LINE"

+.34 +.32 +.30 +.28 +.26 +.24 +.22 +.20 +.18 +.16 +.14 +.12 +.10 +.8 +.6 +.04 +.02 0

+

—

1967 · 1968 · 1969 · 1970 · 1971 · 1972 · 1973 · 1974 · 1975 · 1976 · 1977 · 1978 · 1979 · 1980 · 1981

UPDATED THRU AUG. '81

CHART 3

279

ment. A vicious circle develops of high government debt and borrowing pushing up interest rates, and interest rates pushing up debt further, perpetuating inflation.

Chart 5 shows three short-term rates plotted since 1929: Federal Funds, 90-Day Treasury Bills and the Discount Rate. The interest rate cycle and inflation velocity cycle have been moving together and are very similar to interest rates, led by Federal Funds, moving up with inflation and down during recession (disinflationary periods), as chart 4 shows, the beginning of interest rate volatility, like the inflation velocity, coincides with 1967 when debt expansion began in earnest. As each interest-rate cycle moves higher than the previous cycle, a wide, upward-moving channel is formed. Like the inflation-velocity cycle, the interest-rate cycle also peaks, on average, about every five years (1966, 1970, 1974 and 1980-81). Interest rates are currently forming peaks in the fourth cycle since the mid-1960s.

The interest rate movements over the past 15 years are alarming when looked at in the perspective of a 50-year span. The comparison of rates today versus 1929 show that interest rate volatility is unprecedented, just as is recent debt expansion and inflation. The fact that all three are at record high levels and move together is not a coincidence; debt is the cause, high interest rates and inflation are the effects.

Chart 5 shows a short-term interest rate (4-6 month prime Commercial Paper) plotted with a long-term interest rate (Standard and Poor's AAA Corporate Bonds) since 1911.

In a healthy economic environment, long-term interest rates will be higher than short-term rates in what is known as a positive yield curve. When the opposite occurs, a negative yield curve, short-term interest rates are higher than long-term interest rates. This means that there is a higher and more desperate demand for short-term money due to increased inflationary expectations. It is a sign of economic instability

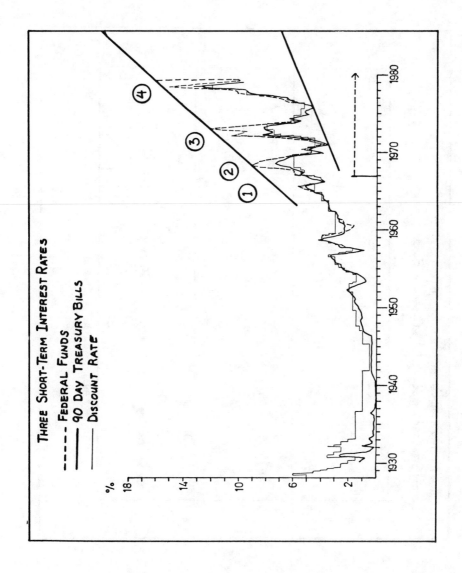

THREE SHORT-TERM INTEREST RATES
- - - - FEDERAL FUNDS
———— 90 DAY TREASURY BILLS
———— DISCOUNT RATE

CHART 4

281

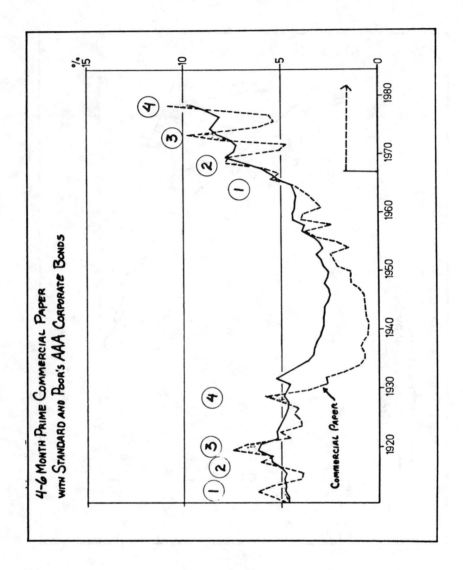

4-6 Month Prime Commercial Paper with Standard and Poor's AAA Corporate Bonds

CHART 5

282

and a credit crunch environment.

Shaded areas on the chart indicate negative yield curve (credit crunch) periods; notice that this phenomenon occured four times in the 20 years preceeding the depression. throughout the 1930s to the mid-1960s the yield curve was positive, generally indicating a time of growth and prosperity with an adequate credit supply. The first negative yield curve in 36 years occurred in 1966 and was the first of four since that time. Since 1966, negative yield curves have coincided with the cyclical interest-rate "peak areas" and positive yield curves have coincided with interest rate trough or bottoming areas.

GOLD IN THE ECONOMIC CYCLE

What does all this have to do with the price of gold?

Gold is the keystone of the economic cycle. Since 1968, when gold began to fluctuate on the free market, this cycle paralleled inflation and interest-rate cycles, generally rising in inflationary phases and declining in recessionary phases. By becoming increasingly more volatile, gold, like inflation and interest rates, has formed a long-term uptrend and channel.

The most outstanding feature about the three, however, is that since 1968, though generally moving together, gold has led interest rates and inflation by several months. This has been true not only at major peaks and troughs, but throughout the cycle.

GOLD: AN INFLATION HEDGE?

You have often heard gold referred to as an "inflation hedge." This is very true, at times. Owning gold is one of the few and most liquid ways to protect your assets. The long-term trend in gold and inflation is up; owning gold is the best way to "beat inflation" and end up with a healthy percentage increase on your investment. It is important, however, to know when to buy and sell; generally speaking, buy near the onset of inflationary phases and sell into recessionary phases. Specific buy and sell recommendations will be discussed in further detail later in this report.

SUMMARY

In the past 15 years each economic cycle begins with an inflationary phase in which rising inflation and interest rates last about three years. By the time rates and inflation are at their cyclical peaks, the economy is in trouble. Inflation is the overriding worry for the majority of people; food and housing costs are rising rapidly. Everyone is concerned about "fighting inflation" and bringing it down to manageable levels (money becomes tight, inflation moves down, as do interest rates). Then comes the recessionary phase of the cycle which generally lasts about two years. By the time inflation and interest rates reach cyclical troughs, recession and unemployment have replaced inflation as the national concern and the government feels it must do something to "get people back to work." The recessionary phase can be thought of as the "correcting" phase since it washes out some of the excesses that have occurred during the previous inflationary phase. Money is pumped into the economy to stimulate a recovery; the economy gains and another inflationary phase begins.

This repeating sequence of events of inflation followed by recession has occurred four times since the mid-1960s. When inflation velocity and interest rates (charts 4 and 5) are at the top of their channels, inflation is of primary concern; when they are at the bottom of the channels, recession is the uppermost concern.

Since 1967, regardless of cyclical ups and downs, the primary long-term trend has been and continues to be up for both inflation and interest rates. Reaching peaks about every five years, each cycle begins from a higher base level than the previous cycle and moves to an even higher level, with each progressive cycle becoming increasingly more volatile. Why?

Debt. It is quite evident that 1967 is a key time period and turning point for the U.S. economy; the dramatic expansion of government debt since that time has caused not only higher inflation and interest-rate levels, but has caused economic cycles to become more and more volatile. As long as debt continues to grow, interest rates and inflation will ultimately continue higher.

People often have the impression that fluctuations in gold are unpredictable, lacking in order. Nothing could be further from the truth. The gold market is one of the most orderly of markets. Once you are aware of its cyclical pattern and have the ability to interpret what it is saying, gold can be used as a gauge of current economic conditions. Because of gold's leading-indicator qualities, future changes in the major economic cycles surface several months prior to occurrence. Gold not only leads interest rates and inflation; it leads other aspects of the economic cycle as well, which also directly affect the quality of life.

THE CRIME/UNEMPLOYMENT GOLD LINK

It is interesting to note that when gold was at its high of $850 an ounce in January 1980, there was a greater probability of being robbed or murdered than when it was $200 an

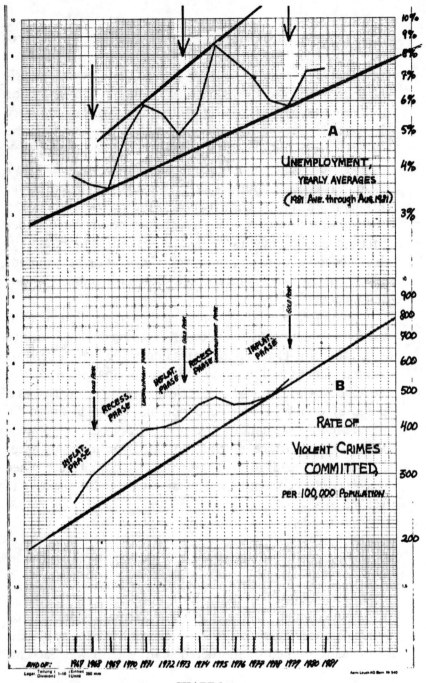

A

UNEMPLOYMENT,
YEARLY AVERAGES
(1981 Ave. through Aug. 1981)

B

RATE OF
VIOLENT CRIMES
COMMITTED,
PER 100,000 POPULATION

END OF: 1967 1968 1969 1970 1971 1972 1973 1974 1975 1976 1977 1978 1979 1980 1981

CHART 6

286

ounce in 1978. Today, the probability is even greater. More people are buying guns than ever before and security businesses are booming.

Charts 6A and 6B tell a powerful story. First look at 6A, the unemployment rate, and then look at 6B, the rate of violent crimes committed (a compilation of occurrences of murder, robbery, rape and assault). Both charts are plotted on a ratio scale and begin in 1967. At first glance it is evident that unemployment and violent crime are both moving in an uptrend and follow the economic cycle, but a closer examination reveals another, little-known correlation.

It is apparent that the unemployment cycle relates closely to the cycles we've seen previously. However, unemployment lags gold. When gold peaks (note arrows), unemployment is at its cyclical trough. The unemployment peak occurs about two years after the gold peak. This lagging relationship means that shortly after gold peaks and the recessionary phase of the economic cycle is started, the unemployment rate begins to rise in earnest. As mentioned previously, rising unemployment is a result of recession as businesses cut back.

Crime lags gold, but a close look at 6B shows a major difference in comparison to the other charts. Crime has longer cyclical upmoves and shorter downmoves than the others. Since 1968, about a year after gold had begun its major upmove, crime began to move up from its cyclical trough and continued up during the inflationary phase. As gold peaks and begins to fall, unemployment begins to rise, marking the beginning of the recessionary phase. Crime, however, continues rising with unemployment, throughout the recessionary phase. It does not reach its cyclical peak until unemployment peaks, a clear correlation with rising unemployment and rising crime. What makes crime different is that it rises in both inflationary and recessionary phases. Once unemployment moves down, crime stabilizes at the higher level or declines slightly. This stabilization period, however, has only lasted about one year within each of the two previous cycles; the rest of the time the crime rate is rising.

In September 1981, the FBI Crime Report was released giving recent statistics, which are not plotted on this chart. They state, however, that crime was up 9% from last year, there is a murder committed every 23 minutes in the United States and that crime in general is now rising four times faster than the population growth. This indicates two things: that the current cycle's sequence of events is moving in line with previous cycles and there is still a way to go until the crime peaks for this cycle.

A depressing thought, true, but an awareness of the social repercussions of debt-caused problems is essential. People routinely blame the crime increase on television violence, drug use or the decline in morality. The point is that never do you hear of the government's unique contribution to the problem, that debt increase parallels crime increase. As long as debt continues to grow, perpetuating inflation, crime too will continue to rise. Economic unrest invariably leads to social unrest.

OIL AND GOLD

Chart 7 shows the price of oil since 1970. The arrows mark the gold peaks and again there is the familiar pattern which has formed since then. During the inflationary phases, oil moves up sharply and tends to stabilize during the recessionary phase.

There is something else worth pointing out, however, regarding oil's relationship to gold. In mid-1970 when gold was $35 an ounce and oil was $2 a barrel, their ratio was 17.5 (35 divided by 2). Since that time, based on market extremes, this ratio has fluctuated between approximately 8½ to 27, but the

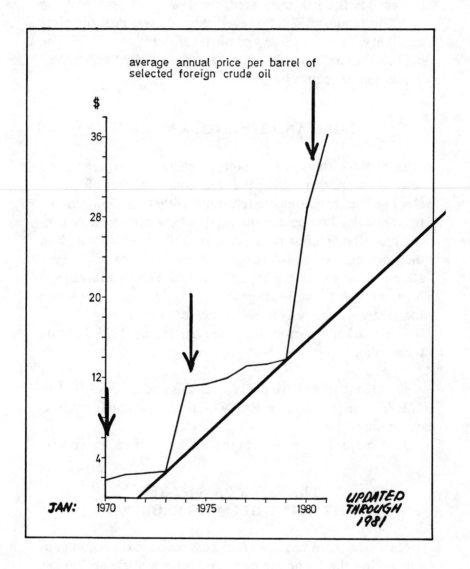

average annual price per barrel of
selected foreign crude oil

UPDATED
THROUGH
1981

CHART 7

289

17.5 level seems to be the average. For example, the 1976 gold trough was the low ratio area; the 1980 gold peak was the high. By January 1981, however, the ratio was near the average level with gold at $625 and oil at $36, a ratio of 17.36. The point is that neither gold nor oil are historically "expensive" in relation to each other.

GOLD AND THE STOCK MARKET

Since 1968, the stock market in general has experienced a severe bear market during the recessionary phases of the cycle. The important thing to remember is that the Dow has suffered about a 30% decline during thee bear markets which occur just after interest rates peak. A major cyclical trough in the stock market then develops about six months to one year after rates peak. Some argue that most stocks will outperform the Dow, and this is generally true. However, in major bear markets nearly everything "washes out."

The market down-moves since early July 1981 indicate three things:

1. Interest rates have peaked for this cycle.
2. The sequence of events within the economic cycle is continuing.
3. A major bear market in the stock market is under way.

TRANSFER PAYMENTS:
THE OVERWHELMING PROBLEM

Now that there has been a discussion of various components within the economic cycle and how debt expansion has caused higher and more volatile cycles. What can be done? The fact that the Reagan Administration is the first to not on-

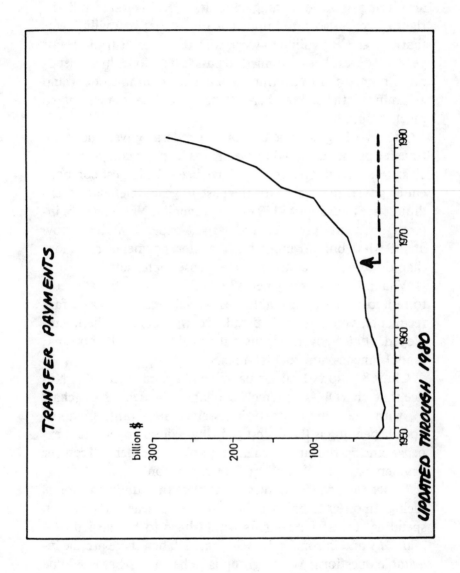

CHART 8

291

ly publicly acknowledge the problems and their cause, but also trying to do something about it, is the biggest step in the right direction so far. Important too is that it finally seems that Congress is willing to work with the Administration. For years Congress has continued to pass legislation which spends more money than government takes in, adding to debt and enlarging deficits. So where is the government spending so much money?

The two largest expenses of the federal government are transfer payments and defense. Transfer payments, currently close to $300 billion annually, have been the largest component of government debt for the past 10 years. Defense expenditures are now about $130 billion annually. National debt interest payments are the third largest expense and are now about $100 billion annually. Transfer payments are more than double the second largest expense, defense.

What are transfer payments? It is the money "transferred" to retired civil service employees, social security and welfare recipients, veterans, retired railroad workers and the unemployed. It also covers expenses for medicare, public housing, school lunches and food stamps.

Chart 8 shows transfer payments beginning in 1950. Notice that chart 8 is extremely similar to the debt chart (chart 1), with the same dramatic rises since 1967 quite obvious. Social spending is the fastest growing federal government expense and is the uncontrollable part of the debt. Transfer payments are the "why" of debt expansion.

This is the primary domestic problem the administration is facing. In order to balance the budget or at least cut down on spending, transfer payments would have to be slashed *dramatically* and in some cases eliminated. Then there are the inevitable questions: Which group is to be cut? What would be the social repercussions?

In September 1981, between 250,000 and 500,000 people in

what was perhaps the largest political protest in Washington in the past 20 years, staged a demonstration to oppose Reagan's social and economic policies. At the time, no major reductions in benefits had occurred, yet workers and people from all public sectors gathered at the capital to protest what one speaker called taking away of the "bare necessities." Coretta Scott King, widow of slain civil rights leader Martin Luther King, accused the administration of being selfish and was quoted as saying, "American people of all races will not suffer in silence while the architects of reaction (the Reagan Administration) seek to shatter the hard-won social and economic gains of the last 50 years." This protest exemplifies how social programs are not limited to any one group; they have, in fact, become integral bread and butter issues to millions of Americans.

It is doubtful that this demonstration will be an isolated incident, instead it is further confirmation of existing long-term cycles. Turning around transfer payments, thus debt expansion, is obviously going to be extremely difficult.

SUMMARY

Because the national debt is so out of control, it is doubtful that a substantial turn around will be possible, at least not in the near future. In the meantime, keep an eye on transfer payments since they are the key. Until there are significant and unprecedented changes in this area it is safe to assume that debt expansion and the cycles of inflation, interest rates, gold, crime, unemployment, oil and the stock market will continue as they have since 1967.

GOLD PURCHASE TIMING

The first half of this report establishes the general background of the economic cycle and explains gold's relationship to other economic variables. By leading interest rates and the economic cycle in general, gold is able to give early warning signs of inflationary and recessionary pressures in the economy. Gold purchase timing, therefore, is vital for anyone who is concerned about their economic future.

Once knowing and understanding that the gold cycle does exist, you must be able to identify when major price reversals occur in order to invest and plan accordingly. Therefore, an understanding of gold's cyclical timing is imperative.

GOLD TIMING TOOLS: PRICE CYCLE, VELOCITY AND THE MOVING AVERAGE

If what has been said up to now sounds pessimistic, there is some good news: the cycle is predictable. Following are explanations of some of the tools used in analyzing the gold market, the current cycle position and what can reasonably be expected in the future.

Our core analysis of gold is based on a three-faceted approach: the Gold Price Cycle, the Velocity Indicator and the Confirming 65-week Moving Average.

THE GOLD PRICE CYCLE

First, the basic gold cycle and constant cyclical similarities that have occurred since 1968.

Chart 9 illustrates the weekly gold price in U.S. dollars, on a ratio scale, since 1968. There have been three major cy-

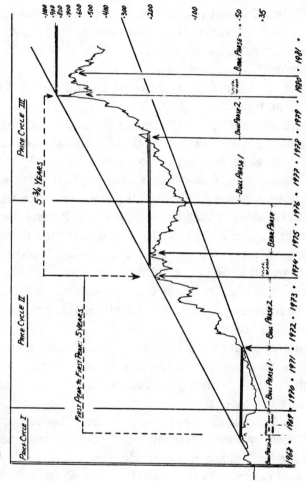

GOLD PRICE CYCLE

WEEKLY GOLD PRICE IN US.$ SINCE 1968
LONDON PM FIX

UPDATED THROUGH SEPT. 25, 1981

CHART 9

295

cles since 1968, which are identified on the chart as cycles I, II and III. (A complete gold cycle has occurred twice since 1968 and it is currently ¾ through a third cycle.) The vertical lines mark the trough area which completed one cycle and begins the next. Cyclical peaks have occurred approximately every 5½ years, measuring from first peak to first peak. Within all three individual cycles, there has been a significant price movement similarity, defined as phases. These recurring phases are identified on the chart as Bull Phases 1 and 2 and the Bear Phase.

Bull Phase 1 begins the cycle with a basebuilding period in which gold rises slowly from the trough and ends at the previous cyclical peak level (see horizontal lines extended from the previous peak). This phase lasts about two years. Cycle I did not have a Phase 1 due to gold's newness in the free market.

Bull Phase 2, which lasts about 1½ to 2 years, begins at the previous cyclical peak level and ends with the forming of the first gold peak. This phase has consistently experienced an average 340% rise. (In Cycle II, gold rose from $44 to $197, a 348% increase. In Cycle III, it rose from $197 to $850, a 331% increase.) Bull Phase 2 identifies the most dramatic and profitable move in the gold cycle.

In combination Bull Phases 1 and 2 take about 3½ to 4 years. These two phases identify the major bull market within each cycle. A second peak occurs within a year's time, completing the cyclical top.

The Bear Phase begins with the second gold peak which is followed by a decline to the major cyclical trough, thus ending the bear phase and individual cycle.

Gold is currently in Cycle III's bear phase, which began at the second gold peak in September 1980.

STEP 1: BULL MARKET

Step 1 begins when the velocity crosses above the zero line and moves into "positive territory." During this step, it reaches the highest level of all steps and touches or overshoots the upper boundary of the widening velocity range.

This step begins by *confirming* a major bull market. At the onset gold is just beginning its major cyclical uptrend. Step 1 parallels and identifies the major cyclical bull market and keeps you invested with the trend. Therefore, while step 1 is in force, so is the gold bull market.

Toward the end of step 1, there will be a cyclical top forming. Step 1 ends when velocity breaks down and penetrates ascending trendline A. Velocity remains in positive territory throughout this step. In cycles II and III, step 1 ended within weeks after the second price peak had formed, thus confirming the end of the bull market for that cycle.

Step 1 of the velocity cycle lasts for approximately four years. This is using an average of cycles II and III, which have proved to be more reliable and consistent in timing. Step 1 has occurred three times since 1968.

The guidelines recommendation for Step 1 is: buy, accumulate and hold gold throughout most of these four years.

STEP 2: BEAR MARKET BEGINNING

Step 2 begins when velocity breaks down and penetrates through ascending trendline A. It then moves down sharply and consolidates at a lower level. Whether this consolidation occurs above or below the zero line is irrelevant; its lower level in relation to step 1 is the definitive characteristic of this step. Step 2 ends with the beginning of another sharp break down from this second tier level. This step has been extremely consistent, lasting eight months.

The beginning of step 2 confirms that the bull market is over for that cycle and identifies the beginning of the bear phase. This is the first major sell signal and a warning sign of a major cyclical trend reversal. During this step gold moves lower; however, the end of step 2 preceeds another sharp breakdown.

In all three cycles the timing of step 2 has been remarkably uniform in lasting eight months—a model of consistency. Although velocity and price are becoming more volatile per cycle, the timing of this step has been extremely consistent. Step 2 of the velocity cycle has occurred three times since 1968.

The guideline recommendation for step 2 is: sell preferably at the beginning of this step, but throughout it as well.

STEP 3: BEAR MARKET

Step 3 begins with a sharp move down from the step 2 base area. Velocity reaches the lowest level of all steps and touches or overshoots the lower boundary of the widening velocity range. This step ends when velocity penetrates upward through descending trendline B. Velocity is in negative territory throughout this step.

Step 3 parallels the major cyclical downtrend and identifies the bear phase. While step 3 is in force, so is the gold bear market. Throughout most of step 3 gold was low and stable in cycle I, while in cycle II it was falling. The end of step 3 indicates that gold's cyclical decline is at, or near, an end. The actual "bottom price" will occur now or in step 4. Notice that in cycles II and III when velocity's lower boundary is touched for at least two to three weeks or is overshot, it represents an oversold situation and indicates that a bear market rally is likely. This recently happened in August 1981.

298

This step has consistently lasted ten months. At the end of June 1981, cycle III began step 3, right on schedule, with a sharp move down from the $450 area; in August 1981, gold rebounded in a bear market rally. However, keep in mind that step 3 is still in process; therefore, the bear market can be expected to last until about April or May 1982. Since 1968, step 3 of the velocity cycle has occurred two times with the third now in process.

The guideline recommendation for step 3 is: do not buy.

STEP 4: WARNING, PREPARE TO BUY

Step 4 begins when velocity penetrates upward through descending trendline B and ends when velocity crosses above the zero line into positive territory. This is the shortest of all four steps.

The beginning of step 4 is a warning sign of a major upward cyclical trend reversal. It indicates the coming of a major bull market. During this step, gold moves higher from its cyclical low. The end of step 4, however, confirms that the cyclical price trough has formed and the bear phase is over.

The consistency of step 4 is its short-term duration of one to four months. This step has occurred two times since 1968.

The guideline recommendation for step 4 is: prepare to buy.

In finishing the explanation of the individual steps per velocity cycle, it is noteworthy to point out that by using a combination of these steps there are other impressive consistencies.

"The Complete Bull Market" is composed of steps 4 and 1, in that order; these are warnings to buy and gold's bull market, respectively. The combined timing of these two steps has been about four years, four months and has occurred twice.

"The Complete Bear Market" is composed of steps 2 and 3; these are the first major sell signal and gold's bear market, respectively. In both velocity cycles I and II, this combination of steps has lasted one year and six months. The bear market of velocity cycle III began with step 2 on October 17, 1980. This bear market can be expected to last until about April 1982.

Timing consequences began with step 2 of cycle I, therefore, use these as a starting point to combine all four steps. Step 1 of cycle I has been the only exception since 1968. From this point to the beginning of step 2 of cycle II to step 2 of cycle III, timing was consistent, taking about six years. Step 2 of cycle III began October 17, 1980; therefore, it can be reasonably projected that October 1986 will begin step 2 of the next cycle, which will mark the end of the next major bull market.

In concluding, velocity is performing currently in step 3 of velocity cycle III which began at the end of June 1981. Gold had a sharp decline at the beginning of step 3; this occurred in late June 1981 when it fell from the $450 area to around $390. By early August 1981 velocity had overshot its lower boundary (indicating a good-sized bear market rally was likely) and it did rally from that level. As of this writing, the bear market rally is still in force with gold at $455.

Because this step lasts ten months, it can reasonably be expected the bear phase will end in approximately April or May 1982. Remember that the cyclical low can occur toward the end of step 3 or during step 4; this translates into a gold trough of March to July 1982.

Some may feel that these steps are too mechanical, that life is not that way and that the gold market is an emotionally and politically motivated market. This is true to a point, but also true is that the velocity indicator has been one of the most reliable tools; the steps are orderly and they work. They give guidelines that would be very costly to ignore.

The three main points of the individual velocity steps can be summed-up as follows:

Step	Function	Duration	Guideline Recommendation
1	Buy signal: confirms and identifies major bull market	4 years	Buy/Hold
2	First major sell signal: marks the beginning of major bear market	8 months	Sell
3	Identifies major bear market	10 months	Do not buy
4	Warns of a major upward reversal	1-4 mths.	Prepare to buy

THE 65-WEEK MOVING AVERAGE: A FINAL CONFIRMATION

For those who feel ambitious enough to follow the major trend, the 65-week moving average is a simple, yet powerful tool when used with gold. Chart 10 shows gold in U.S. dollars plotted with its 65-week moving average on a ratio scale since 1968. This moving average has proven to be the most reliable when used as a final confirmation; it identifies major cyclical reversals and confirms major bull or bear market trends. Notice that the price consistency penetrates the 65-week moving average only at major top and trough reversal areas.

Toward the beginning of the bull phase of the gold cycle, it will move above the 65-week moving average; this confirms a major upward trend reversal. Gold will then stay above the moving average, confirming a bull market until the bull phase is over. It has consistently remained above the 65-week mov-

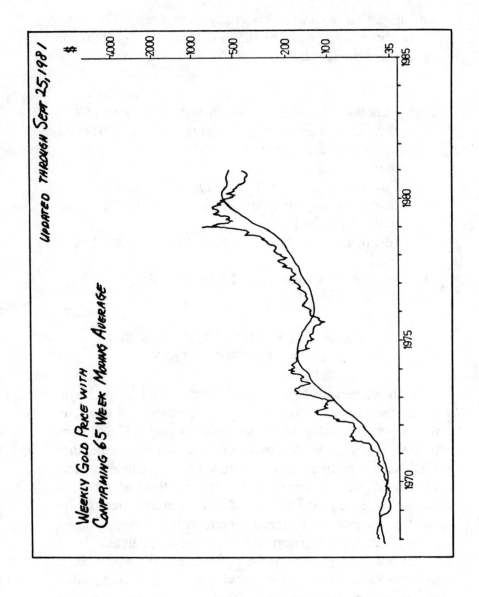

CHART 10

ing average about four years, four months in the last two cycles.

On the other hand, when gold moves below its 65-week moving average, a major downward reversal is confirmed. It will then stay below the moving average, confirming the bear market until the bear phase is over.

Gold has remained below the moving average in the past two cycles between fourteen to eighteen months. It is currently below the moving average and has been since January 1981. Therefore, in March to July 1982 it is expected that gold will cross above the moving average, thus representing a final confirmation of a new gold bull market.

In combining the moving average indicator with the velocity steps, a consistent correlation has emerged. At the cyclical top area, gold has consistently penetrated the moving average on the downside in the middle of step 2 (the "sell" step). At the cyclical trough area, gold had consistently penetrated the moving average on the upside at the beginning of step 1 (the "buy" step). Because the velocity indicator anticipates and confirms reversal areas before the moving average does, this indicator serves as a final confirmation.

The three tools discussed have been, and continue to be, extremely valuable in identifying and timing the major turns in the gold cycle. This also shows the current gold cycle position.

THE FUTURE: WHAT PRICE GOLD?

The cycles described will not continue indefinitely. Sooner or later the economic cycle will probably break out of its channel. Complete cycle destruction will more than likely happen in one of two situations, both equally catastrophic: hyperinflation, if the cycle breaks out on the upside at a

303

major cyclical peak, or depression, if there were a downside break at a major cyclical trough. The stated objective of the current administration is to reduce debt, which would possibly moderate, but not end, the cycle and reduce the danger of a hyperinflationary breakout.

In the meantime, the cycle's repeating sequence of events is expected to continue. Following a likely overall scenario for the next cyclical gold trough and peak determined by combining technical analysis and results of the three indicators. These projections should be thought of as the approximate time and price parameters for a general guideline in planning to buy and sell.

Begin the scenario knowing that the gold cycle is currently in a bear phase, below the 65-week moving average and velocity is in bear step 3. The gold timing tools indicate that the bear phase will last until approximately March to July, 1982; at that time the cycle III gold trough should begin to form. This trough is identified on chart 15, the gold projection chart. Technical analysis indicates that the price at the trough will be within the approximate range of $300 to $325. The long-term uptrend will intersect with the $300 to $325 range at the cyclical trough, based upon the projected time frame of March to July, 1982.

Once the major gold trough has been confirmed it would be time to buy. Any price attained within this trough area will prove to be immensely profitable. Confirmation of the trough will not only mark the beginning of a new gold bull market, but because gold leads, it will also indicate entering another inflationary phase in the economic cycle.

Although the next cyclical peak appears to be about five years away, its approximate timing and price levels can be estimated using the regularities in the gold cycle.

For the first two years of the bull market, gold will be in a steady but quiet uptrend. In early to mid-1984, it will probably reach a high of $850; by this time, there will be rising inflation, interest rates and oil prices. Soon after gold rises above $850, price movements will become much more dramatic until gold reaches its first peak. Gold timing tools indicate that this peak will occur between September, 1985 and September, 1986. This time period is identified on chart 11.

Figuring a 340% increase from the $850 level for the next cyclical peak, a price of about $3,750 is projected. Technical analysis indicates that gold will peak within the approximate price range of $3,750 to $4,900. The upper side of the long-term widening channel will intersect with the $3,750 to $4,900 price range, at the cyclical peak, based on the projected time frame of September 1985 to September, 1986. By October, 1986, there should be confirmation that the gold bull market is over; sell at that time. Waiting for confirmation assures

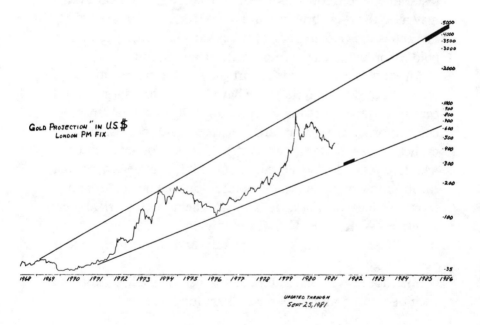

CHART 11

305

staying with the major trend; although it may not be possible to sell at the very highest price, you will be invested for the majority of the move.

Why expect the cycle to recur? Because none of the fundamentals have changed. Unless transfer payments can be slashed dramatically, the federal debt will continue to grow. Murray Weidenbaum, Reagan's chief economist, recently said, "I think you need a multiyear time horizon to see the full Reagan program work out." The chances of a major reduction in the near future is highly unlikely. Unless there are significant changes, it is safe to conclude that the debt-caused cycles in the economy will continue to be progressively more volatile.

Our perspecitive is a long-term overview. Historical momentum is so strong that as long as there is economic instability, the trend will continue to be up. Political events may alter the cycle briefly, but gold continues to be an orderly market as the velocity indicator has shown; velocity identifies gold's "order", its consistent pattern and timing.

Although much of this report may not appear optimistic, we are not "doom sayers". We have brought to your attention certain observations made of leading/lagging relationships, correlations, increasing growth rates and consistency of cyclical movements, among other things. For now and the next five years, keep an eye on gold, debt, transfer payments, the inflation rate and interest rates. Don't be misled by short-term declines or rises, rather put them in historical perspective. Watch the U.S. economy in general and follow major trends. Then make person and investment plans accordlingly.

For those investors willing to impose these disciplines on their decision-making the rewards should be generous.

CHAPTER TEN

TAX AVOIDANCE

Tax evasion is very illegal, but tax avoidance (doing everything you can to avoid paying excessive taxes) is very smart. Judge Learned Hand, the famous New York State jurist, once said: "Anyone may so arrange his affairs that his taxes shall be as low as possible. He is not bound to choose that pattern which best pays the Treasury. Everyone does it, rich and poor alike, and all do right; for nobody owes any public duty to pay more than the law demands."

And Mortimer Caplin, former director of the IRS, had this to say about the powerful organization he once headed: "There is one difference between a tax collector and a taxidermist; the taxidermist leaves the hide."

Over 150 hidden taxes are included in the price of a single loaf of bread. There are 116 indirect taxes levied on a suit of clothes and 100 such taxes are surreptitiously attached to a carton of eggs.

Federal, state, regional and municipal taxes are to blame. There are federal, state and city income taxes—both corporate and personal. We pay property taxes, excise taxes, sales taxes, inventory taxes, special district taxes, estate taxes, intangible taxes, capital gains taxes, payroll taxes, franchise taxes, gift taxes and unemployment insurance taxes. Then there is Social Security as well as license fees, fines and permits.

While it only costs ten cents to produce *one barrel* of Arabian crude oil (that's less than a quarter cent per gallon), we pay over a dollar a gallon at the pump. Most of the price increase comes from taxes.

The Arabian government oil cartel (OPEC) tacks on a stiff

307

royalty tax which accounts for the biggest chunk of the high retail prices at the pump.

When more dollars are chasing fewer goods, prices rise. Inflation is a cost which is involuntarily inflicted on the American citizenry. Inflation, like regulation, is yet another example of a devastating hidden tax.

Ultimately, the consumer foots the bill for every single tax government forces us to pay. *Everyone* is a consumer. We are *all* hurt by excessive taxes.

A wide spectrum of taxes—of just about every sort and variety imaginable—has foisted higher prices on the American consumer. The price tag on every automobile, comb and jellybean includes a long string of buried taxes and *no one* can escape paying them.

The cost of the gas you burn in your car is mostly tax. You must pay registration and license fees. You may have to pay a toll to get on a state thoroughfare. When your car isn't running, there are parking fees, parking meters, meter maids and tickets.

The government taxes the interest you earn from your savings account, the dividends you receive from stocks and the income you make from a wage, salary or capital gain. You pay taxes every time you turn on a light, pick up the phone and turn up the heater or air conditioner.

You pay taxes every time you pour yourself a drink, light up a cigarette or turn on the stove; every time you take in a play, go to a movie or go out to dinner.

A good part of the mortgage or rent is earmarked for taxes. You pay taxes when you buy a diamond, sell a diamond or keep a diamond. You pay taxes whenever you fly on an airplane, travel by train or cruise on a ship.

You pay taxes when you earn money, when you save it and when you spend it. You pay taxes if you give someone a generous gift.

They'll get you when you work, when you play, when you drive, fly or ski. They will tax your home, your investments, your clothes, your family heirlooms, your property, your working time and the things you eat.

To repeat once again, there are federal, state and city, personal and corporate income taxes. There are personal and commercial, state, county and municipal property taxes. There are assessments on people living within special districts and there are forced exactions levied by regional governmental entities. There are excise taxes on gasoline, alcohol, tobacco, motor vehicles and automobile parts.

There are sales taxes, inventory taxes, estate taxes, intangibles taxes, capital gains taxes, payroll withholding taxes, franchise taxes, gift taxes, unemployment insurance taxes, value-added taxes, social security taxes, license fees, fines, permits, tariffs, regulatory costs, inflation...

Preventing your hard-earned dollars from taking a one-way journey to Washington is worthy of your most dedicated attention. Few other endeavors will add more to your net worth. The only money you'll ever have for investing and spending is what the government lets you keep.

Why pay the IRS money you are allowed to keep? You do have a choice as to whether you pay a small or a large amount of income tax. But you must learn the rules each year and abide by them strictly. You will find them always changing, often contradictory, rarely simple, difficult to understand, and challenging to apply. Winning the money game will be very difficult unless you understand how to play and win the tax game. And this game is definitely "hard ball."

KNOW THE IRS

Be forewarned the IRS wants as many of your hard-earned dollars as they can extract. Its your job to legally protect yourself against their efforts and to arrange your financial affairs to keep taxes paid to an absolute minimum.

While the tax agency has 80,000 agents in its employ and towers above the pygmy-sized taxpayer in financial resources, information retrieval abilities, legal expertise and experience, you shouldn't lose sight of the fact that the IRS is dwarfed by the 1,000 taxpayers that exist for every IRS employee.

Only one out of every five IRS employees is an outside agent, and only a very small fraction are auditors. While it is true that the IRS could gun down any one of us if it took the notion to marshall all of its vast resources in our direction, it should be of some solace to you that the IRS is even more badly outnumbered than is the starcrossed tax payer.

The intimidating choice of psychologically terrorizing words inside the instruction manuals to IRS forms is another example of the bluff behind the Internal Revenue Service. No word is peppered throughout the manuals with greater frequency than is "must." Following close behind for a photo-finish second is "required." Then comes phrases like "does not," "shall not," "may not," and "never."

While the instructions talk about the financial drubbing you can see starting to take form, the tone is very authoritative. When reflecting on what the pallid taxpayer can do to minimize the riptide of taxes, the language takes a sudden turn and becomes ambiguous, loose and tenuous. One way to circumnavigate the biases riddled throughout IRS instructions is to read their information with these thoughts in mind:

Whenever you see the word "never," substitute in your mind the word "rarely." The word "must" is translated to mean "according to the IRS." And "may" is interpreted to mean "this is what to do to save taxes."

MONEY LOST FOREVER

The tragedy of your paying a dollar in taxes is that you not only lose that dollar, but you also lose what that dollar would earn for you if you were allowed to keep it.

Technically, the IRS never forgives a tax, but our tax laws do allow you to defer a tax until a later date. If you've chosen certain investments, perhaps you will also convert ordinary income into capital gains, taxed at a maximum of 20 percent.

You may be tempted to say, "If I'm going to pay the tax someday, why don't I just pay it now and that way I won't have to worry about it?" There are five reasons to always defer a tax:

1. *Inflation.* Every year you postpone paying a tax you not only continue to receive the earnings on that money, but when and if you ever do pay the tax, you can pay it with cheaper dollars for which you have worked fewer hours. If you have $1 of taxable income today in a 40 percent bracket, you lose 40 cents of purchasing or earning power if you pay the tax. But if you can postpone the tax for ten years, and if by some miracle the government does change its printing press mentality and inflation slows to 7.2 percent, you can pay the tax with one-half of the purchasing power that you would have to use if you paid it today.

Perhaps you can attain a better grasp of what is happening if you realize that if the printing presses double the amount of money in circulation, the value of your money is cut in half. So when you pay your 40 cents of tax in ten years, it only has the value of 20 cents.

2. *Convert to Capital Gains.* Often over this period of time you can convert ordinary income into capital gains. If you can accomplish this you can then reduce your tax liability to 8

cents of purchasing power in ten years—that is, if you quit the money and tax game at that time. You may want to begin the game all over and postpone the tax again.

3. *Time Value of Money.* Money has tremendous earning power, so strive to keep it working for you. For example, let's assume you can postpone paying $10 of tax for five years and that you can invest it at 10 percent (and surely we can do better than that). Your results would be as follows:

	Before 50% Tax	*After 50% Tax*
After Year 1 $10 =	$11.00	$10.50
After Year 2 10 =	12.10	11.03
After Year 3 10 =	13.31	11.58
After Year 4 10 =	14.64	12.16
After Year 5 10 =	16.11	12.77
Pay Tax 10 =	6.11	2.77

4. *Declining Tax Rates through 1984.* Not only would you be able to continue to receive return on your money but the tax rate is scheduled to decline through 1984.

5. *Stepped-up Basis.* If your goal is to build an estate for your heirs, on death there is a step up in your basis and there is a strong possibility that the tax can be completely avoided and it will be a whole new game for your heirs.

So, never pay until it is absolutely necessary. Put your tax dollars to work as long as you can. At only 7 percent return, in ten years each dollar can gain another 97 cents for you, which would still have a purchasing power of 47 cents even after the erosion of a 7 percent inflation rate.

Once you pay the IRS, that money is lost forever.

312

TAXABLE INCOME

Taxable income is the portion that you have left after you've made all your permissible deductions.

Before the passage of the Economic Recovery Tax Act of 1981 (ERTA) there were two classifications of income: personal service and passive income, which could be further dissected into tax-free, tax-deferred and tax-sheltered income. Passive income was taxed as high as 70 percent. Under the new act, this has been reduced to a maximum of 50 percent. Since the distinction between earned and unearned income has been changed for taxation purposes, we won't need to discuss them, so let's look at tax-free, tax-deferred, and tax-sheltered income.

TAX-FREE INCOME

You can receive tax-free income from municipal bonds, municipal bond funds, and municipal bond trusts. I cover these in another chapter and you should study the tax-equivalent tables. For example, a 10 percent municipal bond equates to a 20 percent pre-tax yield in a 50 percent tax bracket. (Most tax-favored investments that I consider viable produce greater than an after-tax rate of return of 10 percent.)

I'll have to admit, I never buy municipals, even though we make them available to clients who want them, for in my opinion, there is no such thing as tax-free income. The spread between the interest I could receive on a municipal bond and the return I could receive on other investments, I believe is my tax. I would have just paid my tax in advance.

In these inflationary times, the economic viability of having to earn $20,000 in a 50 percent tax bracket in order to have $10,000 left to invest in a municipal bond—which in ten years at only 7 percent inflation would have a purchasing power of $5,000—does not seem to be a promising way to increase true net worth. Do note also what I have to say about the possibility of losing interest deductions if a certain percentage of your portfolio is composed of municipals.

TAX-DEFERRED INCOME

Insurance companies have introduced the single premium tax-deferred annuity. In this type of investment an insurance company guarantees your principal plus a minimum interest rate, and your tax on the interest is deferred until you withdraw the principal. You may withdraw your original investment without tax because after-tax dollars were placed there, so the tax has already been paid. (There may be a penalty imposed by the insurance company on the interest portion for early withdrawal.)

The chief advantage of tax-deferred annuities is that your interest is compounding tax-deferred. Because there is no immediate loss to taxes, you are compounding dollars that would not have been in your account had they been siphoned off by taxes. Again, the tragedy of taxes is not only that you lose the dollars, but you lose the dollars the dollars would earn if they were still in your possession. Also, you have more control over when you can withdraw these funds and pay the tax.

Tax-deferred income is also available through the tax-managed trust funds. These funds usually are invested in high-yield securities that allow income to compound tax-free inside the fund.

In a tax-managed fund dividends and capital gains are not paid to you, but are allowed to compound automatically. When you redeem your shares, they are taxed as long-term

314

capital gains if you have held them for a year. These shares can also fluctuate in value.

Most mutual funds elect to be taxed under the special provisions offered to regulated investment companies. As a result, most funds do not pay corporate taxes on dividends or interest as long as they pass along at least 90 percent of income to their shareholders. In turn, the shareholders pay taxes at their individual rates. Tax-managed funds are operated differently. They have elected corporate tax status and do not plan to distribute realized income and capital gains to shareholders. Since income is not distributed, there is no tax to the shareholders. The funds pay taxes on only 15 percent of dividend income less operating expenses. This is possible because tax law excludes from taxation 85 percent of preferred and common stock dividends paid from one U.S. corporation to another.

You may find that tax-managed funds offer other features that meet your needs. If a regular cash flow is desired, most funds allow for a monthly or quarterly check through a systematic withdrawal plan. Some funds allow for telephone redemptions, which improve liquidity. Social Security (Tax I.D.) numbers are not requested by most funds and no forms are sent to the Internal Revenue Service, because annual income tax reports for the shareholders are not necessary. However, you are responsible for reporting capital gains once shares are redeemed.

TAX-SHELTERED INCOME

You can receive tax-sheltered income from various limited partnership investments and certain individual investments. This type of income, though probably incidental to the reason you made the investment, will most likely become your favorite type of income. The tax is deferred, but you'll remember how important it is to defer a tax and how you can often convert at least a portion of your return into long-term capital gains with the more favorable tax rate.

INVESTING BEFORE BEING TAXED

It's essential to your financial planning that you wisely invest your before-tax dollars.

Tax-favored investments all contain some degree of real risk. You could lose your entire investment. However, you most certainly will lose the entire sum you send to the IRS.

The risks are there. This is the very reason that Congress has provided the tax incentives. They want to encourage you to invest in high-risk areas that provide for the social good of our country.

There are pitfalls in tax-sheltered investments. These consist of economic risks—such as dry holes, cattle deaths, fluctuating markets, unsuccessful research and development projects, lack of sales, and poor management. There is also the risk of being a passive investor. As a limited partner, you cannot participate in the management without losing your limited liability status. This is why it is so important to evaluate management carefully. Because of the risks involved, you should never invest more than you think you are emotionally prepared to lose. You should always analyze the economics of the investment carefully and you should not be tempted by a tax overkill at the price of eventual returns.

DEDUCTIBILITY

Let's look at deductiblility as it applies to a person in the 50 percent tax bracket:

316

A. *0 Percent Deductible.* All of the investment was made with your money; none of it was IRS's. A good example of this would be a municipal bond or a stock investment.

B. *50 Percent Deductible.* If it's 50 percent deductible, 75 percent is your money, and 25 percent is the IRS's. Good examples of this would be agriculture, marine containers, and certain leasing programs.

C. *100 Percent Deductible.* If its 100 percent deductible, 50 percent is your money, and 50 percent is the IRS's. Good examples of this would be programs of oil and gas drilling, cattle feeding, certain real estate, horse breeding, etc.

D. *200 Percent Deductible.* In this instance, none of it is your money; all of it is the IRS's. Cable television, mining, research and development, and certain two-tiered real estate programs would be good examples.

E. *Over 200 Percent.* In this investment not only have you not used your money, but you've actually been paid not to do so. Certain mining, video, energy management, medical-related franchises, research and development using recourse financing, and two-tiered real estate investments.

PROGRESSIVE INCOME TAX RATES

Taxes begin at the 12% level on your first dollar of taxable income, over and above the "no tax" bracket. The current "no tax" bracket is $2,300 for a single person and $3,400 for married people who file jointly.

You reach the 50 percent rate at $55,300 in 1983, and $81,800 thereafter if you are single, and $109,400 in 1983,

317

and $162,400 thereafter if you are married and filing a joint return.

We all have some hard dollars and some soft dollars. However, most of the tax-favored investments discussed in this chapter require that some portion of your income be in the 44-50 percent bracket and that you have varying amounts of net worth for investment to be "suitable" in the eyes of the regulatory agencies. I know that if you are in, say, the 40 percent bracket, you don't like paying taxes any more than the person in the 50 percent bracket, but your financial planner's hands will usually be tied by the regulatory agencies, and he'll have to abide by the suitability requirements. But do read on and take hope. We do have some tax-favored investments for the 33 percent bracket investors, and more and more are being added all the time. Qualifications on some are as low as $30,000 of income and $30,000 net worth. With inflation and the tax-bracket creep, you may cross the magic 50 percent mark before you realize it.

DEDUCTIONS AND HOW THEY WORK

Most of the people for whom we do tax planning do not understand why or how deductions (write-offs) are allowed against taxable income or against their tax liability. Since this may be true of you also, let's look at some of the characteristics of deductions. These cannot be treated comprehensively in just one chapter, so you'll need to do some in-depth study on your own. I especially recommend that you obtain and read booklets on the Economic Recovery Act of 1981 from your C.P.A., a reputable C.P.A. firm, Prentice-Hall, the Research Institute, or the Commerce Clearing House.

First of all, you need to understand how limited partnerships and, in some respects, subchapter S corporations are treated for tax purposes. The limited partnership investors are treated as individuals, so that all of the tax deductions flow through to the limited partners. The most common sources of these deductions are investment tax credit, depreciation, interest deductions, depletion, royalty and lease payments, and losses due to various causes.

INVESTMENT TAX CREDIT (ITC)

The investment tax credit is a credit against your tax liabilities that is allowed on qualified investments on certain depreciable tangible personal property used in a trade or business or for the production of income in the first year the taxpayer places the property in service. In a 50 percent tax bracket, ITC has twice the value of a write-off. In lower brackets it may be worth three times a write-off. A tax deduction is applied against your gross income and lowers taxable income. An investment tax credit is a credit against the tax itself, so you are allowed to subtract it after you come up with the amount of tax due on your taxable income.

The Economic Recovery Tax Act of 1981 liberalized incentives to encourage investment in both new and used property (with limitations) by establishing new investment credit rules. The new rules apply to property placed in service after 1980.

A 6 percent credit applies to qualified property in the three-year depreciation class; and 10 percent applies to all other qualified property. If you cannot use the credit this year because of lack of taxable income, you may carry it back three years and carry it forward for fifteen years for credits arising in taxable years ending after 1973.

You should become familiar with the various at-risk limitations and recapture provisions.

Energy conservation properties are eligible for an additional 10 percent energy tax credit. Certain expenditures may qualify for both the regular investment tax credit and the energy investment credit if they meet the qualifications for both.

If you dispose of property on which you have taken ITC prior to the close of the recapture periods (generally the first full year after the property is placed in service and the succeeding four years, except for three-year property in which the period is reduced by two years), your tax liability will be increased. (Look at the act, for it states exactly what your liability will be.)

QUALIFIED REHABILITATION EXPENDITURES

A new investment credit for qualified rehabilitation expenditures of certain buildings and certified historic structures was added by ERTA. The exact percentages are clearly defined in the act.

RESEARCH AND EXPERIMENTATIONS

A new credit for research expenditures made after June 30, 1981, and prior to January 1, 1986, was made available by the act. Special rules and percentages are presented in detail. Generally, any unusued portion of the credit may be carried back three years and forward fifteen years.

CHAPTER ELEVEN

FINANCIAL PLANNING

In this chapter we will discuss many aspects of personal financial planning. Hopefully, you will gain insights into what you can do to adjust your money affairs in the most advantageous manner.

CHOOSING YOUR BANKER

Take the time and effort to carefully choose the bank you will deal with. And remember, a bank is only as good as the people who work there. A close friendly relationship with your banker can be a major asset. You want someone who is friendly, cooperative and whose institution can provide you as many services as possible, including sufficient assets to finance any reasonable project you undertake.

NOW ACCOUNTS

Negotiated order of withdrawals (NOW) accounts are much like a regular checking account, available from both savings and loans and banks. What makes a NOW account different and seem better than a traditional checking account is the 5¼ percent interest it pays on the balance in your account.

Although NOW accounts may seem attractive compared with checking accounts that earn no interest, you must consider what they are costing you in terms of opportunity to earn a higher return if you placed the dollars required for your minimum balance in some other investment that may yield a far higher rate of return. Also, the service charges for such accounts (if you don't maintain a minimum balance) may be higher than the rather small amount of interest you will earn.

CERTIFICATES OF DEPOSIT

A certificate of deposit (CD) is a deposit account that is usually opened in a minimum amount of $1,000-$5,000 and has a fixed rate of interest that will be paid if the certificate is held until maturity. Certificates of deposit are issued by both savings and loan associations and backs, and the maturities range from fourteen days to any number of years.

While short term CD's may be a place to store cash, I'm skeptical of stashing cash there for the long term. I believe other vehicles offer a much better ROR (return on investment.)

FEDERAL GOVERNMENT OBLIGATIONS

The federal government offers investors numerous possibilities, including savings bonds, Treasury bills, Treasury notes, Treasury bonds, and various federal agency obligations. All of these (with the exception of some federal agency obligations) are guaranteed by the federal government.

Series EE bonds. The government obligation with which you are probably most familiar with is the Series EE bonds. The bonds are issued on a discount basis, which means you pay less than their face value, and their value gradually increases. The difference between what you paid for and what you receive at maturity or redemption is your interest. If you hold the bonds until maturity, which is five years, you will have earned 9 percent a year compounded semiannually. Taxes on the interest are deferred until you cash them in. The interest is usually exempt from state and local income taxes. You have to hold bonds for six months before you are permitted to redeem them. If you redeem them before five years, you will earn less than 9 percent. If you own some Series EE bonds at present and plan to hold some of them, it will be to your advantage to redeem the ones you bought most recently.

Tax deferral does have value, even though the return is meager when you compare it with other fixed-dollar alternatives.

Tax-free savings for children are also made possible by buying the Series EE bonds in the child's name to build a fund for, say, college costs. (Not that I recommend them as a good way to build funds for college. Never try to make a fixed dollar accomplish a variable-dollar job.) File a return the first year establishing the interest as the child's income. If the amount is small, no tax will be due. Also, no state or local taxes are due on government bond interest.

T-Bills. Treasury bills have either three or six-month maturities. The minimum denomination is $10,000, with $5,000 increments thereafter. Bills are issued in original maturities of thirteen, twenty-six, and fifty-two weeks. The first two are auctioned weekly (on Mondays unless that is a holiday, in which case the preceding Friday is used), while the year bill is auctioned every twenty-eight days. A simple way to purchase them, for a small fee, is through a stockbroker or bank.

Treasury bills are issued weekly on a discount basis, under competitive bidding, with the face amount payable at maturity. The investment return on bills is the difference between the cost and the face amount. Bills may be sold prior to maturity at a competitive market rate, which can result in a yield greater or less than the original acquisition rate. The yield on bills, like other short-term money market instruments, can fluctuate greatly.

Treasury Notes. Notes have a fixed maturity from two to ten years and bear interest payable semiannually at fixed rates. They are available in minimum amounts of $1,000 for longer maturities and $5,000 for shorter maturities. Selected notes are auctioned competitively through the Federal Reserve System on a periodic basis. Buyers can subscribe through a commercial bank or a broker. Yields on notes are determined by the acquisition price. These notes may be sold prior to maturity at the current market rate and may result in a yield greater or less than the original acquisition rate at a long- or short-term capital gain or loss. Yields on Treasury notes generally are lower than their corporate counterparts because of the excellent marketability and credit rating of government securities.

Series HH Bonds. Series HH bonds produce current income, and interest checks are sent every six months. If you were buying this type of bond, you would pay the face amount in denominations of $500, $1,000, $5,000, and $10,000 and they would yield 9 percent if held until maturity.

If you own Series E or EE bonds, you may exchange them for HH bonds and continue your tax deferment on the interest that has been accumulating. You'll owe taxes on the HH bond interest that is paid currently, but the tax on your increase in the original value won't be payable until you cash in the HH bonds.

Treasury Bonds. Treasury bonds have a fixed maturity of over ten years and are the longer counterpart of Treasury notes. Yields on Treasury bonds, because they are of longer maturity, are sometimes higher than on Treasury notes, if we assume a "normal," positively sloped yield curve.

MUNICIPAL BONDS

Municipal bonds are issued by local governments (states, cities, various districts, and political subdivisions). Usually, municipal bonds have lower yields than government bonds because of one special feature: the interest paid on these municipal obligations is exempt from federal income tax and usually from state income tax if the owner of the bond is a taxpayer in the state that issued the bond.

Yields on municipal issues are determined by the current level of interest rates, the credit rating of the issuer, and the tax laws.

Most municipal bonds are issued in the serial form, some maturing each year for several years, with maturities as high as thirty years. Interest is normally paid semiannually. Investors tend to buy them as they are issued and hold them until maturity. However, municipals, like other bonds, can be sold prior to maturity in the secondary market at the prevailing market rates.

There has been talk from time to time about Congress eliminating the tax-exempt privilege inherent in municipal bonds. If such a change should be legislated, it should not affect those bonds issued prior to the legislation, and their scarcity could easily enhance their value. Before the onerous Tax Reform Act of 1976, we always assumed that the government would not change the rules after the game had been played. Now retroactive legislation has become a reality and a future threat. However, federal taxation of state and municipal bonds does require an amendment to the Constitution ratified by two-thirds of the states. Heavily indebted states are not likely to look favorably on such an amendment.

Another important feature of municipal bonds has been their relative stability. Next to U.S. government bonds, municipal bonds have been the "safest" of all securities. The

New York City and Cleveland fiscal debacles placed a cloud on bonds of cities that do not practice prudent financial policies. Puerto Rican bonds also have received lower ratings in recent years.

TYPES OF MUNICIPAL BONDS

There are three main types of municipal bonds.

Full faith and credit bonds of a state or political sub-division of the state have the full taxing power of the issuing local government available to pay both the principal and the interst.

Special Tax bonds have a designated tax (gasoline, liquor, cigarettes) specifically pledged to pay the interest and princi-pal.

Revenue bonds are backed by the earnings in a particular facility and do not have the taxing power of a local govern-ment upon which to draw. Many of those bonds are of a very high quality and are often rated equal to or higher than some bonds backed by taxes.

A limited number of hybrid bonds are also paid from both taxes and revenues. As well, industrial revenue bonds have appeared in recent years. These bonds generally are secured by a corporation that has entered into a lease agreement with a community. The bond issuer is normally a public authority that issues the bonds under its municipal title but receives an-nual installments sufficient to pay the principal and interest on the bonds from the corporation that is using the facility.

CORPORATE BONDS

Since inflation transfers wealth from the money lender to the borrower, Corporate bonds are not on my recommended list as either conservative or aggressive investment vehicles

Bonds give us one of the clearest examples of how inflation creates and destroys wealth. Let's take the example of a AAA-rated American Telephone and Telegraph (AT&T) bond issued in 1946 at par ($1,000) with a rate of 2-5/8 percent, maturing in 1986. True to its promise, AT&T has never missed paying $26.25 annually on this bond and in 1986 it will faithfully pay the owner $1,000. However, if the widow needs her funds today, its market price is only $740.

What happened? Why did the AT&T bonds that were recommended as "prudent" investments by banks and trust companies turn out so dismally? AT&T was not trying to take advantage of anyone. It didn't force investors to buy 2-5/8 percent bonds. The corporation itself didn't realize what a bonanza it would reap. The real reason that the widows were hurt and AT&T was helped was that inflation greatly accelerated, bringing disastrous results to the bondholder.

Inflation transfers wealth from the lender to the borrower. The bondholder is hurt in three ways. He receives less in terms of interest than he could on newly issued securities. Also, when the market value of the bond falls, he suffers a decline in wealth. And when he receives back his principal, his purchasing power is less.

Under the Poor Richard rules of yesteryear, bonds were investment vehicles that you put at the bottom of your safe-deposit box; you clipped their coupons semiannually, and you redeemed them on redemption date. Although not exciting, bonds were fine when prices were stable.

History shows that bonds have been a bad buy even if your investment horizons are relatively short. Periods when inflation has accelerated have lasted longer than periods in which inflation rates have decelerated.

ANNUITIES

Insurance salesmen have been busy pushing Annuities for some time. Is this a good way to save for your future? Should you invest in an Annuity and hope for a secure financial future?

The best answer to this question can be found by looking at the past advertisements of insurance companies trying to entice you to buy an annuity. Go to your local library and request back issues of *Life* magazine. You might start with the February 1, 1943, issue. There you will find a half-page ad with a bold headline that reads, "$150 a Month as Long as You Live." The familiar logo at the bottom reads, "_____ Mutual Retirement Income Plan Guarantees Your Future." The fine print does not say how much you would need to invest to retire at 60 with $150 per month, but it does hint that the smiling couple in the picture began at age 40, twenty years previous to the time it showed them in happy retirement. Now ask the librarian for the January 16, 1950, issue of *Life*. It also carried an ad by the same company headlined, "How We Retired with $200 a Month." The ad shows another mature, well-dressed couple. There is a sandy beach with waving palm trees in the background. This one also does not mention the amount of investment that they would have had to make over that period of time. The same logo appears, however: "_____ Mutual Retirement Income Plan Guarantees Your Future."

Now ask for the January 1, 1951, issue of *Life*. It carried a picture identical to the January 16, 1950, ad and the same copy, except the headline had been changed to, "How We Retired with $250 a Month." Yes, it had the same guarantee at the bottom. The January 23, 1956, *Life* ran another ad by the same insurance company. This headline read, ,,How a Man of 35 Can Retire at 55 with $300 a Month." This time

328

they did not even bother to change the picture of the smiling, delighted couple. The inflation train continues to run faster and faster, but the ad department seems to be able to keep up by increasing the ante each time.

"Retire on $150 a Month" sounded pretty god, so this dollar figure was commonly used in offering fixed-dollar retirement plans. But the story kept changing. The changes in these figures provide evidence that there is no such thing as a "guaranteed, riskless" way to achieve financial independence.

Have you ever wondered why the annuity ads often show a man fishing? Maybe its because he needs something to eat!

Try to imagine what such an ad would be like today. What if someone today guaranteed that you would receive $1,500 a month when you retired twenty-five years from now? Do you really think that amount is going to be enough a quarter century from now? Will it be enough during the twenty to thirty years after you retire? Come on; do you really think that sum will put you on easy street?

SINGLE-PREMIUM DEFERRED ANNUITIES

Single-premium deferred annuities are a different breed entirely from the old annuity contracts, and they can play a part in your "guaranteed" dollar investment program. Income is accrued to your account tax-deferred. For example, if you invest $10,000 in a single-premium deferred annuity that is earning 10 percent, at the end of a year your account will be $11,000. Until you withdraw the $1,000, no tax is due, and it compounds tax-sheltered.

If you want some of your funds guaranteed and do not want the income from these funds to be taxed currently, you may want to consider a single-premium deferred annuity. It offers:

1. Guaranteed principal.

2. Interest guarantees.

3. Tax deferral.

4. Special tax treatment at retirement if annuitized. (I do not recommend annuitizing.)

5. Tax-free exchange from one custodian to another.

6. No tax is payable until the withdrawals equal the full original investment.

7. Probate, with its publicity, delays, and costs, is avoided, with proceeds being paid to the beneficiary.

MONEY MARKET MUTUAL FUNDS

We've looked at the various ways in which you can lend your money and found that although many of them carry some guarantees and can offer stability, many of them offer guaranteed losses because they have a low rate of return after taxes and inflation, or because money market conditions would force you to take a loss if you sold before maturity.

Where should you put funds that you need for cash reserves or while waiting for the right investment? In my opinion, the best place is in money market mutual funds.

I've previously described them, but for a brief review, these are mutual funds that invest only in large-denomination short-term money market instruments issued by the Treasury, government agencies, banks, and corporations. The first money market fund was started in 1972. There are now 111 funds with approximately $200 billion of assets.

For years many Americans had no choice but to accept the small return on savings accounts because of a law known as Regulation Q. The only competition for the saver's funds was in the number of teflon skillets and fuzzy-wuzzy blankets offered for new accounts.

The money market funds have come to the rescue of the small saver who does not have enough money to buy a $10,000 Treasury bill or a $100,000 certificate of deposit, which carry market interest rates.

The money market funds offer four major advantages: higher return, instant liquidity, more safety (in the opinion of many), and more privacy.

How do you open a money market mutual fund account? You can go to your financial planner or stockbroker or call one of the 800 numbers given in the ads on the financial pages of your daily newspaper and ask for a prospectus and application blank. Some will accept as little as $1,000, and all as little as $5,000. There is no charge for depositing or taking out funds, the interest compounds daily, you receive approximately the rate of a million dollar certificate of deposit, you can write a check for $500 or more, and even draw interest until your check is processed.

In my opinion, all of these characteristics make the conventional savings accounts and regular certificates of deposit obsolete.

LIFE INSURANCE

Your life insurance policy should be designed to fit your needs at this particular time and under today's conditions. Since your needs will change, you should review your policy on a regular basis. A good insurance program need not be expensive, and being over-insured is not good for astute personal financial planning.

WHAT KIND OF INSURANCE?

We feel that the best insurance overall is low-price term insurance. Term life insurance is pure insurance and does not try to mix insurance with investments as other forms of insurance, especially whole life attempts to do. Don't ever confuse investing with insuring. Cash value life insurance makes a darn poor savings vehicle. The small pittance in cash value that your policy will yield (and usually only after you drop the policy, and therefore surrender your benefits, is almost always far less than any other type of investment, including the most ordinary money market fund.

Remember, insurance is for dying, investments are for the living. A decent term insurance policy will give most people adequate protection at the absolute lowest price. That makes good sense.

SHOULD YOU REPLACE YOUR POLICY?

As more and more folks become aware of what a poor investment cash-value life insurance is, they are anxious to replace their present life insurance policies and find more productive ways to put their dollars to work. In an attempt to slow this tide of change, some companies have waged very successful campaigns to get regulations passed to require that agents complete and submit lengthy, detailed, and often difficult replacement forms if they recommend the replacement of any policy, regardless of which mortality table was used.

Replacement forms in some states have become so tedious and time-consuming that many a conscientious financial planner has left his client's present insurance program alone, even when it was grossly inadequate and unnecessarily expensive, rather than spend the many hours required to complete these forms.

Some insurance companies, when they receive a notice that one of their cash surrender value policies is going to be replaced, send a dire warning letter and pamphlet to the policyholder, warning him of the serious mistake that he is about to make. Many of the large insurance companies have marshaled their forces to try to put an end to replacement of their policies. Nevertheless, in most cases, replacement is probably a better idea.

WHEN SHOULD YOU NOT REPLACE?

Are there circumstances when you should not replace one or more of your insurance policies? Yes, and here are some of the reasons:

1. You are uninsurable.

2. You cannot lower your cost per thousand by obtaining a new policy.

3. Any of the nonforfeiture provisions of your present policies are important to your current financial planning. These provisions may include paid-up additions and extended-term provisions. Extended term provides that if you quit paying premiums, the company uses the cash surrender values in the policies to extend the period of your coverage. For example, let's say that your cash value was enough to buy you term coverage for ten years. You chose this option and died in the eleventh year. Your family would receive nothing. If you died in the second year, they would receive only the extended term amount and the insurance company would keep the nine years of prepaid insurance premiums. There may be income options and annuity options in your present policies that you should examine carefully. Determine if your financial planner can provide you with better alternatives.

4. You are planning to give false information on your new insurance application. There is a two-year contestability period that could result in your heirs receiving only the amount of coverage those premiums would have purchased had you given accurate information.

5. You bought your policies from a friend, and you feel that you would lose him as a friend if you replace them, and a friendship based on his economic benefit is more important to you than the economic future of your family.

6. You cannot withstand the pressure that may be brought to bear on you by your present insurance company or its agent if you attempt to replace. Did Uncle Charlie sell you the policy?

YOUR RETIREMENT

I believe you owe it to yourself, your loved ones and to society to do everything possible to retire with dignity when your working days are through. Here we will explore the pros and cons of different kinds of retirement planning.

CORPORATE RETIREMENT PLANS

If you are incorporated or work for a corporation, one of the best tax-sheltered ways to prepare for your financial needs at retirement is through either a profit-sharing plan or a pension plan, or a combination of the two. This allows you to put before-tax dollars into the plan and then compound them tax-sheltered. If you are the chief operating officer of a corporation, you will find it most advantageous to have a comprehensive study made by a specialist in the field. He can do a study to determine which type of plan is most advantageous to you while keeping within the IRS guidelines. If you are an employee, however, you may not be permitted to offer any input into that decision.

Technically, profit-sharing and pension plans are designed to attract and hold good employees, which they do if employees are kept adequately informed. However, let's assume you are the chief operating officer or head a closely held corporation. You probably receive higher pay than most of your employees, and the greatest advantage will usually accrue to you. An even greater advantage may accrue to you if you are older than your employees and set up a defined pension plan.

I want to try to make you pension smart. Here are a few of the options you and your planner may want to consider.

DEFINED BENEFIT PENSION PLAN

If you are much older than your employees and you pay yourself a relatively high salary compared to theirs, you may want to have a defined benefit plan. This plan can be designed by your specialist to allocate a higher percentage of the contribution to you so that under certain circumstances it is possible to shelter in the plan more than you earn. The only limitation on the dollar amount that can be set as the annual deductible contribution is the amount required to fund the allowable intended annuity when you retire, as determined by an actuary.

If you have employees, the plan cannot discriminate in your favor. Because your employees will generally be younger, however, the cost of funding the pension plan for them should be far lighter proportionally than for you, without being discriminatory.

Your corporation may set aside and deduct sufficient money to fund a straight life annuity on your retirement equal to the lesser of (1) $136,425 or (2) 100 percent of your compensation for your highest consecutive three years of plan participation.

At present there can be provisions in the trust document to permit you to borrow from your own plan under IRS guidelines. This privilege is now being discussed in Congress, so you'll need to check the status of this legislation before making a loan from your plan. If you or your employees do make such a loan, the plan must have a legal note with a definite repayment schedule, and you must also pay the going interest rate! (The cost of interest may also be deducted from your taxable income.)

DEFINED CONTRIBUTION PLAN

Another possibility for you to consider is the defined contribution participant plan with an individual account. The balance in the account determines the benefit a participant will ultimately receive. Subject to adjustments for vesting provisions, the amount contributed remains stable.

These plans include profit-sharing, money-purchase, and target benefit plans. The benefits are derived solely from the contributions made to the various individual accounts. The amount of the contribution is generally based upon a percentage of the annual compensation of each participant or upon a specified dollar amount. The benefits are increased by the earnings attributable to investment of the account and by forfeitures from other participants. The benefits are decreased by the losses attributable to investment of the account.

Profit-Sharing Plan. This plan has a contribution formula that permits the employer to allocate a percentage of its profits to the plan. The actual contribution to the plan is then determined by the employer on the basis of the available profits. If there are no profits, no contribution can be made by the employer.

Most profit-sharing plans have discretionary formulas. A profit-sharing plan may specify, however, that a stated percentage of your company's profits will be contributed to the plan each year.

Once the amount of the contribution is determined, the total contribution is then allocated to the individual account of each participant in the plan. There are a number of possible formulas for determining allocations. The simplest, and perhaps the one used most often, allocates the contribution to the participants on the basis of compensation of each participant compared to the compensation of all participants.

Forfeitures are allocated to the accounts of each of the participants on the same pro rata basis on which contributions are allocated.

The maximum amount that may be added to a participant's account in a profit-sharing plan is the lesser of 25 percent of each participant's annual compensation or $45,475 adjusted for the cost of living. Included in the annual additions that are to be within this maximum amount, are employer contributions, certain employee contributions, and forfeitures.

The amount of contribution deductible may not exceed 15 percent of total covered compensation of all participants.

Money-Purchase Pension Plan. Unlike the profit-sharing plan, the money-purchase pension plan always specifies the formula in the plan document. The formula cannot be discretionary. The contribution formula is stated as a rate or percentage of compensation.

Like the profit-sharing plan, this plan allocates the amounts contributed on a predetermined pro rata basis among the participants. Unlike the profit-sharing plan, the money-purchase plan allows all forfeitures to reduce your company's future contributions.

Generally, the amount deductible in a money-purchase plan is equal to the amount of the required contributions under the provisions of the plan. The annual amount that can be added to a participant's account is the lesser of 25 percent of the participant's compensation or $45,475 adjusted for the cost of living. Included in the annual additions that are to be within this limit are employer contributions, certain employee contributions, and forfeitures.

Target-Benefit Plan. The target-benefit plan is a combination of the defined benefit and money-purchase pension plans. It targets a particular benefit for participants but does not promise to deliver it, as the defined benefit plan does. The company's contributions can thus remain level each year, regardless of the turnover of personnel and the performance of the portfolio.

All of the retirement plans that I have discussed can be integrated with Social Security. This means that you can exclude from the plans all covered compensation up to the Social Security limit and the exclusion may be set at a lower figure. This has the effect of favoring the company's more highly paid employees.

OPTIONS WHEN YOU TERMINATE YOUR PLAN

As you approach that day when you want to "hang it up" or you want to become an employee of another corporation, for example, you have three options on termination:

1. You can take your funds in an annuity or other installment payout method that will be taxed at ordinary income. At your death, any remaining balance would escape estate taxes if it is properly set up. (This I do not recommend.)

2. You may roll over the entire amount into an Individual Retirement Account (IRA). The entire sum, unreduced by taxes, continues to accumulate tax-deferred until you begin withdrawals. At age 70½ you must start withdrawing.

3. Take the entire balance as a lump-sum distribution. This entitles you to use a special ten-year averaging.

IRA ROLLOVER

You will have only sixty days after receiving a distribution from a retirement program to decide whether to do an IRA rollover or to pay your tax to the IRS.

The rollover was originally designed to give portability to employee pension plans; that is, if you had been working for a company with a retirement program and you decided to move to another company, you could take your vested interest with you and transfer it into an IRA rollover and not be currently taxed on the distribution. The people who have used it most, however, are those who are retiring and want to postpone taxation.

When you receive your distribution, you must first subtract any contributions that you have made. These were contributed with after-tax dollars and are therefore recovered without tax. If you want to withdraw some of the remaining funds, you may do so, but you must pay the tax on these withdrawals at ordinary income rates. The remainder you can roll over without tax and have the funds compound tax-deferred until you begin your withdrawal. You must wait until you are 59½ to start your withdrawal without penalty and you must start at 70½.

You will have a large number of investment choices, but you will be required to use a custodian or trustee that is acceptable to the government. Your choices are:

1. Mutual fund custodial account.

2. Custodial account with a trust company.

3. Commercial bank or savings and loan.

4. Fixed and variable annuities provided by life insurance companies.

Of these choices, I would recommend the first and/or second ones. Let's consider the first option. If you choose a mutual fund that is a part of a family of funds that has a money market fund, you can always have the choice of being in stocks or in a cash equivalent position. You can divide your funds between their growth funds, middle-of-the-road funds, special situation funds, bond funds, and so on, and you can move from one to the other without commission and without tax.

If you choose the second option, you can use any investment that is acceptable to the trust company. This lends itself to a wide array of limited partnerships in oil and gas, real estate, individual stocks, and mutual funds. You can also direct the custodian to increase or decrease these areas as you see fit. I do not recommend the last two options listed above.

Until recently a fifth choice was an Individual Retirement Plan Bond. The Treasury Department has now stopped offering these bonds, but bonds issued prior to April 30, 1982 will still be governed by the terms under which they were issued; that means you are locked in and can't move them.

If you choose a particular custodian and later want to change to another, you may do so. This is called a "transfer of assets" from one custodian to another. This is not a taxable transaction because no "constructive receipt" has occurred. For example, if you previously rolled over your pension plan into certificates of deposit at a bank or savings and loan, you do not have to leave it there. You need only have your financial planner prepare a transfer of asset form for your signature. He can do this easily if you'll give him a copy of one of your confirmations from your present custodian, or you can take receipt of your assets once a year and redeposit them within sixty days with another custodian without tax consequences.

INDIVIDUAL RETIREMENT ACCOUNT

The Economic Recovery Tax Act of 1981 (ERTA) expanded the amount and eligibility for Individual Retirement Accounts. Under this act every person under the age of 70½ can contribute 100 percent of earned income up to $2,000, deduct that amount from his taxable income, and let the amount compound tax-deferred.

If there is an unemployed spouse, $2,250 can be contributed if no more than $2,000 is placed into any one spouse's account. If both spouses are earning, each can have a $2,000 account. This applies even if the spouses earn only $2,000. The whole amount can be placed in an IRA. If the amount earned is less, then the total amount can be contributed.

IRA can be considered an admission by the Congress that adequate Social Security may not be there when you are ready for it, or it may be in ailing health, but you'll have no complaint, because you had an opportunity to provide for your own retirement income outside of Social Security.

If you average 15 percent per annum on your money, your results will be:

Years	$2,000	$4,000
10	$ 46,699	$ 93,398
20	235,620	471,240
30	999,914	1,999,828
40	4,091,908	8,183,816

341

In addition, your contribution will be deductible. In a 33 percent tax bracket ($29,900 joint), your tax savings will be $600 if $2,000 is contributed, and $1,320 if $4,000 is contributed. If you invest this tax savings at 10 percent net after taxes, your results will be as follows:

Tax Savings

Years	$660	$1,320
10	$ 11,570	$ 23,140
20	41,582	83,164
30	119,423	238,846
40	321,322	642,644

If, for example, a working couple age thirty-five establishes an IRA with the above averages, they will have $1,999,828 plus $238,846 or $2,238,674 in their retirement program at age sixty-five. That amount should put a bit of nutritious food on tne table and, if the Love Boat is still sailing by then, provide the opportunity for a bit of enjoyable diversion.

WHEN SHOULD YOUR IRA BE INVESTED?

If you haven't made your IRA contribution for this year, do it today. Your funds should be compounding inside your IRA tax-deferred rather than be diluted by taxes outside of the plan. You are allowed to make your contribution up to the time you must file your tax return for the past year.

HOW SHOULD YOU INVEST YOUR IRA?

We recommend that our clients begin with a well-managed family of mutual funds that has in its stable an aggressive growth fund and a money market mutual fund. Although we offer clients other alternatives, we recommend this approach for three reasons:

1. An account can be opened with as little as $250 (even less in some funds) and can be added to in amounts of $50.00; all dividends and capital gains are automatically reinvested. The custodian fee is modest, usually around $6.00 per year.

2. When the account grows to $10,000, we recommend that the timing service discussed earlier be superimposed on the fund so that the timing service can move the funds as market conditions indicate from the growth fund to their money market fund, or vice versa. There would be no commission for doing this and no tax consequences since the funds are under the tax shelter umbrella of the IRA account.

3. Later, we recommend opening a trust account and using limited partnerships. These partnerships do not usually have reinvestment privileges, so the fund will be a good depository for these cash distributions. In this way, we have all the funds compounding without any funds remaining idle.

After your account has been established, you can use a wide range of acceptable investments.

KEOGH PLANS

Are you self-employed as a professional person, a proprietor, or a partner of an unincorporated business? If so, you probably work longer hours than your friend who works for a corporation, but you probably enjoy your freedom and independence. However, when you sit down at the beginning of each year to assess your financial progress and begin to make plans for the new year, you may become painfully aware that the tax bite left you with very little to invest for the golden years of retirement.

At that time, you may look with envy at your friend who vorks for a corporation with a pension or profit-sharing

343

plan, or who has incorporated his business and set up such a plan. Contributions have been made for his benefit in a retirement plan with before-tax dollars, while you, if you are in a 30 percent tax bracket, had to earn $1.41 to have $1.00 left to set aside to invest for your retirement; and if that $1.00 produced income, you also lost 29 percent of that amount to taxes.

Congressman Eugene J. Keogh considered this an inequitable arrangement, so in 1962, he succeeded in getting Congress to enact the Self-Employed Individuals Tax Retirement Act, HR-10. With the passage of this legislation and later amendments, it became possible for you, if you are self-employed, to establish a Keogh Plan for your retirement.

YOUR CONTRIBUTIONS

The plan allows you as a self-employed individual to set aside 15 percent of your earned income (after expenses and before income taxes) or $15,000, whichever is the smaller of the two. A minimum contribution (and deduction) of the lesser of 100 percent of earned income or $750 is allowed if your total adjusted gross income is $15,000 or less. These contributions are fully deductible, and all earnings accumulate over the years tax-sheltered.

If you have employees, you must also include all full-time employees who have been in your employ for three years. A full-time employee is defined as one who works for you at least 1,000 hours per year (but may drop below this number without elimination).

If you have had your self-employed status less than three years and are setting up a plan for yourself, you must also do the same for each employee who has worked for you the same period of time. Here is a rule that may help you to answer questions you may have with regard to contributions you must also make for employees: "You must do for your employees what you are doing for yourself, if all conditions are the same."

The amount you must contribute for them must be the same percentage you contribute for yourself, with certain variations.

KEOGH CALCULATIONS

As an example: if your earned income from self-employment is $100,000 for the year, if you have been in business for two years, and if you have a full-time employee who has worked for you for those two years, you must include him. If you pay him $12,000 per year, your Keogh contributions would be:

$$\$100,000 \times 15\% = \$15,000 \text{ contribution for yourself}$$
$$\$\ 12,000 \times 15\% = \underline{\$\ 1,800} \text{ contribution for your employee}$$
$$\$16,800$$

In a 50 percent bracket, Uncle Sam contributes $8,400 of the $16,800 and you contribute $8,400, making it possible for you to invest $15,000 for your benefit at a cost to you of $8,400.

If, however, you are netting $200,000 annually, and have one employee whom you pay $12,000, you may contribute $15,000 on your behalf, and only have to contribute 7½ percent of the employee's income, or $900, because your $15,000 contribution for yourself is only 7½ percent of your $200,000 income. (When the 15 percent limitation is applied, no more than $200,000 of your self-employed earned income may be taken into account.)

Your investment choices are the same as those under IRA, and in addition, one real estate limited partnership has a leveraged program especially designed for pension/profit-sharing and Keogh plans that qualifies under the new rules of ERTA. This should prove to be an excellent investment medium and well worth your study.

You have the freedom to move from one investment to another under a Keogh Plan without tax consequences. This gives you the flexibility needed for the dynamic world of change.

If you have chosen the mutual fund route, you may want to consider investing monthly as you earn. This gives you the possible benefits of dollar-cost-averaging. For example, if you are contributing $3,600 to the plan, you might invest $300 per month.

You may also consider a lump-sum investment at the beginning of the year, so that your dividends and capital gains, if any, can be compounding throughout the year. Market conditions each year will determine which approach is best.

REAL ESTATE

Before ERTA, it was difficult to effectively invest in real estate in a pension plan, especially if you had only relatively small amounts to invest and if the real estate was leveraged, because the IRS held that such investment produced "unrelated business taxable income." ERTA now exempts Keogh and corporate qualified plans from taxation on income from mortaged real estate as long as certain acquisition rules are followed. An excellent management group whose multi-family limited partnerships we have used for years now offers a limited partnership that invests in a managed portfolio of equity real estate using leverage. The group's investment objectives are:

1. Provide an inflationary hedge by employing conserva-

tive investment policies and sound management practices.

2. Provide capital gains through potential appreciation.

3. Provide quarterly cash distributions from partnership operations.

4. Build up equity through the reduction of the principal portion of permanent mortgages on partnership properties.

5. Exclude from unrelated business taxable income the entire portion of any allocations.

Because the partnership will acquire primarily developed commercial and industrial real estate, the fund should enjoy a number of potential advantages. In particular, it will avoid the risks of new construction, the difficulties of obtaining permanent financing, and the uncertainties related to initial leasing. Actual, rather than projected, operating results and engineering studies can be obtained on prospective purchases.

Most properties are expected to be purchased with existing financing in place, often at more favorable terms than are available on new construction today. Rents may be lower than on comparable newly constructed projects, so that existing properties are more likely to be competitive, both now and in the future, as rents and construction costs continue to rise.

It is expected that the partnership, under full capitalization, will own approximately thirteen to sixteen properties throughout the United States. To reduce the risk inherent in the ownership of a single property, the partnership will spread its capital over several properties in different geographical areas. Such diversification will tend to decrease the effects of any local economic fluctuations on the entire partnership.

Investment units are $1,000 with a minimum in corporate

plans of ten units or $10,000, and in Keogh Plans of five units or $5,000.

Real Estate Investment Trust. Some excellent real estate investment trusts designed especially for pension plans are also available. One that we use is managed by a team that has a long record of successful registered limited partnerships in real estate. Each share is $25.00, the minimum number of shares is 40 ($1,000), and the minimum additional investment is $100 (4 shares). The funds are invested in land sale or lease-back transactions and participating mortgage loans on improved, income-producing properties.

Miniwarehouses. Limited partnerships investing in mini-warehouses are another viable pension fund investment. They should pay a good cash flow, which can be reinvested in the mutual fund you have in your plan to keep your compounding going, and also offer the potential for land appreciation. The partnerships finance these warehouses once you've received your original investment back through cash flow. When your original funds are returned, they can be invested in another miniwarehouse partnership or another viable investment vehicle.

Wraparound Mortgages. Some limited partnerships invest in a diversified mortgage portfolio consisting primarily of wraparound mortgage loans (a form of junior loan) that are structured to provide equity build-up normally associated with equity ownership. Such loans are selected by the general partner and are placed in the limited partnership for investments by pension and profit-sharing trusts and other organizations exempt from federal income taxes.

Today's market abounds with underleveraged properties that create a demand for mortgage funds at a time when those

348

funds are in short supply.

The object of the wraparound mortgage is not only to generate a high current return but to receive a higher total return over the life of the partnership when the equity build-up is realized in later years.

In wraparound financing, the borrower is offered a new mortgage loan on an existing property (the wraparound loan); the principal amount of this new mortgage equals the balance outstanding on an existing prior mortgage loan on the property plus the amount of the new money loaned.

You may be wondering why the owner of a building would be willing to have his property wrapped in a new mortgage. There can be considerable advantages to the borrower and the lender. Let's assume the borrower is in the 50 percent tax bracket. As you know, interest payments are deductible and principal payments are not. The wraparound mortgage is also being used to fund cost overruns. Let's say that the developer of an enclosed mall shopping center obtained a forward commitment from an insurance company when interest rates were lower than they are at present. It is two years after the original commitment and the developer finds that he is able to lease his space at a substantially higher rent than originally projected. Under the ratios typically used for debt service coverage, he is able to borrow an additional $2 million. When the developer goes back to the original lenders, they will provide the additional funds, but want to increase the rate from 10.5 percent (the original commitment) to 16 percent plus participation. The registered limited partnership management we have been using was able to provide a new $14 million wraparound that gave the developer an additional $2 million to fund cost overruns. The wraparound was at a point higher than the first mortgage (11.5 percent) and so provided sufficient leverage for the partnership to achieve its overall current yield and deferred interest of 19-20 percent.

ENERGY

Another investment that I believe in is the oil and gas income limited partnerships. Again, "own the thing that owns the thing." Investments in products that everyone wants and needs and that are in short supply should be profitable to supply.

This has been a profitable investment not only in the past, but I believe it will continue to be one. There may be temporary gluts of oil on the market from time to time, but worldwide consumption is increasing and should continue to increase as the Third World countries become more industrialized.

MONEY MARKET MUTUAL FUNDS

Every pension fund should have a money market mutual fund. In periods of very high interest, it is a safe depository in which funds can compound at good rates. In periods of lower rates, the main portions of the account should be invested in other areas, but the account should be kept open for new contributions to your plan. It can be a depository for the quarterly distributions from your real estate partnerships that do not have reinvestment privileges, or for the funds from stocks you have sold when you have not yet decided what stock to replace it with or when the timing may not be favorable to be in the market at all.

The money market fund also provides liquidity for a retiring or departing employee who has vested interest in the plan.

OTHER INVESTMENTS

Be on the lookout for other "prudent" investments for your plan, whatever "prudent" may mean today. The race horse Seattle Slew is in a pension plan and all his tremendous earnings have accrued to the benefit of the plan holders and have not been taxed. Remember, however, that if you do use the more exotic investments, they may not turn out to be the bonanza Seattle Slew has been and you may have a government clerk standing in judgment against you and helping your employees sue you for your lack of "fiduciary" behavior.

CABLE TELEVISION

Cable television offers considerable potential if the program is structured properly and has top-quality management. Although cable television is a relatively new industry, it has exhibited a consistent growth profile and a remarkable record of stability, and it may offer you a unique investment opportunity. Some analysts project that cable television will be a $20 billion business by 1990.

Traditional cable systems have been in towns that do not have good television reception because of mountainous terrain or long distances from TV stations. A cable system receives TV signals by using a tall tower and distributes the signal throughout the town on a coaxial cable. Subscribers are charged a monthly fee for the service. After the cable system is built in a community, the maintenance and operating expenses are very low in relation to income. The business is generally very predictable and operates much like a utility company.

The capital required to construct or purchase a cable system is substantial, but the investor can leverage his equity investment by using an institutional lender specializing in making first-lien mortgage loans on good cable systems. The collateral on this loan is the cable system itself, and in many cases the personal guarantee of the investor is also required.

The tax shelter is created primarily by the depreciation of the system, the interest on loans, the investment tax credit earned on purchasing the system, and, in the case of a new system, actual operating losses in the first year or two.

A high-quality cable television limited partnership may offer you an investment period of two or three years with an equivalent tax write-off of 200 percent during that period, and with an additional two or three years of tax write-off with no additional investments.

In this same limited partnership, you may look forward to a cash flow starting in the second or third year and continuing throughout the life of the partnership. A total cash return of 200 percent or 250 percent may occur over an eight- to ten-year partnership, in addition to the tax advantages.

One major technological change that has improved the investment's profit potential is the use of satellites and earth receiving stations, which provide additional TV programming. This additional programming attracts more subscribers and so brings in higher monthly revenues.

Some of these programs include uncut movies without commercials, commercial-free entertainment, and sports specials. Because of these Pay-TV channels, cable is proving to be very attractive to residents of larger cities. The demand for cable television is growing in larger metropolitan areas where the housing density and family incomes are higher.

Cable television is regulated by the Federal Communications Commission, and in the past few years there has been a noticeable trend toward deregulation, as there has been in the transportation and trucking industry.

AGRICULTURE

Agriculture tax shelters include cattle feeding, cattle and other livestock breeding, crops and timber. With the exception of cattle feeding and breeding, none are widely available as *public programs.*

CATTLE FEEDING

Young "feeder cattle" are purchased with partnership *proceeds.* These cattle become collateral for resource loans to purchase more cattle and grain for the feeding period. Interest and feed costs push total first year deductions to 50% to 100%. When "finished cattle" are sold after 4 to 6 months, bank loans are repaid and the general partner's share is deducted. Any balance is ordinary income to the limited partners.

Because the holding period for cattle is 24 months, there are no capital gains. Disease and price fluctuations are major risks. Risks, however, can be partially offset, but not eliminated, with hedging and insurance.

BREEDING PROGRAMS

In addition to cattle, "breeding" refers to fur-bearing animals, other farm animals and fish or shellfish. Although the "livestock" varies, program operations are similar. An initial "herd" is purchased. First year tax losses can equal up to 50% to 90%; feed costs and depreciation are the principal deductions. Depreciation and investment tax credit is available on the initial herd but not on offspring.

Sale of offspring generates income. Except for fish and shellfish programs, most females and superior males are retained to increase herd size and quality. Capital gains are

353

available on livestock held more than 12 months (24 months for horses and cattle). Disease and price fluctuations are major risks. *Recapture* may reduce profitability.

CROPS

The list of potential crop partnerships covers virtually anything grown in an orchard, field, grove or vineyard: fruits, nuts, grains, vegetables, etc. Wine grapes, nuts and citrus are the most popular program types.

Labor costs, interest and operating expenses are deductible. By using leverage, first year tax losses may approach 50% to 90%. Crop sales generate ordinary income. Depreciation may offer partially tax sheltered cash flow. Risks depend on weather, price fluctuations and whether new or mature properties are involved. Capital gains, subject to recapture restrictions, are primary investment objectives when the land on which the crops are grown is finally sold.

HORSE BREEDING

Another tax-advantaged investment is the breeding of race horses—thoroughbreds, trotters, pacers or quarter horses for racing, and Arabian horses for their beauty.

RACE HORSES

The demand for well-bred horses was further enhanced by ERTA. Under the new tax law, the purchase of (or fractional interest in) a race horse over two years old with good breeding potential lends itself to the following tax treatment:

1. You are allowed a 25 percent depreciation write-off when you place the horse in service during the year; 38 per-

cent depreciation write-off the next year; and 37 percent the next. The rates are subject to certain short taxable year rules.

2. If you start breeding a race horse that is over two years old before the three-year depreciation period is up, you do not have to change to the five-year depreciation period.

3. The capital gains rate has been reduced to 20 percent. If horses are held for at least twenty-four months, some portion of the sales proceeds can be treated as long-term capital gains, except for sales of offspring that will produce ordinary income unless they also are held for twenty-four months and are used for either racing or breeding purposes that will again result in capital gains. Breeding horses over twelve years old when placed in service are also included in the three-year class for depreciation. The younger ones can be depreciated over five years. A two-year-old race horse can be depreciated in three years.

The first-year depreciation rate applies regardless of when you place your horse into service during the first year, be it January or December (unless you have a short tax year). Salvage value is completely eliminated from any computation of depreciation and you are allowed to depreciate them to zero.

Additional incentives are the residual income provided through the state aid programs to thoroughbred breeders. California, Florida, Louisiana, New Jersey, and New York have state-wide organized programs. It is estimated that over $8,000,000 will be available each year to breeders of horses racing in New York State.

Owning race horses was once only for the very rich and was called the "sport of kings." Today, through limited partnerships, the units can be small enough so that even if you only have a small amount to invest you can participate in the fun while enjoying some good tax shelter. (Or you can buy an individual horse and keep it on a farm where there are experts to breed, raise, and race your horse.)

You should select a partnership that is managed by a general partner with a proven record in racing, breeding, and training. The partnership should have the facilities and personnel necessary to breed and raise a foal from a weanling to a yearling or two-year-old.

Racing is a sport, but breeding is the business. Generally, the first two years of an operation are unprofitable. Profits start in the third year when the broodmares drop their foals. Well-bred mares should produce good weanlings, and good weanlings offer the possibility of financial success.

Racing is the other facet of the partnership activities. A winning filly can be worth millions on retirement as a broodmare. The same is true of a winning colt.

ARABIAN HORSES

Investing in Egyptian and Polish Arabian horses can also provide you with tax advantages and an opportunity to build real capital growth. Owning Arabian horses was once only for the very rich, but, again, through limited partnerships the units can be small enough so that even if you only have a small amount to invest and are only in the 44 percent bracket, you can participate in the fun and at the same time enjoy tax advantages.

As in the case of race horses, you should select a partnership that is managed by a general partner with a proven record in breeding and training. The partnership would have the facilities and personnel necessary to breed and raise a foal from a weanling to a yearling or two-year-old. Here, too, the business requires careful planning, diligent effort, and intelligence.

Generally, the profits start in the third year, as for race

horses. The breeding rights for a stallion can be a tidy sum. The breeding rights for Seattle Slew, a thoroughbred, currently run $200,000, and last year I attended a quarter horse sale where the lifetime breeding rights for one stallion syndication brought $30 million.

Because of the complexities of the industry, it can offer an opportunity for substantial risks as well as large rewards.

Most tax shelters are rather boring and you don't get to participate, but this one can be great fun, especially if you can visit the horse farm or go to the races with the hope of seeing your colors pass the finish line first!

EQUIPMENT LEASING

Equipment leasing is another area with which you will want to become familiar. You may want to consider becoming a direct purchaser or acquiring an indirect ownership of equipment by investing in a registered limited partnership or in a private placement.

Your potential benefits come from tax savings, cash flow and ending value. Tax benefits come through investment tax credits, depreciation of the equipment, and interest deductions on loans. Gains can come from rental payments during the term of the lease. In addition, you may receive residual values when the equipment is sold.

A registered partnership can provide you with the opportunity to pool your capital with a large number of investors. Such a partnership would be able to purchase more equipment than you would be able to acquire on your own. Of course, the number of different purchases that the partnership could make would depend on the funds available to it from the offering.

In the early years it is possible that depreciation may generate tax losses for you in excess of your tax-sheltered distributions. These may be used to offset other taxable income that could defer some tax liability into the future.

Many partnerships have little or no cash flow during the first three years, if they are highly leveraged. If little or no leverage is used, cash flow occurs earlier.

This type of investment is mainly a deferral and should allow you to move some of your income and tax problems from a year of high tax liability to one that is not as high, perhaps after retirement, or this investment may buy you time to carry out additional tax planning. It does not give you the added time-use of money. The investment tax credit, however, is not a deferral; it is a credit against your taxes, and thereby reduces the taxes you pay in the year of purchase. Equipment leasing can offer a dual advantage—tax deferral and tax elimination.

You'll want to check thoroughly the quality of the equipment, the creditworthiness of the lessee, and the possibility of sudden obsolescence. The most promising opportunities for good equipment leases will be in periods of tight and expensive money.

There are three parties to a lease transaction:

1. The *manufacturer* or seller of the equipment.

2. The *user* of the equipment.

3. The *lease company* or an *investor group* acting as the lease company.

All three parties benefit from a lease transaction: the manufacturer or seller is able to make a sale—as a cash transaction; the user puts the equipment to work in his business—sometimes at a better cost to him than available through other financing sources; and the lease company or pool of investors receives some major tax saving and a return on their money.

A registered limited partnership we have used for several years has had a consistently good performance largely because of excellent management, which is a vital part of any leasing partnership. The partnership selects the portfolio of equipment and evaluates the creditworthiness of the users (lessees). Balance is necessary for the added safety of diversification because different types of equipment have different useful lives and tax benefits. The portfolio of equipment might include corporate jets, copy equipment, race cars, oil rigs, over-the-road trailers, and the like. The lessees would usually be one of the Fortune 500 companies or companies that have comparable creditworthiness. The management is responsible for seeing that the equipment is maintained and that all the rental payments are made on time.

Computers. The numerous private placement programs available on computer equipment provide excellent income tax deferral benefits in combination with varying degrees of residual value risk of the equipment. Because of the dynamics of the new technology and ever-improving manufacturing techniques, consider those programs that minimize the amount of residual value needed to yield a good economic investment. Those that require material residual value have higher risk. You will find offerings that are structured for an individual and for limited partnerships.

ORCHARDS AND VINEYARDS

Another area to consider for your tax-sheltered investing is orchards and vineyards.

ERTA introduced some changes in cost recovery that have had a favorable effect on the tax advantages of income-producing tree and vine crops. It is now possible to completely depreciate the original cost of the trees or vines over

359

five years rather than the twenty-five to thirty years, as has been the practice in the past several decades. Likewise, irrigation systems including pumps and wells have a short cost-recovery period of five years. Since the tree or vine components represent the greatest allocation proportionate to the total value per acre, the tax advantages are substantial. This shortened cost recovery period coupled with ITC credit, which is also available for trees or vines and the irrigation systems, can offer you a 150 percent write-off of your original investment over a five-year period.

If you are a first user, you can also take ITC of 10 percent of the total value of your trees or vines or irrigation system. First user is determined by when the asset is put into service, which is represented by the year of installation for the irrigation system and the first year of commercial production for the trees or vines. For most trees and vines, this means the fourth year of production.

TIMBER

Another area to consider on an individual or partnership basis is an investment in timber. Some of its profit-potential characteristics are:

1. Low management costs

2. Continuous physical growth

3. Replenishable natural resource

4. Excellent hedge against inflation

5. Actuarial predictability

6. Favorable marketing outlook

A well-tended commercial forest can be a safe and rewarding investment that can provide you with ample cash flow and the potential for excellent capital gains. Trees grow constantly, both in height and in width. One economic benefit of timber is that when the price of timber dips temporarily, the growth in physical volume continues and before long can overcome the effect of the price decline.

It is predicted that the demand for timber will double in the next twenty-five years. By purchasing uneven-aged stands of timber, you may benefit from a harvest of mature trees every five years while benefiting from their growth; with stands of 1,000 acres or more, 100-acre parcels can be scheduled for cutting each year at annual yields of 8-12 percent.

Apart from the future impact of inflation on timber prices, the demand-supply outlook for timber is very favorable and should lead to a rise in prices. The increasing demand for timber for such conventional uses as building materials, as well as for energy needs, is putting additional pressure on the timber industry. Studies are now being made on the possibility of using "energy plantations" as a cheaper source of fuel.

Timberland offerings are usually structured with agricultural cropping activities to produce a 100 percent write-off, and this form of offering would be more attractive to you as an individual or a major owner of a corporation because of the tax write-off and the tax-free buildup of the investment. A straight timber investment without agricultural cropping activities offers a low tax write-off, usually 10 percent. This type of offering could be a viable consideration for a pension plan.

It can be a conversion shelter in that your gains will be subject to long-term capital gains taxes at a maximum rate of 20 percent. It is usually a one-time investment with no letter of credit or recourse note.

It can also be a comfortable estate builder because it will steadily grow in size and value. Pine trees, for example, grow at an annual rate of 12 percent. Anything that grows at 12 percent, as you will remember from our rule of 72, doubles in size every six years. Should you need income, a cash contract can usually be obtained in thirty days and the lumber cut within ninety days.

As you can see, investing in timberland has some interesting potential. Work with your financial planner and determine if this is an area about which you should be better informed. Carefully examine the offerings, for a strong and experienced general partner is important.

BLENDED WHISKEY

It is possible to buy the Scotch at the stage where it is already blended with both malt and grain whiskey. But it is difficult to sell except back to the blender who sold it to you!

Generally, the better investment is an aging malt whiskey.

Since scotch is a commodity not sold on a commodity exchange, there are no daily price quotations, so that a speculator must subscribe to and read British Scotch Whiskey trade magazines; or have a good whiskey broker do all the buying and selling for you.

A speculator must not sell the scotch for at least the full four year period and must have purchased a large enough batch to interest the buyer in blending companies in buying from you. Here is where the whiskey broker can give good advice.

Increases in your scotch investment are greatly dependent upon increased worldwide demand for scotch whiskey.

The possibilities for losses are huge. If too much whiskey is produced you could be forced to hold onto your scotch in storage without a buyer.

The insurance and warehousing costs must be paid by you each year.

The commission costs are very high. Reputable whiskey brokers charge a 5% to 10% commission when buying **and again** when selling, plus insurance and storage costs per gallon each year the whiskey ages.

These storage and insurance costs are not tax deductible and trading too often makes the Treasury Department require you to buy a permit as a wholesale liquor dealer.

Be cautious in choosing a broker. The whiskey brokerage field is mostly unregulated by the American government and almost everyone can call himself a whiskey broker and charge any commission for selling you whiskey warehouse warrants.

Reputable brokers will usually not buy or sell in units under $2,000.

The sale of your whiskey results in long-term capital gains for you, and England levies no tax on non-English residents.

TAX LOSSES

If you are approaching the end of the year and have losses in your stock or bond portfolio, you probably should establish the loss. You may charge off $1.00 of capital loss against $1.00 of capital gains. If you still have losses you have not used in this manner, you may charge off $2.00 loss against $1.00 of ordinary income up to a maximum of $6,000 of loss against $3,000 of ordinary income. Any excess you have may be carried forward to be used in future years.

MUNICIPAL BOND SWAPPING

If you own some municipal bonds and interest rates have risen since you made your purchase, but you still want to own municipals or corporates, you might consider swapping bonds. You must be sure that the bonds you repurchase are either from a different issuer or of a different issue date or coupon maturity.

The swap could work like this. You own bonds with a par value of $10,000, a coupon rate of 4 percent that is due in ten years, and a market value of $7,200. You sell these bonds and replace them with $10,000 par value bonds carrying a 6.5 percent coupon rate, due in twenty years at a discounted price of $7,200. Your net results would be (1) your yearly income is increased $250 per year; (2) you have established a capital loss of $2,800; and (3) you will recoup your loss in 11.2 years by the increased income of $250 per year. If you have a long-term capital gain to charge your loss against, you'll recoup it sooner. If you do not have a long-term capital gain or if your loss exceeds the gain, $6,000 of your excess can be applied against $3,000 of ordinary income. If your gain is short-term, $3,000 can be applied against $3,000 of ordinary income. If your losses are greater than this, they can be carried forward indefinitely to be applied against future gains and/or applied against $3,000 per year ordinary income.

If your capital loss is considered long-term for each dollar of loss, only one-half can be offset against ordinary income, subject to the $3,000 limitation.

ALL-SAVERS CERTIFICATES

In the government's efforts to provide more funds for housing mortgages, ERTA included the provision that for the taxable years ending September 30, 1981, there is a $1,000 ($2,000 for a joint return) lifetime exclusion from gross income for interest earned on qualified depository institution tax-exempt savings certificates. In order to qualify, the certificate must: (1) be issued between these dates by a qualified savings institution (which generally includes banks, mutual savings banks, cooperative banks, savings and loans, credit unions); (2) have a maturity of one year; (3) have a yield equal to 70 percent of the yield on fifty-two week Treasury bills, as determined a week before the certificate is issued; and (4) be available in $500 denominations. With a bit of intelligent planning, surely you can do better with your money.

PENSION AND PROFIT-SHARING PLANS

If you own or are one of the higher-paid employees of a corporation, an excellent way to shelter funds from taxes is to establish a pension or profit-sharing plan. Have a specialist design the plans that give you the greatest advantage. These are covered in detail in a later chapter.

If you own a closely held corporation and all the conditions are right, probably no other vehicle will provide you with such good shelter without the IRS questioning your deduction. If you follow all the rules, it will give you the flexibility to play the game to your maximum tax advantage. You can balance the funds between the corporation, yourself, and the pension plan.

When you establish a plan, not only are your contributions deductible to the corporation, but also all the earnings in your plan compound as tax-sheltered income. Under certain circumstances, it is possible to contribute more than 100 percent of your salary to a defined benefit pension plan. You can be the trustee of your plan and can decide how it is to be invested.

At retirement, you can roll over your IRA to postpone taxes. Funds that are not withdrawn are permitted to continue to compound tax-sheltered. Also, if death should

365

occur, inheritance taxes can be avoided if the plan is set up properly.

These plans can be funded in a variety of ways through the use of mutual funds, stocks, oil and gas income programs, wraparound mortgages, certain real estate partnerships, and so forth.

I have covered only a smattering of the more popular legal tax avoidance investments available. The reader should realize that all reasonable means to avoid taxes should be explored and all "too good to be true" tax shelters, usually are just that. Investigate before you invest. After all, paying off Uncle Sam probably won't burn you up as much as having a con artist run off with your hard-earned money.

SUMMARY

If you are in a 22 to 29 percent tax bracket, you should consider making investments that give you tax-sheltered income, such as registered limited partnerships investing in triple-net leases of commercial real estate and oil and gas income programs. If you are in the 29 to 44 percent bracket, you will also want to consider registered oil and gas income programs and add to those registered offerings of multi-family housing, office buildings, shopping centers, mini-warehouses, motels, and hotels. If you are in the 39 percent bracket, you may want to look at registered programs such as cattle feeding, marine-container leasing and movies. If you are in the 44 percent bracket and above, you will have a wide variety of both registered and private placement instruments to choose from.

THE MORALITY OF TAX AVOIDANCE

"Since man has to sustain his life by his own effort, the man who has no right to the product of his effort has no means to sustain his life. The man who produces while others dispose of his product is a slave."

Ayn Rand

DEPRECIATION

If you acquire property for use in your trade or business or for the production of income and the property does not fall within one of the enumerated Accelerated Cost Recovery System (ACRS) classes, you may deduct the entire cost of the property in the year of purchase. However, the cost of machinery, equipment, buildings, or other similar items that do fall within an ACRS class must be deducted over the period of time and in the manner specified by the code and regulations. The amount you deduct each year is called depreciation. You are allowed depreciation on the total cost, even though you may have borrowed part or all of the money to make the investment.

The most important thing you need to know about depreciation is that it is a bookkeeping entry. You do not send anyone a check, though you are permitted to deduct the amount of the allowed depreciation on your income tax return. (Actually, if you are a limited partner, the general partner sends you a K-1 stating your proportionate part of the deduction, and your C.P.A. puts this information on Schedule E of your tax return.)

Depreciation is allowed because buildings, materials, and so on have a limited useful life and must be replaced. Depreciation allows you to set up a reserve to replace the asset.

367

ERTA attempted to make socially desirable or economic investments more appealing through quicker depreciation or write-offs.

ACCELERATED COST RECOVERY SYSTEM

ERTA greatly liberalized depreciation schedules by introducing a new system of depreciation called the Accelerated Cost Recovery System (ACRS) effective January 1, 1981. In general, you are allowed to recover your costs on the basis of statutory periods of time that are shorter than the useful life of the asset, or the period for which it is used to produce income. The cost of eligible property is recovered over a three-year, five-year, ten- or fifteen-year period, depending on the classification of the property.

Any of the booklets on ERTA will give you the various depreciation schedules that are now allowed. Especially note the provisions regarding real property.

With regard to real estate, our tax laws put it on a pedestal as a favored investment because nonrecourse debt can be used without the disallowance of deductions.

INTEREST EXPENSE

If you are an investor in a limited partnership, sole proprietorship, or partnership, you may be allowed to deduct your proportionate part of the interest expenses incurred for the investment. Prepaid interest is not deductible. Interest expense occurs any time leverage is used by borrowing funds. (Your deduction for investment interest is limited to your net investment income plus $10,000 if it is not incurred in a business. This limitation may seem grossly unfair to you, as it does to me, since my father didn't set up a multimillion dollar trust from which to receive investment income, as is the case of a particular senator who pushed for this limitation. What about the hard-working entrepreneur who is still trying to make it?)

Let's think about leverage, for the use of leverage generates interest expense and larger depreciation and other deductions per dollar invested.

LEVERAGE

Deductions can usually be greatly enhanced by the use of borrowed dollars. This is referred to as leverage and is a very important tool in many tax-sheltered investments. Leverage can entitle you to tax deductions in excess of your cash contributions, but you must be "at risk" (except for real estate) meaning you must pay on the due date if the cash flow from the investment has not paid off the indebtedness or if the due date is not extended.

Your basis in your investment determines the amount of deductions that you may take and includes your equity investment, your undistributed revenues, and the proportionate part of any partnership debts for which you are personally liable.

Repayment of the debt principal creates a call on the shelter's revenue which is not deductible for federal income tax purposes; thus, as the shelter progresses, phantom income is created. These are dollars you don't see because they have gone to repaying funds that were borrowed on your behalf, but they are taxable to you. The taxable income will eventually exceed the cash flow that is available for distribution to you. Despite the high initial deductibility, the excess deductions do not create a permanent tax shelter for you, which leaves only your soft dollars at risk.

Also, you should be aware that the day of reckoning for excess deductions cannot be avoided by making a gift of the

369

property or permitting the loan to be foreclosed. This will be treated as a sale.

This is the reason you should also invest the funds you would have sent to Washington. Do not treat these as spendable, but only as assets to build your net worth and to pay a tax when it becomes due.

DEPLETION

Certain assets such as timber, oil and gas, and mineral royalties can become depleted. An oil well, for example, will not flow or pump forever. The oil reserves will become depleted. You may qualify for depletion on the basis of the amount of cost or statutory depletion; statutory depletion is generally the higher of the two.

LOSSES

Although investment and business losses are almost always deductible, there are certain limitations on the timing if they are capital losses. These limitations are covered in the section "Municipal Bond Swapping" in this chapter. The purpose of investing is rarely to obtain real losses. The tax laws are structured to give you the incentive to invest in areas of need that may show losses at the beginning but that have hopes of gains at a later date. Real losses are to be avoided whenever possible.

DEFERRAL vs. PERMANENT SHELTER

Permanent. Certain forms of tax-sheltered investments generate deductions that are "permanent" in nature. These are: investment tax credit, if the equipment is held for the required time; energy tax credit; research and development

370

credit; and rehabilitation credits.

Deferral. Such items as depreciation, interest, and certain losses defer your taxes, but as we've seen, deferral can be very important. It may permit you to shift to another year and allow you to pay with a cheaper dollar and it may also give you added time to do tax planning. Deferrals reduce your cost basis and when the property is sold, your taxable gain will be based on the difference between your sale price and your adjusted cost. If you are an investor in a partnership, the general partner will provide you with a K-1 form to be used for your tax return and from which you can calculate your cost basis.

DIVERSIFICATION

A vital requirement for any successful investment program you ever undertake should be diversification—the not-all-your-eggs-in-one-basket rule. This rule applies especially to tax-favored investments since most of them are definitely higher risks than investments without tax advantage. It is prudent to spread this risk within the investment area itself as well as among various area. For example, if you have chosen a general partner who offers a number of oil and gas exploration programs throughout the year, spread your investment throughout several of his programs. Also, spread your tax-favored investments into a wide a variety of industries as is practical.

Spreading your dollars into several offerings allows you to lower your risks and increase your potential for profit. If one tax-favored investment goes sour—and you should go into each of them with the full knowledge that this could and probably will happen sooner or later—don't spend your time crying and moaning and saying, "I'll never use another tax-advantaged investment." You'll really lose if you do that.

You're a "big kid," so act like one. You're smart enough to have earned enough money to put you in a higher tax bracket, so do as you've been doing in your business—dust yourself off, and go out and try again. If you do your homework, you'll win most of the time. You know you are going to lose if you capitulate to the IRS.

Most of the tax shelters you will be considering will be structured as limited partnerships, either registered or private placements. Under the limited partnership arrangement, the pooling of funds by a large number of investors provides more funds and thus more diversification. However, the partnership can be structured as a sole proprietorship if the amount of the investment is not too large for one investor.

The advantage of the limited partnership arrangement is that all the tax benefits and revenues flow through the partnership to the individual limited partner. This makes it possible for a person who has investable funds but little or no expertise and who wants to avoid liability beyond his investment to put to work a general partner with expertise who is willing to take liability.

REGISTERED LIMITED PARTNERSHIP

In a registered offering, the general partner has gone to considerable expense and time to register the partnership with the Securities and Exchange Commission (SEC), or perhaps if all sales are to be made within one state, only with state. Even after going to this expense, the partners must also go to each state for clearance. In some states, it may be impossible for citizens living in that state to participate in some excellent investments. Registration allows the general partner to offer the investment through a financial planner or other individuals registered with the National Association of Security Dealers, who are allowed to make public offerings to those who meet the suitability requirements. The offerings are usually quite large and may be for amounts in excess of $100 million. Each unit is usually $500 or $1,000, although some may be as high as $5,000, and the minimum amount of investment is usually from $2,500 (5 units) or $5,000 (10 units) in an individual account and $2,000 (4 units) in an Individual Retirement Account. The offerings are usually open for several months, so you should have ample time to become familiar with an offering, unless you wait until its closing date.

PRIVATE PLACEMENTS

These are limited partnerships that the general partner has not registered with the SEC. From June 10, 1974, to June 1982, these offerings were made under SEC Rule 146, which exempted from registration certain offerings made to thirty-five or fewer "suitable investors." The burden of determining suitability was placed on the general partner and the financial planner.

Be careful. As an investor you had to be rich and smart, or be rich and have a smart friend (technically called an "offeree representative"). Because the number of investors was limited to thirty-five (most states did not make you count those who invested $150,000 or more), the size of each unit was often too large for the prospective investor, or the total amount of money to be raised was so small that the whole offering would be placed within a few days and you may not have had time to study its potential in depth.

The SEC has now issued Regulation D to replace Rule 146. The number of permissible investors has been expanded and some of the restrictions removed. You will find more details of this regulation in a later chapter. I am pleased to see some relaxation of the rules in private placements. With the increased scarcity of venture capital, they may prove to be absolutely essential to the maintenance of the free enterprise system. A system that works!

In order to solve your tax problem you must have a product. This product must be a business that is "engaged in for profit" to pass the IRS nose test. Large volumes have been written on the various tax-shelter programs available in the marketplace. In this chapter I will cover a few of the ones you are most apt to encounter. The fact that I have not covered a particular shelter does not mean that the one you are offered is not a viable one. Nor does the fact I've covered it relieve you and your financial planner of the responsibility to do your "due diligence," which means try to become as informed as you can.

REAL ESTATE

Traditionally real estate has been a great tax-sheltered investment, and it is also the one most favored by our tax laws. We've already discussed in the real estate chapter the potential for investing your after-tax dollars in registered limited partnerships to produce tax-sheltered cash flow and often excess deductions to save your taxes on your other income. You may want to reread that chapter now to review the various tax advantages that investing in commercial income-producing real estate can offer. Chief among these are the fact that nonrecourse debt can be used without disallowance of deductions. Recourse means that the lending company has a mortgage on the property and must look to the property for obtaining funds rather than having a claim to your assets.

Most of the investment you'll be using for tax-shelter in real estate will be private placement.

You will only have the diversification you do in a public

offering because the placement will usually only be one apartment project, rather than the fourteen to fifteen in the public offering, or one shopping center, or one office building.

ERTA PROVISIONS

ERTA has eliminated the use of component depreciation, which was allowed under prior law. This may be a blessing in disguise since the new law eliminates litigation over depreciation methods. Be sure you avoid accelerated depreciation on commercial nonresidential properties because otherwise your gains will be taxed at ordinary income rates on sale. (If the property is held until death, there will be a stepped-up basis.) You can avoid this by using straight-line depreciation over a period of fifteen years. Straight-line depreciation will enable you to get back the depreciation as long-term capital gains with a maximum effective tax rate of 20 percent.

Be sure to read the portion of the offering memorandum that deals with the method of depreciation to determine if it meets your objectives. All depreciation on commercial property is subject to recapture at ordinary rates if ACRS is used. The amount of depreciation in excess of straight-line depreciation is subject to the recapture rules if ACRS is used for residential property. (Subsidized housing has its own set of special rules.)

SUBSIDIZED HOUSING

A disturbing factor about Section 8 housing is that costs are higher when the government is involved in housing. Average gross rents for Section 8 units are $362 a month compared to $291 for private unsubsidized units. In other words, it would appear that government involvement costs taxpayers

$71 a month per apartment unit compared to what the tenant would be able to rent the same apartment for in the private market.

If you are considering a Section 8 offering, be careful to check out the following:

1. Is the developer selling the property to the syndication at a substantial premium?

2. What depreciation schedule is being used?

3. What occupancy rate must the property have to break even? (I've seen those that would require a 98 percent occupancy rate year-round, with the renters paying on time. Unfortunately, many of those renters have no money. That's why the government is taking care of them.)

4. Check out the area. Is it declining or growing?

5. Find out what other Section 8 housing already exists.

6. What are the recapture problems on sale?

If you are a sophisticated investor with a large tax problem and have a battery of sharp advisors and a keen eye for the real estate business, you may be able to profit from a well-structured Section 8 offering designed for the elderly under Section 515 of the Department of Agriculture Farm Home Loan Bank program.

If you don't fit this description, you would probably be happier avoiding subsidized housing.

RENOVATION OF HISTORIC BUILDINGS

Although qualifying structures are less plentiful with each passing year, the Economic Recovery Act of 1981 substantially lowers the after-tax cost of rehabilitation of certain older or historic structures. The law allows a 15 percent investment credit for costs of rehabilitating commercial buildings that are thirty to forty years old, a 20 percent credit for buildings that are at least forty years old, and a 25 percent credit for rehabilitating residential or commercial structures that are certified as historic and worthy of preservation by the secretary of the Interior Department. These rules require rehabilitation to be substantial and 75 percent of the existing external walls to be retained.

The credit claimed vests over five years and is claimed in lieu of any regular investment or energy tax credit. Taxpayers claiming the rehabilitation credit must use the straight-line method of depreciation. For other than certified historic structures, the depreciable basis is reduced by the amount of the credit. You may also be entitled to other tax breaks from the city, county, and state.

OIL AND GAS

Oil and gas accumulate in pore spaces of underground rock formations. A given "reservoir," as these accumulations are called, may be small or may contain millions of barrels of oil or billions of cubic feet of natural gas.

Because of the technology required, and because of "dry holes," the search for oil and gas is expensive. Industry statistics indicate that only about one exploratory well in ten finds a new field and only one out of 40 or 50 is a significant commercial success. Because of high costs and risks, oil and gas companies are often forced to look outside for cash to finance drilling. Individual investors supply much of this drilling capital through tax shelter limited partnerships.

Oil and gas investment represent perhaps the best all-around tax shelter. It offers opportunities for high first year tax losses, partially tax sheltered cash flow and capital gains. Oil and gas is also the riskiest tax shelter because of "dry holes." However, diversifying partnership proceeds among numerous wells spreads the risk.

TYPES OF PROGRAMS

Limited partnerships that drill for oil and gas may be blind pool programs or specified property programs. Blind pools are most popular. Drilling programs are further classified according to risk. A few drill only exploratory or "wildcat wells." The majority seek to diversify risk by combining wildcats with 10% to 75% "development wells"—the wells which must be drilled over the extent of the reservoir before it can produce its maximum yield. Development drilling is considerably less risky. Roughly eight out of ten are completed as producers according to industry statistics: however, remember that a successful well may not be a profitable well. Development well sites result from someone's wildcat discovery. As you might suspect, they are expensive, limiting potential profitability of a balanced drilling partnership while lessening the risk.

These oil income partnerships are based on a simple concept. A series of limited partneships acquire existing, producing oil and gas properties for the income that they generate. The production from these wells is sold, and the income flows back to the limited partners and to the managing general partner. They offer good income potential, which is substantially tax-sheltered in the early years, and a continuing partial shelter in later years, as well as opportunity for appreciation to stay abreast of inflation; some provide first-year deductions that may be used to reduce your other taxable income.

As in real estate limited partnerships, you, the limited partner, have limited your liability to the amount of your investment. The general partner who possesses the management expertise has unlimited liability. He secures the proper producing properties and has the responsibility of operating them on a profitable basis. For doing so, the general partner usually shares from 10 to 15 percent of the costs and the revenues.

Despite the oil business's reputation for riskiness, in my opinion a well-managed oil income program has less risk than most stock investments. This is true because oil income programs are not particularly subject to short-term market fluctuations. The value of the programs depends upon the value of their reserves and the level of income that they produce. The value of the reserves usually stays abreast of inflation. The true income fund partnership does no drilling. If an opportunity exists for in-field drilling, such drilling is contracted for by the general partner on a farmout basis. This means that none of the limited partners' money is subjected to any drilling risk.

The structure of this type of partnership is similar to the diversified concept of a mutual fund, and the oil income programs acquire a variety of already producing oil and natural gas wells for the income or profit they can generate as the natural resource is produced over the economic life of the properties. The properties acquired by the general partner for these programs have generally experienced several years of production. This is desirable because after sufficient time has passed, oil reservoirs have enough production history and reservoir data to allow reasonably accurate estimates of the reserves. Such producing properties can be evaluated within an acceptable margin for error, usually in the 10 percent range. It is at that stage that oil income programs become buyers of producing properties.

If you become an investor in oil and gas income limited

partnerships, the major portion of the revenues will flow directly to you. You will receive the depletion and depreciation allowance that shelters part, and sometimes all, of your cash flow. You'll pay taxes only once on the remainder that is not sheltered. To date, we've had almost all of the cash flow sheltered.

CASH FLOW INVESTMENT OPTIONS

Some programs offer three options for the disposition of your quarterly distributions.

The first option is to reinvest all of your quarterly distributions into subsequent partnerships. This gives you the opportunity to increase your capital base if your objective is asset growth rather than current income. If your financial objective changes, you are always free to choose one of the other two options.

A second option is to receive a portion of your distributions quarterly or monthly in cash and to reinvest the balance into future partnerships. This method is designed to provide you with a way to use a portion of your income currently while maintaining your capital base. We have found that if you limit your cash withdrawal to no more than 10 to 12 percent, you should be able to maintain your capital and also experience considerable growth on your original investment.

But you might say to your financial planner, "I think my ball of twine is about to unwind, so just send me the total cash distribution." If you choose this third option, you will receive all your distributions in cash quarterly. Each distribution will contain a portion of original capital as well as income earned on the capital.

PAST PERFORMANCE

How would you have fared if you had made an investment of $10,000 in the October 1970 partnership of a typical management company and were appraising your results on December 31, 1981 (see illustration)? (I always use $10,000 in my examples because the math is easier, but you may invest as little as $2,500 on an individual or corporate purchase and as little as $2,000 in an IRA account, and in some of them add as little as $50.)

Hypothetical Investment of $10,000
in an Oil and Gas Income Program
(As of December 31, 1981)

Option I—All distributions reinvested:	
Distributions reinvested	$ 92,647
Purchase price	182,097
Option II—Accepting 12% withdrawal:	
Distributions in cash	$ 13,200
Distributions reinvested	60,812
Total distributions	74,012
Purchase price	137,931
Option III—All distributions in cash:	
Distributions in cash	$ 50,931
Purchase price	58,083

Investors generally experience a gradual increase in distributions over the first two or three years of a partnership's life. This is due primarily to the amount of time required to invest the partnership's funds in producing properties plus the need to dedicate a part of the cash flow to repay loans made by the partnership to acquire their properties if you are

381

investing in one of the leveraged programs. Since each partnership is a depleting entity, once it has reached its maximum distribution level, you see a gradual decline in your distributable cash flow over its remaining economic life. As the table illustrates, to date not only have the reserves not declined in value, but they have increased as has your cash flow (see following hypothetical illustration). This has been due to increases in the price of oil and gas sold, improved recovery techniques, and expert management of the partnerships.

Should you expect to do this well if you were to invest in an oil and gas income limited partnership today? I really don't know. I do know that the 1970 timing was exceptionally good. There is no question that they have reaped the advantage of greatly accelerated oil prices, for which they cannot claim credit. I truly hope that oil prices won't accelerate as rapidly in the future; however, it appears to me that there will still be significant price increases.

RESTORED LIQUIDITY

Restored liquidity is a difficult concept to understand. This means the amount of your original investment that has been "restored" to you—in other words, how long did it take you to get your money back? For example, if you had invested $10,000 in the program previously, your restored liquidity would be as shown in the following mentioned illustration.

	$10,000 Investment		
Year	Annual Cash Flow	Cumulative Cash Flow	Restored Liquidity
2	1921	1921	19.21%
3	1614	3535	35.35
4	1400	4935	49.35
5	3625	8560	85.6
6	3475	10,335	103.3
7	2700	14,735	147.3
8	6484	21,219	212.2
9	6484	27,703	277.0
10	6484	34,187	341.8
11	8104	42,291	422.9
12	8644	50,935	509.4

Perhaps you did not need current income, chose not to reinvest in the next program, and could not think of anything more constructive to do with your checks than to put your quarterly distributions into a passbook savings account at your bank. If you did, by the first quarter of your fourth year you would have put all of your funds back into your savings account, where it would be drawing interest; in addition, you would be receiving cash flow from your oil and gas program.

To this example we can now add two additional columns. Column I would show earnings on your cash flow from your program plus 5¼ percent interest in your savings account all compounded annually, and Column II would show restored liquidity from the program plus interest from your savings account (although I've used 5¼ percent passbook savings, I can't think of anything more obsolete today than a passbook savings account):

383

	Column I	Column II
1971	0	19.2
1972	100	36.3
1973	190	52.2
1974	274	91.2
1975	478	130.7
1976	686	164.6
1977	864	238.0
1978	1,249	315.3
1979	1,655	396.7
1980	2,082	498.5
1981	2,617	611.1

It's interesting to note that your cash in your savings account would now be $61,130 and your repurchase price for your oil program would be $58,083, for a total of $119,213. You now have the potential for two incomes from the original $10,000. Had you chosen to reinvest in future oil and gas programs instead of withdrawing the cash, your repurchase price would be $182,097, or an additional $62,884. It rarely pays to take a working dollar and make it become a loaned dollar that works for a savings institution.

Compare this restored liquidity with an investment of $10,000 in a corporate bond paying 10 percent. It would have taken you ten years to receive interest checks totalling $10,000 (to say nothing about the loss of purchasing power that has occurred to your principal owing to two-digit inflation). Always keep indelibly pressed on your mind the time use of money. Money received today is always more valuable than the same amount received in the future.

BUYING RESERVES

How does the general partner determine how much to pay for oil and gas properties? Since oil and natural gas are found in sand and rock formations, the energy cannot be extracted from beneath the earth's surface in a matter of days, months, or, for that matter, sometimes many years. Because of this natural delay, the expected revenue to be returned over time is discounted to present worth when petroleum engineers are determining the price that should be paid for an acquisition.

The first thing the engineers determine is the amount of oil or gas a reservoir will produce annually and the estimated cost of producing that reservoir. They must then determine what price they expect to receive per barrel or per Mcf, which allows them to calculate the gross revenues to be realized over the property's economic life. By subtracting the operation costs from the gross revenues, the operating profits may be determined for each year of the well's economic production.

You wouldn't invest a dollar today for a dollar to be paid back to you at some time many years later. Neither would a petroleum engineer. Consequently, after the general partner has determined his objective rate of return for the partnership, he must discount each year's revenue by that factor to a present worth figure. The total value of each year of revenue's net worth becomes the price that may be paid to achieve the target result. This is the "time-use of money" concept that we've already discussed.

Discounting is nothing more than compounding in reverse. When you learned the "Rule of 72" earlier, you learned that money that is invested and compounded at 12 percent per year will double every six years. Conversely, if we wish to see our money compound at 12 percent per year, we would pay only half today what we would expect to realize in six years. With this in mind, we would be willing to pay only 50¢ for a dollar of net revenue to be realized in six years. If a dollar of revenue would not be realized for twelve years, we would be willing to pay only 25¢ today for that future dollar of revenue. If the dollar of revenue is not to be realized for eighteen years, we would pay only 12½¢ today for that future dollar of revenue. With this formula, we would be willing to pay only 87½¢ for $3 of future revenue that would be realized, $1 in each of the sixth, twelfth, and eighteenth years.

DEPRECIATION AND DEPLETION

Depreciation in an oil and gas program is similar to that obtained in a real estate investment. The depreciation schedule allowed by the IRS.

Depletion allowances are unique to natural resources and have been allowed because the resource is being depleted; therefore, a portion is considered to be a return of capital.

As you are probably aware, percentage (statutory) depletion has been under attack by Congress constantly for several years. With the Tax Reduction Act of 1978, percentage depletion is no longer allowed for those buying already producing oil and gas properties. However, investors are allowed cost depletion.

If Congress continues to chip away further at percentage depletion allowance, then you should anticipate paying even more for gas at the pumps.

Since the oil and gas income funds now use cost depletion instead of statutory or percentage depletion, their tax-shelter benefits should not be greatly affected, particularly in the earlier years.

TAX-SHELTERED CASH FLOW

What should you anticipate in the way of cash flow if you should invest in an oil and gas program? The figures we presented when we first started recommending these programs are as follows. (We still use the same figures even though results have been far superior to our projections.)

	Cash Flow Investor	Write-offs
1st year	7—9%	Sufficient to shelter cash flow
2nd year on	10—12%	Sufficient to shelter cash flow 2nd year

If your cash flow is greater than 12 percent and you take all your distributions in cash, a portion of your cash flow probably represents a return of your own capital, and you may be gradually liquidating your holdings in oil and gas.

The goal of any investment program is to obtain cash flow, tax-sheltered with appreciation potential. To date, tax-sheltered cash flow has been a delight to many owners of previous income programs. They must realize, though, that the IRS never truly forgives a tax. The limited partners are reducing their tax basis and will have a capital gains tax on selling if the sales price is above the cost basis that is left. My philosophy is to take the tax-sheltered cash flow now. In the meantime, you'll have the time-use of your money, and we will surely be able to think of a way to avoid paying the tax later, or at least reduce it when and if that time should come.

INVESTMENT UNITS

Most states require a minimum investment of $2,500 ($2,000 for IRA accounts). New partnerships are available for investment monthly, quarterly, or yearly, depending on the programs selected. Some states require that the minimum be invested in each new partnership one wishes to invest in, while other states let you add as little as $50 into new partnerships as you go along, once you've met the original minimum in at least one offering. The wells in each partnership are selected for a broad blend of payouts. Some wells may have a high cash flow and deplete more rapidly. Others may deplete over a much longer period of time. The operators work continuously to increase production. The reason for this is that the general partners' interests in these programs parallel those of the limited partners. As they increase productivity for you, they increase their own revenues.

MINIMUM REPURCHASE PRICE

Some programs offer you the guarantee that if within ten years after you invest in one of their partnerships your total distributions plus your repurchase price do not equal 100 percent of your investment, they will add an amount necessary to reach that minimum repurchase price. In my opinion, the general partners should never have to dip into their coffers to meet this guarantee.

DISADVANTAGES OF OIL AND GAS INCOME PROGRAMS

There are two disadvantages to oil income programs of which you should be aware. These are investment lag time and liquidity.

Oil income programs may raise all of their money before they identify the properties that they intend to buy. (They may also have properties inventoried and ready for placement.) If they do not have the property available, the funds are usually invested in Treasury bills, certificates of deposit, or money market mutual funds while the program management searches for suitable purchases. They may be able to find the right properties immediately, or it may take as long as a year to do so. During that year, you would not be receiving oil income, although you would be receiving interest on your funds. However, in recent years as the amount under management has grown, very large purchases have been made in advance.

A more important disadvantage of some oil income programs is their limited liquidity, since there is no ready market for the limited partnership interests in the absence of a "bug-out" provision by the general partner.

You should always view your investment as a long-term one, but of course, you never know when you might need to convert your investment into cash. The general partner of one of the largest of these programs is contractually obligated to repurchase your program from the partnership's inception, subject to its financial ability to do so, at their determined purchase price.

After the acquisitions are completed, the general partner may give you a cash selling price each quarter or each year, depending on the program involved. You may choose to cash in your interests or continue to retain them. Our clients usually choose to retain them, since they do not know of another investment that has offered them a comparable cash flow, with tax shelter and potential for appreciation.

OIL AND GAS DRILLING LIMITED PARTNERSHIPS

Historically, oil drilling programs have raised far more money than income programs. In recent years, public and private drilling programs have attracted more than $1.5 billion per year, whereas the newer income programs have attracted less; but the amount is increasingly rapidly as many more investors have received pleasing results as energy prices have risen.

You may be asking, "Isn't it risky to drill for oil and gas?" The answer is, "Yes, it is." Searching for oil does involve considerable risk. (Paying taxes does, too.) Most oil programs attempt to reduce your risk by drilling a large number of holes in different areas on which a large amount of geological study has been done.

Should you invest in a drilling program? Your answer should be determined by your tax bracket, the source and regularity of your income, your temperament, and other tax-sheltered investments that are available to you.

In a drilling program you are usually allowed to write off 60-100 percent of your investment. This means that if you invest $10,000 in a drilling program that entitles you to eventually write off 100 percent, you will be investing $5,000 of your money and $5,000 of the IRS's money. Your question now is, "Am I willing to risk my $5,000 for the potential of keeping IRS's $5,000 and possibly a larger return?" If your answer is "yes," go ahead and make the investment. If it is "no," then you'll be more comfortable paying the tax or seeking other ways to turn your tax liabilities into assets.

Always keep in mind that striking oil is not simply a matter of drilling a hole in the ground whereupon the oil gushes out like a broken water main. Nothing could be further from the truth. Despite the high level of U.S. petroleum technology, there remain many situations in which trial and error is the only method that can be used to determine whether there is oil at that location and whether it can be raised to the surface and transported to the refinery economically.

TAX BENEFITS

There are three important tax benefits available to you if you invest in an oil drilling program. These come from the deduction of intangible drilling costs, the depletion allowance, and the potential for partial longterm capital gains treatment upon the sale of the investment. Your program may also be structured in a way that will provide additional tax benefits through investment tax credits and depreciation of capital equipment.

Your major costs in drilling can be expensed as intangible drilling expenses. These include well-site expenses and actual drilling costs. This should mean that from 60 to 90 percent of your investment may be deducted in the year you make the investment and up to 100 percent within two to four years.

The extent of your tax benefit will depend upon the type and amount of your income.

DEPLETION

The best-known tax benefit is the depletion allowance. This allows for a portion of your income from the sale of oil and gas production to be tax-sheltered provided that you qualify as a small producer. As a limited partner in both the income programs and in the drilling programs, you will usually be classified as a small producer and will also qualify for the minimum "windfall profit" tax. This illustration shows the depletion allowance rate by year and by production volume.

Depletion Allowance Rate

Year	Production	Exempted	Depletion Rate
1982	1000 barrels a day	6.0 million cu.ft. gas	18%
1983	1000	6.0	16%
1984 and thereafter	1000	6.0	15%

To determine your tax-sheltered amount, apply the depletion rate to your gross income before separating expenses that will result in the tax-free amount (assuming they do not exceed 50 percent of the net income). Typically, 30 percent or so of the cash flow in a drilling program would be tax-sheltered, as the following example illustrates:

Gross income	$2,000
Less separating costs	600
Net income	$1,400
Depletion allowance (18% of gross income)*	360
Taxable income	$1,040 (74.29% of net income)

* 18% in 1982,
16% in 1983, 15% thereafter.

In this example, you would receive a check for $1,400, with $360 or 18 percent of gross income being tax-free because of the depletion allowance. The maximum amount of the depletion allowance that would have to be included as a tax preference item would be $360. But it would not be taxed at the minimum tax rate unless you had other items of tax preference that when added to this would exceed the exclusions ($10,000 or 1/2 tax liabilities). In certain types of program structures, an even larger percentage of income may be tax-free because of depreciating capital expenditures.

STRUCTURING DRILLING PROGRAMS

There are many ways to structure a program in terms of who bears the cost, who receives the tax advantages, and who receives the income.

The structure of your program is important, but it may not be as important as the strength and technical qualifications of the general partner and the partner's ability to find and develop profitable reserves.

The most frequently used sharing arrangements you will encounter are: (1) functional allocations, (2) reversionary interest, and (3) promoted interest.

Functional Allocation. In this structure all items that are immediately deductible for income tax purposes are paid for out of investor funds, and the general partner pays for all nondeductible (capital) items. Oil and gas revenues are usually shared 60 percent to investors and 40 percent to the general partner. Because investor funds are used only for deductible items, this structure results in the highest deductibility, usually 100 percent of the initial investment. Deductible items are primarily intangible drilling costs, including dry holes and abandoned acreage. This structure transfers all of the deductibility, a disproportionately large share of risk, to the investor. Therefore, it is important that the general partner be required to make some minimum risk investment. Usually this minimum risk is set at 15 percent of the investor subscriptions if the general partner is to earn 40 percent of oil and gas revenue.

Reversionary Interest. Investor subscriptions are used to pay for all costs. The general partner pays for a small portion of the program, usually 1 percent. Investors receive a high percentage of oil and gas revenues (usually 99 percent) until they have recovered their investment on some basis, at which time the investors' share of revenues decreases and the general partner's share increases. The key to this structure is the basis on which investors achieve payout before the sharing of revenues changes. The most desirable basis from the investors' point of view is for the interest to change only after the investors have recovered their entire investment in the program. From the general partner's point of view, the interest reversion should occur as the investors are paid out on each well. As a compromise, most programs are written so that the interest reversion occurs on the payout of each prospect. The difficulty with this is that the general partner decides what constitutes a prospect and will generally lean toward defining each well as a separate prospect. If you are interested in a reversionary interest program, be sure that the payout point is on a prospect or program basis and that the definition of prospect is clearly set out.

Promoted Interest. Investors and the general partner each pay a share of the cost and risk of drilling and acreage, and share oil and gas revenues on a disproportionate basis. Typically, investors pay for 75 percent of all initial drilling and acreage costs to earn 50 percent of revenues, while the general partner pays for 25 percent to earn 50 percent. The general partner is more at risk in this type program, and in return earns more equity.

The following summarizes some of the significant characteristics of these three structures.

Table of Three Types of Drilling Programs

Type of Structure	Deductibility % of investment	General Partner at Risk	% Investor Equity	Remarks
Functional allocation	90–100	Moderate	50-60	Frequently used by established program sponsors for exploratory or balanced programs.
Reversionary interest	50-80	Low	99 before payout	Used mostly by new or financially weak program sponsors for developmental programs.
Promoted interest	50-80	High	50	Frequently used by established program sponsors for exploratory or balanced programs.

We have spent considerable time on oil and gas investments because of their popularity with investors seeking tax shelters. Now let's turn our attention to some other unique investments with high risk and high tax-sheltering possibilities.

WHAT ABOUT MARGIN?

On the surface, buying securities on margin sounds real good. On many investments (especially real estate) leverage is important. However, margin-buying has lost countless billions of dollars to investors. While some have become wealthy using this form of leverage, I think ten times as many have lost their shirts. I find that it is usually best if you discipline yourself to the use of only your investable funds. To lose some of your savings in the market is one thing. To lose your future savings in the market is another. Yes, I know if it goes the other way your potential for gain is greatly enhanced. It's not that I don't believe in leverage. I believe very strongly in using leverage in real estate and other areas, and in using stock as collateral for funds to purchase capital items.

If after these warnings you still want to open a margin account, here is how it works. First, the Federal Reserve Board sets the margin requirements. These requirements have ranged from 50 to 100 percent in the post-World War II period. For example, if the margin rate is 70 percent, it means that if you want to buy $10,000 worth of stock you would need to put up $7,000 in order to make the purchase. You would deposit the required cash or securities with your broker within five business days after the purchase.

You will pay interest for the amount you have borrowed. This has ranged from 6½ to 20½ percent. The amount of interest will be posted on your statement monthly.

To open the account you deposit $2,000 or whatever minimum your brokerage firm requires, and sign a margin agreement and a securities loan consent form. This agreement gives your broker the power to pledge or lend your securities. Your securities will be held in what is called "street name," meaning that you are registered in the name of the brokerage house and you do not receive delivery of the certificates. Your broker will, however, credit you with all the dividends received, send you all the reports, and vote your stock in the manner that you direct. You must also abide by the margin maintenance requirements. This usually requires that your margin equity be at least 25 percent. For example, if you bought $20,000 worth of stock with an initial margin requirement of 70 percent, you put up $14,000 and receive credit of $6,000. Let's assume the stock drops to the point where it is worth $8,000. Since you owe your broker, your equity in the securities is only $2,000 and you are right at the 25 percent limit. At this point you will receive a margin call and you'll be asked to put up more cash or securities. If you cannot meet the call, he will sell your securities, retain the $6,000 you owe him, and credit you with the balance.

A "call" option is a contract that gives you the right to buy 100 shares of a given stock at a fixed price for a fixed period of time. The period of time usually runs nine months and ten days (for tax reasons), but you can run 30, 90, 120 days or other lengths of time. The premium that you pay for this option usually runs about 10 - 15 percent of the value of the stock.

A "put" option is the reverse of a "call" option. You now have the privilege of selling 100 shares of the stock at a fixed price within the option period. These usually cost a few percentage points less than call options and are not as popular.

Why would you ever buy an option? The main reason is that it gives you a chance to make a sizeable profit on the move of a stock while limiting the amount of possible loss. For example, you think that General Widgets Company stock selling at $40 may surge to $80. It would cost you $4,000 to buy the shares, and you may not want to risk $4,000 or you may not have $4,000 to invest. Still, you would like to take the chance that General Widgets will jump and as a result you'd make a large profit. In this case you might go to the option route, buying an option for $400. Let's assume your anticipations are correct and the stock hits $70 within the option period. You exercise your option, buy the 100 shares at $40, and then turn around and sell the shares for $70. You have received $7,000 from the sale of the shares. From this you would subtract the $4,000 you paid for them, the $400 premium for the option, and about $110 for the brokerage commissions, and you would wind up with a profit of $2,490.

Now let's assume that your expectations did not materalize and General Widgets goes to $30. What do you do? You do nothing. You simply let your option expire. You are out $400. Your loss is limited to the cost of the option and you are thankful that you didn't buy 100 shares at $4,000 and watch your investment shrink.

"Put" options work in reverse. (There are also some very fancy devices called "straddles" — a combination of a put and a call; "strips," which are composed of two puts and one call; and "straps," which are one put and two calls.)

What is a call option? It is a contract that allows the buyer of the option the right to purchase a particular stock at a specific price during a defined period of time, regardless of the market price of the stock. A covered call option is an option written by a seller who owns the underlying security. When you write a covered call option, you receive an option premium and also continue to receive any dividends on the underlying portfolio stock.

The combination of the income from the option premium plus the dividends from your stock may be two or three times the amount of the dividend alone. Option writing can substantially increase your income from the stock without a commensurate increase in risk.

You may also lock in a profit. If you have bought a block of stock with the goal of making $5 per share profit and sell an option at $5, you lock in that profit.

Your overall objective when you sell call options is to utilize various strategies to produce higher current income, lessen your portfolio's volatility, and reduce your risks in down markets.

Now let's return to portfolio basics.

398

DIVERSIFICATION

Don't put all your eggs in one basket or all your faith in only one company, for it may disappoint you. You may be well informed on sales figures, competitive situations, or whatever, but always be prepared for a disaster. Going for broke on a winner could make you rich, but no one knows which stock will be the big winner. If you buy a diversified group of fundamentally sound stocks with good earnings, the chances are that in a good market you will catch at least some of the big winners. Most big money in a diversified portfolio comes from one or two big winners.

Don't be deceived into thinking that ten oil stocks is diversification; it is not. You should have a portfolio covering a wider range of industries. For example, you may have some stocks in the soft drink industry, the retail area, drugs, home furnishings, electrical equipment, brewing, agricultural machinery, gold mining, and others.

When managing your own portfolio, you may find it extrememly helpful to limit yourself to ten stocks regardless of the amount of money you have to invest. I'm surprised to find that investors think they can only own 100 shares of each company's stock. If the capital you have available for investing is sufficiently large, perhaps you should consider owning 1,000 shares of each stock.

TIMING

There is a time to plant and a time to harvest, and a time to buy and a time to sell. Buy stocks only when you think you can make a profit. The only reason to be in the market is to make money. Buy only when you anticipate a substantial rise within one year. Look for 25 percent appreciation per year.

Buy for investment gain, not dividends.

To make money in the market, you may have to learn to buy ice cubes in the winter — in other words learn not to run with the pack. Learn to buy the stocks others are selling and sell what others are buying. You may find it extremely hard to go against the crowd.

Selling a stock is no easy task for many. But you'll never be a winner in the market unless you learn to sell, as well as buy. As mentioned earlier, a 20 percent drop in the value is my definite "consider selling at one" signal. Another consideration is this: If I had the money I would receive by selling this stock, would I reinvest in this company or invest elsewhere? If you cannot say truthfully that you would use the money for that stock, you ought to sell it!

AVERAGING

Many stock brokers are fond of recommending that their clients "average down." This, in my judgement, is not sound advice.

Let's say you bought 100 shares of a stock at $30 per share and shortly it plunged to $20 value per share. There are many who will recommend that you buy another 100 shares at $20. This would give you an average cost per share of $25 on the 200 shares.

I feel you can average yourself right into the basement of the poorhouse. I never mind paying a higher price than my original purchase price if there is earnings justification. It just means that the market has confirmed my own good judgement. I do not like to continue to buy a security that is falling.

There may be exceptions to this rule, so go back and redo your homework and monitor this stock very closely.

CHAPTER TWELVE

YOU CAN BE A MILLIONAIRE

There is a great personal power in positive financial planning. Power to do good for yourself, your loved ones and society. Profit investing and solid money management can make your life better.

Money will give you many options in life that are impossible without it. Wealth can never buy spirituality, mental or physical health, or true love, but it can help with almost everything else.

Do you want to be rich? Would you like to be a millionaire, or even a multi-millionaire? If you answer "yes!" with deep conviction, you can rest assured that it is possible. Strong desire, unrelenting faith and sufficient time can make your wealth dreams a reality.

By putting "wealth power" in your financial planning, you can achieve amazing results. Your wealth-building goals can come true. First, rid your mind of "the poverty consciousness" and replace it with the powerful "prosperity consciousness."

Following are some very valuable excepts from the life-changing, Profit Ideas book, *How to Achieve Total Success* by Russ von Hoelscher that may both inspire you and give you a totally new outlook on wealth.

Bless and give thanks for who you are and what is now yours, and use daily affirmation treatments to bring more benefits and more abundance into your experience. Affirmations work wonders for increasing wealth, building better relationships, maintaining or restoring health, attracting love and for all other desired conditions and good things. They should be an integral part of your personal positive mind programming strategy for success.

THE LAW OF ABUNDANCE

All people in love with life and who practice prosperity thinking seek more abundance. They affirm increases in both quantity and quality in food, clothing, transportation, housing, knowledge, health, luxury, leisure, peace and satisfaction. These are not selfish, egotistical desires but normal, positive goals for anyone who is aware of the laws of abundance. How beautiful to live in accord with our true nature and use the miraculous law of abundance rather than to succumb to the false prophet that is lack and limitation and decreased expression.

The law of abundance always promotes expansion. There is a Universal Law for increase. There is no such law that upholds decrease. Abundance is what the Universe is all about, and to experience it in our life we need only united with this Truth. Lack and limitation are foreign and unknown effects to the Principle of Life; nevertheless, as creative beings with free choice, we can experience them as an individualized expression if we so choose. This choice, of course, can be (and usually is) subjective and not objective.

Abudance is real and it is truth in the Universal sense. Limitation is not recognized in the Universal sense. It is a false condition, yet we can give it undeserved power if we transfer our energy to it. In effect, we can make it our truth.

Here's an illustration about what is universally true and what is true for the person.

The earth has always been round. That's the way it is and always has been and always will be. Just five hundred years ago, most people did not believe the world was round. Almost everyone then believed the world was flat. So in effect

402

their lives and activities were governed by this belief. Although universally erroneous, the belief did assume power in their lives. They made it their truth, and their mode of transportation, especially be sea, was governed by their belief.

The truth is always the truth and can never be other than the truth. At the same time, the individual may uphold a false notion and allow it to be "ture" in his or her life. In so doing, a person can allow himself to be governed by a false premise and live at its effect. We become what we think we are!

Man is not a machine. Freedom of choice allows us to align ourselves with That Which Is or to live at the effect of something that isn't truthful, harmonious or life-expanding. The choice is ours. Just remember—the truth about your life is that you deserve only the best of everything, complete, unlimited abundance. To live in poverty you must convince yourself that lack and limitation is the way things are. If you convince yourself that there "isn't enough," you will soon be lacking things that you desire, and you will most certainly be limited. Outward appearances (abundance or lack) must always be the reflection of what you believe to be so.

AVOID TOUGH TIMES TALK

To reach abundant wealth and total financial freedom, only think, talk and act prosperous. When others tell you about impending "bad times" or how "the economy is in bad shape," do not align yourself mentally with such tales of woe. Likewise, don't buy into the sea of negativity available from television and radio news programs or your local newspaper. Anything opposed to rich thinking must not be allowed space in your conscious or subconscious. I am not telling you not to listen to what's happening in the financial world, positive and negative. I am saying that you should not

403

"buy into" the negative. Don't let yourself make financial or life decisions based on negativity.

You may have heard the story about the hamburger shop owner. Joe sold the biggest and best hamburger in town from a busy downtown corner location. Business was so good, Joe sent his son, Joe, Jr., to college to learn business and marketing. After four years in a leading institution of higher learning, Joe, Jr. returned. His father greeted him. "Great to have you back, Son. Business is better than ever. Now, I want to expand the business, rent the spot next door, knock down the dividing wall and really cash in big."

"Wait, Dad," Joe Jr. says. "Don't you know we are in the middle of a terrible recession? Times are tough. What we have to do is cut back. We'll reduce the size of our hamburgers twenty percent, stop giving away all these condiments and close earlier!"

Joe Sr. shook his head in disbelief, but decided his educated son must know what to expect from the economy. Soon business fell by nearly fifty percent, and old Joe sadly had to admit to his son, "You were right, Joey, times really *are* tough."

Good, bad, terrific or tough, it is all really a state of mind. Human beings have too often developed a perverted "love affair" with bad news. The front page of your daily paper is filled with stories of murder, rape, robbery, wars, threats of wars and impending disasters—all in big black headlines. In small print on page twenty-three, if you're lucky, you might read something about man's positive achievements or an inspiring story about love or human kindness. Do you still wonder why mankind appears to be in less than a desirable state?

What you think of and talk about, you will act upon. For the sake of your prosperity, avoid "tough times" talk.

DIRECT YOUR MONEY FLOW WITH GOALS

Goals can lead you up the stairway to Total Success. In the exciting arena of wealth-building, they are indispensable to be rich in record time. You should set daily goals and weekly goals, along with long-range big goals. Always remember—once money begins to materialize and circulate in your life, you must self-direct it for best results, forever increasing the flow. Become a "money magnet" by using self-direction and goals. Once you have begun to create more prosperity in your experience, it is time to direct and increase the money flow with the wealth strategy of the very, very rich—wealth pyramiding.

Even if you do not desire millions, you still will greatly benefit and enjoy more rich-living by making your money work for your good. The Law of Increase is in perfect harmony with this principle.

THE LAW OF INCREASE

Life is forever expanding and creating more, and this fact also can apply to your prosperity.

Life is cyclical, full of peaks and valleys, but overall movement is always forward. The Law of Increase, as it applies to money-making, states that things will always get better and increase in value—good stocks and bonds, precious metals, real estate, etec.—they will always go up in value and be substantially higher five years from now than they are today.

Making, saving and investing money should be a routine in our lives without a do-or-die urgency to it. It is not conducive to prosperity living to procrastinate or refrain from making decisions. At the same time, it is not wise to rush into things or attempt to accomplish everything at once. Use your business or job as your source of day-to-day living, and use your investments to increase your overall wealth. Above all, never forget that the real riches *are inside your mind!*

The basic idea behind the creation of wealth is this: You can't be rich in your pocketbook until you're rich in your mind. Mind is the creator of all that is in the physical world. In dealing with this unlimited power that is Mind, it behooves us to sharpen and use every mental tool at our disposal.

Intutition is a powerful mental tool to use in attracting riches. It may be a good idea to point out here and now, this author does not believe one gets rich, although this is a common way to state it, but rather that one attracts wealth through becoming rich on the mental level. Real wealth is always within.

THE TEN COMMANDMENTS OF PROSPERITY

To achieve total wealth and enjoy unlimited riches, many new attitudes concerning prosperity must be cultivated. These "Ten Commandments of Prosperity" will help you rid yourself of negative concepts that actually prevent you from living abundantly. It is only positive affirmations that will attract wealth to you. Try the following ten daily and expect positive results!

I. *THOU SHALT NOT THINK PROSPERITY IS EVIL. Rather, think and proclaim: "Prosperity is right and good for me, and I graciously accept it as proper and beneficial for me and others in my experience. I want and use ever-increasing wealth for good purposes. I thank God for my prosperity."*

II. *THOU SHALT NOT SPEAK OR THINK NEGA—*
TIVELY ABOUT PROSPERITY.
Do not say that "It is difficult to be prosperous" or
that "It is hard to obtain enough money." Rather,
think and proclaim: "I see myself surrounded with
wealth. I see myself enjoying more and more beauti-
ful, green money. I am deserving, open and receptive
to greater abundance, and I use my ever-increasing
wealth wisely."

III. *THOU SHALT NOT MISUSE THY PROSPERITY.*
All negative ideas about money originate from the
premise that money/wealth is often made at the ex-
pense of others. Think and proclaim: "I have the right
attitude about money and prosperity. I do no wrong
with my wealth or no evil to obtain wealth. Right-
thinking and right action draws ever-increasing pros-
perity to me like a magnet."

IV. *THOU SHALT SHARE THY PROSPERITY.*
Hoarding wealth is contrary to the Law of Abun-
dance. You must give more so that you can receive
more. Think and proclaim: "I give money to worthy
causes that reflect my beliefs. I plant money seeds and
I reap an ever-increasing prosperity harvest. I give
with a joyful heart, knowing as I give I receive what-
ever I give back, multiplied many times over."

V. *THOU SHALT REMEMBER THY THOUGHTS*
ATTRACT THY PROSPERITY.
Wealth is not something "out there" that you must
try to get. Prosperity is a state of mind. Riches begin
in Mind. Think and proclaim: "The Universe is abun-

dantly prosperous and is anxious that I prosper. The more I use and enjoy wealth for good purposes, the more wealth is attracted to me to enrich my life. My mind, cooperating with Universal Intelligence, is my wealth source."

VI. *THOU SHALT NOT WORSHIP THY WEALTH.*
The Bible and other great spiritual books made it clear that great money and wealth prosperity are not enough to bring one joy, peace and true happiness. Think and proclaim: "Money is not my master; it is my obedient servant. I use my prosperity wisely and never allow it to use or manipulate me. I am never at the mercy of greed."

VII. *THOU SHALT LOVE THYSELF ENOUGH TO REALIZE THAT THEE DESERVES UNLIMITED PROSPERITY AND EVER-INCREASING ABUN-DANCE.*
Thoughts that you are undeserving of prosperity will keep you in the quicksand of poverty conscious-ness. As a unique child of God, you deserve all good things, and you deserve them abundantly! Think and proclaim: "I Am that I Am. I love this life that is in me. I am good, loving, creative and kind. I deserve the best of everything, including ever-increasing pros-perity, and I am becoming prosperous right now!"

VIII. *THOU SHALT NOT BE ENVIOUS OF OTHERS WHO ARE PROSPEROUS.*
A person with envy in his heart tends to think and speak negatively about those who have possessions that they desire but believe they lack. This attitude is a huge roadblock to a prosperity consciousness.

Never put down the rich because they have great wealth. Bless them for their wealth demonstration. Think and proclaim: "I give thanks that so many others are expressing so much beautiful prosperity in their lives. I give thanks for all that I now have and all that is being attracted to me, for I, too, am rich in happiness, love, joy, health, self-expression and creativity."

IX. *THOU SHALT PYRAMID THY PROSPERITY. Money making money is "prosperity acting upon prosperity." This is the fastest way to increase your wealth. Think and proclaim: "My money serves me through wealth multiplication. My prosperity increases and expands. I see my money making more money. The law of increase is active in my life. More prosperity is always flooding into my experience. I thank God for the wealth-pyramid I am now building."*

X. *THOU SHALT BUILD A POSITIVE CASH FLOW. Going into debt for anything but the best sound investments can lead to financial suicide. To enjoy great prosperity you must be a good steward with your wealth and not spend money that you do not have. With the possible exception of your home and your automobile, pay cash for the things you want. Going into debt can sabotage you prosperity consciousness. Think and proclaim: "I recreate and maintain a positive cash flow in my life. I pay cash for most things I want and always have enough cash to do so. I know I'll always have all the cash necessary for prosperous living, and I am very thankful this is true. And so it is."*

I hope you can comprehend the value of these words taken from "How to Achieve Total Success." May I suggest that you read and reread this book. If you do, I'm sure you will be enriched. Wealth-building is first and foremost a state of consciousness.

THE COMPONENTS OF A MILLION DOLLARS

$1,000 multipled by 1,000 equals one million dollars. This may sound like an awful lot of money to you, and in spite of inflation, it still is. Just remember it is also very attainable.

It has been predicted that in the next 15 years, 1985-2000, there will be more people reaching millionaire status than the previously created millionaires in the history of the world.

If "money making money" (wealth multiplication) is the key to wealth-building, and it is, then obtaining that first $1,000 is more important than obtaining several tens of thousands of dollars later on.

How do you get that first $1,000? How about saving it! If you save $20 per week, you'll have that $1,000 in less than one year. Great things can start from a very humble beginning.

If you don't want to wait until you have saved a nice little chunk of money, you can start investing as you earn, on a weekly or monthly basis.

TIME, MONEY YIELD

After deciding to save and/or invest on a regular schedule, the second requirement in wealth-building is to do everything possible to receive a nice, aggressive return on your money while still employing sound investment principles. The third requirement is having enough time to make your invested money yield a rich harvest.

When we speak of "yield," we ordinarily think of income (dividends or interest) as an annual return on the sum invested, expressed in the form of a percentage. For instance, if you receive $5 at the end of a year on a $100 investment, your yield is 5 percent. However, we shall broaden this definition for the purpose of this chapter and use "yield" to describe any distribution, plus any growth in market value. For if $100 grows to $318 in 10 years, we would say its "yield" is 12 percent compounded.

One thing you must be fully aware of is the magic that comes from compounding the rate of return. This means that you are never to treat any income, capital appreciation, or equity buildup as spendable during the period you are building toward your million-dollar goal, but only as returns that are to be reinvested to increase your accumulation. In other words, don't eat your children. Let them produce more children, and before long you'll have a whole army of dollars working for you. Remember Benjamin Franklin's words, "Money is of a prolific, generating nature. Money can beget money, and its offspring can beget more."

For the purpose of our calculations, any taxes that you must pay on your investments are deemed to have come from another source.

One of the most important things you must remember is how important the rate of return you receive on your investment is to your compounding. For instance, if you can put to work $1,000 each year and can average a compound rate of 10 percent per annum, you will be able to reach your million dollar goal in 48 years.

However, if you can increase this compound rate to 20 percent per annum, you can reach your goal in 29.2 years. So you see, it does make a great deal of difference what return you obtain on your money.

BIG RETURNS

What investment vehicles have offered the biggest returns, 20 percent plus, during the recent past? Here's our top ten candidates:

1. Well-located real estate: raw land, croplands, ranches, homes, residential and commercial income properties, using leverage when the timing is right. For every $1 you invest, consider borrowing at least another $4 to put with it through long-term mortgages when funds are available at the right price. Leverage is important to real estate wealth-building.

2. Carefully managed family businesses or closely held corporations. I consider a profitable, closely held corporation one of the best opportunities for tax shelter and creative financial planning that there is.

3. Carefully and aggressively selected and traded growth common stocks in emerging industries. Timing is so important here.

4. Selected growth mutual funds.

5. Selected oil and gas income programs.

6. Antique furniture, art objects, and other collectibles, properly bought and sold.

7. Paintings and sculpture of gifted artists, properly bought and sold.

8. Gold and gold stocks or silver and silver stocks, carefully timed.

9. Entrepreneural activities — new products, services, etc.

10. Investment quality diamonds and precious jewels, with purchases and sales carefully timed and purchased at wholesale.

A MILLION DOLLARS AND YOU

Let's say that you are twenty five years old and have saved that one thousand dollars. Lets also assume you can save $50 a month, and can obtain a 15 percent yield on your investments. Here's what you can accomplish with this modest amount and enough time:

Age 25	$1,000 + $50 per Month
25	$ 1,000
30	8,663
35	18,054
40	40,967
45	87,052
50	179,745
55	466,185
60	741,183
65	1,495,435

If you are thirty years of age and fortunate enough to be able to make a lump-sum investment of $10,000 and can obtain an average return of 15 percent compounded annually, without adding new money to your investment but reinvesting all distributions and paying taxes from another source, your progress report should look something like this over a thirty-five year period:

Age 30	$10,000
35	20,113
40	40,456
45	81,371
50	163,670
55	329,190
60	662,120
65	1,331,800

If you can move up the performance ladder to 30 percent and if you had started with $1,000 and added $50 per month for forty years, your figures would be the following:

Age 25	$*1,000*
30	17,326
35	36,108
40	81,934
45	174,104
50	359,490
55	932,370
60	1,482,366
65	2,964,732

As you can see, at 30 percent you accomplish your goal in thirty years. With a lump sum of $10,000 at 30 years of age and a 30 percent performance, your progress report would look like this:

Age 30	$*10,000*
35	40,226
40	80,912
45	162,742
50	327,340
55	658,380
60	1,324,240
65	2,648,480

You've accomplished your goal here in less than twenty-five years.

Remember, we are not talking about "guarantees." All we are doing here is obtaining a visual picture of what compounding accomplishes over a period of years if you are able to maintain a 15 percent average and a 30 percent average.

We do not know what our future economy will be. Of one thing be can be certain, however: You will never reach your million-dollar goal with this amount of savings using "guaranteed" dollars. As a matter of fact, you won't keep even after inflation and taxes. If you hope to reach your goal, you must save and let your money grow. Investing your money aggressively and intelligently in well-managed and strategically located U.S. companies that are in the right industry at the right time, real estate expertly selected and intelligently leveraged, and natural resources that are in critical demand will not guarantee you growth of capital, but you will have provided your money with the opportunity to work as hard for you as you had to work to get it. The working dollar is an absolute necessity if your goal is to become a millionaire.

Millionaire status is possible. Rich thinking plus "money making money" is the way.